TRAIL OF FEATHERS

Beyond the Devil's Teeth: Journeys in Gondwanaland

Sorcerer's Apprentice

TRAIL OF FEATHERS

In Search of the Birdmen of Peru

Tahir Shah

Weidenfeld & Nicolson

LONDON

First published in Great Britain in 2001 by
Weidenfeld & Nicolson

© 2001 Tahir Shah

Plate no. 1 is reproduced courtesy of the Museum of Fine Arts, Boston. The other
pictures were taken by the author.

A CIP catalogue record for this book is available from the British Library.

ISBN 0 297 64592 7

Typeset by Selwood Systems, Midsomer Norton
Printed in Great Britain by Butler & Tanner Ltd, Frome and London

Weidenfeld & Nicolson
The Orion Publishing Group Ltd
Orion House
5 Upper Saint Martin's Lane
London WC2H 9EA

I am grateful to Richard Fowler,
101st Airborne Division, for keeping his promise.

Perhaps where Lear has raved and Hamlet died
On flying cars new sorcerers may ride.

SAMUEL JOHNSON

Contents

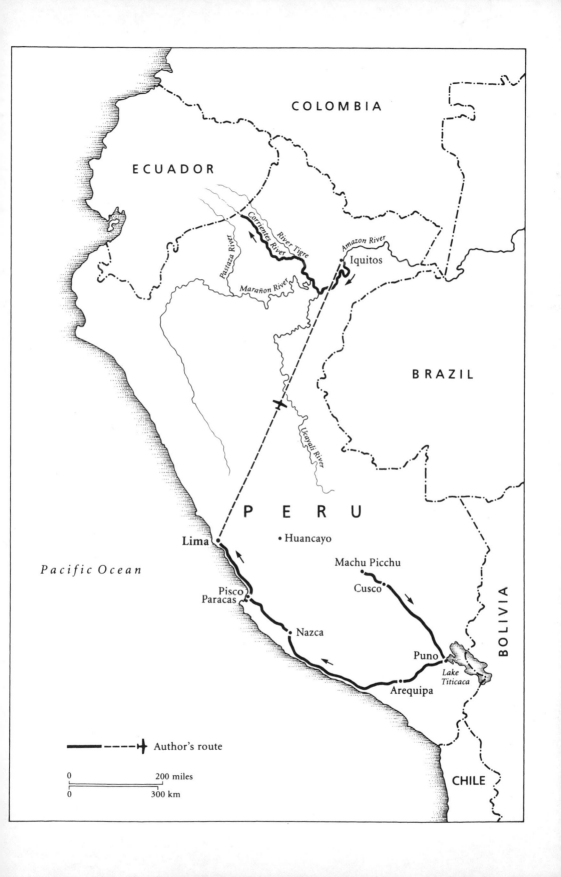

COLOMBIA

ECUADOR

BRAZIL

Pastaza River

Corrientes River

River Tigre

Amazon River

Iquitos

Marañon River

Ucayali River

P E R U

Lima

• Huancayo

Machu Picchu

Cusco

Pisco
Paracas

• Nazca

Puno

Pacific Ocean

Arequipa

Lake Titicaca

BOLIVIA

CHILE

──── ----- ✈ Author's route

| 0 | 200 miles |
| 0 | 300 km |

I

The Feather

The trail began at an auction of shrunken heads. Anxious with greed, a pack of dealers and curiosity-hunters pushed into the library where the sale was about to begin. They had come by strict invitation, as the learned British society was eager to avoid the press. In the current climate of political correctness trophy heads are regarded as an embarrassment, something to be disposed of as quietly as possible. For years I had been an admirer of this unusual handicraft, and was desperate to start a collection of my own. Even though I'd managed to squirm my way onto the underground auction lists, I was lacking the funds of a serious collector. The shrunken head business is a small one, with only a few major players world-wide. I recognised most of them, as they lolled back on their chairs, their wax jackets wet with rain, their hands damp with sweat. All were well aware that such exquisite *tsantsas* are rarely put up for sale.

Wasting no time, the society's secretary held up the first miniature head. Framed in a mane of jet-black hair, its skin was gnarled, its facial features distended. The nose was dark and shiny, and the lips had been sewn together with a magnificent length of interwoven twine. The dealers leaned forward, and swallowed hard, as the bidding began.

Fifteen minutes later the auction was over. All eleven heads had been sold to the same Japanese collector. Well-known and equally well disliked, he'd been trying to corner the shrunken head market for years.

As we filed out, I got chatting to an elderly Frenchman. He was wearing a Norfolk jacket and brown suede brogues, and said he'd come from Paris for the sale. Like me, he was going home headless and empty-handed. We shared a mutual interest in ethnographic curiosities. I lamented that, once again, the crème de la crème in *tsantsas* was going East, to Japan.

The Frenchman looked me in the eye and said that if he were forty years younger, he would drop everything and go to Peru.

'To search for *tsantsas*?'

'Not for shrunken heads,' he replied, 'but for the Birdmen.'

'Who are the Birdmen?'

The man buttoned up his jacket, smiled wryly, and walked off into the rain. I didn't go after him. For, at shrunken head sales, you get more than the usual smattering of madmen.

*

A week later a long manila envelope fell through my letter-box. It was post-marked Paris. Inside was a rust-coloured feather and a slip of paper. The feather was evidently old. Three triangular notches had been cut into one side. It appeared to have been dipped in blood many years before. On one side of the paper was a crude sketch of a man with wings; on the reverse was a single sentence in classic French script. It read:

'. . . and the Incas flew over the jungle like birds. Calancha.'

I assumed that the Norfolk-jacketed Frenchman had sent it, and I wondered what it meant. Was there a connection between shrunken heads and men with wings?

While at the British Library a few days later, I looked up 'Calancha'. There was only one author by this name, Friar Antonio de la Calancha. A single work was credited to him. It was entitled *Coronica Moralizada del Orden de San Augustin en el Perù*. Bound in dull speckled calf, with dented corners, it was a huge book, as long as the Bible. The tooled spine was embossed *Barcelona 1638*. Eight woodcuts adorned the title page. They showed Catholic monks civilising a tribal people, whose bodies were decorated in feathers.

Were these the Birdmen?

From what I could make out, the text rambled on about taming peasants and teaching the Catholic message. I could see no mention of Birdmen.

I left the library but couldn't stop thinking about the flight of ancient man.

*

We all know the tale of Icarus. When he flew too close to the sun, the wax on his wings melted and the feathers fell apart. There's an Arab version as well: Abu'l Qasim ibn Firnas, the ninth century 'Sage of Spain', who made a pair of tremendous wings, cloaked himself in feathers ... and flew. But like Icarus before him, he crashed to Earth.

The more I ran the Frenchman's quote through my mind, the more it teased me. Had the Incas glided over the jungles or had flight begun, as we are always told, a century ago with the Wright brothers? Days passed, and I found myself thinking of little else. I tried to contact the Frenchman, but without luck.

An old fixation was coming to life again. As a teenager I had been obsessed with aircraft and flying. At sixteen I nagged my parents into buying me an air-pass valid for unlimited flights around the United States. For a month I flew from one airport to the next, without ever leaving the aviation system. I slept on departure lounge floors or, better still, took night flights across the nation. I lived on airline food, and prided myself on the fact that I never once paid for a meal. I remember thinking that I'd hit upon a new form of existence, and wondered whether in the future everyone would live like me.

A friend suggested that I check for a mention of primitive flight at the library of the Royal Aeronautical Society. At noon the next day, I cycled through the pouring rain up to the Society's lavish head-quarters, a stone's throw from Park Lane.

By any standards the Royal Aeronautical Society is a mysterious institution. Rather like a gentlemen's club, it is shrouded from the prying eyes of commoners. Once you're inside, you wonder how you could never have known about it before. Strangely, the Society was established in 1866, a full thirty-seven years before the Wright brothers made their first powered flight. The eighth Duke of Argyll, its founder, must have known he was onto a winner. Perhaps, I pondered, he had known of flight in more ancient times.

Pushing open the door to the library on the third floor, I slipped inside. A modest-sized room, looking out onto the gates of Hyde Park, it was laid with maroon carpet and cluttered with desks. Half a dozen wintry gentlemen were sitting in silence, poring over picture books of early fighter aircraft.

I trawled the rounded shelves for a mention of the Incas or Calancha. Most of the books were concerned with twentieth century aviation.

A handful of forward-thinking pamphlets about aircraft had been printed during the 1800s. None referred to the Incas, though. Dismayed at the lack of relevant information, I approached the librarian's office.

From the moment he first saw me, I could sense that the thin, bald librarian had branded me a trouble-maker. He glanced down at a half-eaten Marmite sandwich, in a nest of tin-foil on his desk. Then he looked up and blinked. I explained my interest in the Incas. Had he heard about Calancha's chronicle? Did he know whether the ancient Americans had actually flown? Was there a connection between ancient flight and shrunken heads?

Spreading a single curl of hair across his polished head, the librarian gnawed at the sandwich, and grimaced.

'Incas?'

'That's right, I've heard they flew ... over the jungles of Peru.'

The librarian raised an eyebrow.

'When did all this happen?'

'Oh, um,' I stammered, 'ages ago...'

'*Before* the Wright brothers?'

I did a quick calculation.

'Almost certainly.'

Choking down the last bite of bread, he said he'd see what he could find.

Half an hour later, he stumbled over with a single A3 sheet.

'This is all we have,' he said.

I glanced at the page, a clipping from *The Brentwood Review*, 8 March 1985. The main photograph showed a moustachioed man hurling into the air what looked like an oversized pillowcase. I scanned the columns. The article focused on a retired cash machine repairman, called William Isadore Deiches. A self-proclaimed expert of flight in ancient times, Mr Deiches, so the article said, had cracked a secret code, and could build a flying carpet. He could even make a doormat fly – for Deiches had deciphered aircraft designs from several countries, including Egypt, Japan, Tibet, Mexico and Peru. And, the piece explained, he had even written a book on the secret lore of the Pyramids.

Mr Deiches was my only lead. Somehow he must have worked this out when I called him. His response implied that only desperate people telephoned the Deiches residence.

A child-like voice answered the phone.

'I know how they built the Pyramids,' it said.

'Is that Mr Deiches?'

'You'll never guess how they did it.'

'I want to know if the Incas flew,' I said, changing the subject.

' 'Course they did,' the voice replied easily.

'Are you *sure*?'

'You'd better come round and have a chat.'

2

Valley of the Dead Pilots

William Isadore Deiches opened the door to his Brentwood maisonette no more than a crack. The iris of a single ice-blue eye widened as it observed me. I whispered my name. The door slammed shut. I stood firm and repeated my name. A security chain clattered, and was followed by the sound of unoiled hinges moving slowly. I greeted Mr Deiches. A man of retirement age, he was of average height, with a slender neck, thin lips and an aquiline nose. His hair was concealed by a black Stetson, with a tan leather band; and his skin was oyster-grey, wrinkled like rhino hide.

'Can't be too careful,' said Deiches, leading the way through the hall, into the lounge, 'there are a lot of crackpots out there.'

It might have been a pleasant spring day in Brentwood, but the maisonette's rooms were frigid, dank and smelled of death. Remembering that I'd come in the name of scientific research, I sat down in a low armchair and braced myself. Around me, the scarlet paisley wallpaper seemed to be closing in. Ring-binders were piled up everywhere, and a clutch of mangy soft toys poked out from under a coffee table. Crumbs from a thousand TV-dinners circled my chair.

Deiches handed me a mug of steaming tea, and swept an arm across the coffee table to clear it.

'The Valley of the Kings wasn't that at all,' he said, settling into a rocking-chair, 'it was really the Valley of the Dead Pilots.'

'Egypt?' I said.

'Of course,' he replied. 'Who d'you think taught the Incas to fly?'

I frowned politely.

'Tutankhamen was their best pilot,' he went on, 'but he crashed, poor chap, and died of multiple fractures.' Deiches paused to sip his tea. 'The Egyptians based everything on watching birds,' he said. 'You only ever got a single-seater in Ancient Egypt, because they'd never seen a bird with two heads. Haven't you ever heard of the Saqqara glider?'

I shook my head.

'In 1898,' said Deiches, 'a model of a plane was discovered in a tomb there. No one knew what it was, because the Wright brothers hadn't done their stuff yet, so it got tossed into a box. Then in the '70s someone fished it out and realised it was a prototype of a high-wing monoplane.'

'What about the Americas?' I asked.

Deiches' eyes glazed over. I sensed that it had been a long time since the last visitor had graced his living-room.

'I'm the only man alive who can translate Mayan,' he announced proudly. 'It's a bloody nightmare of a language.'

The expert took a gulp of tea.

'They all had aircraft,' he said, 'the Maya, the Aztecs, and the Incas. What d'you think Mexico's Pyramid of the Moon was for?'

Again, I looked blank-faced.

'For launching gliders, of course!'

A self-schooled authority on ancient flight, Deiches was having a whale of a time. Like a theoretical physicist, he could come out with the wildest ideas and get away with it. Despite my reservations, some of his facts did check out. The Saqqara glider, for instance, well-known to Egyptologists, is on display at the Cairo Museum.

'I'm quite famous in my own little way,' he said, 'everyone knows me in Brentwood. Some people think I'm a crank but I'm not half as cranky as the lunatic who's been calling me with death threats.'

Mr Deiches tugged a tattered folder from an upper shelf and rifled through it. Then he handed me a photocopy. The piece, from a 1934 edition of the *New York Times*, was headed 'Aztec Gliders Flew in Mexico'. I ran my eyes over the article. It reported that an obscure Polish archaeologist, Professor M J Tenenbaum, was claiming he'd found stone etchings of Aztec gliders, which they had called *crirs*. Not unlike King Solomon's fleet of aircraft (known as *rasheds*) the *crirs* had been made of stork feathers. Tenenbaum, the clipping went on, said that the primitive craft had been mentioned in Friar Clausijiro's 18th century book *History of Mexico*, where it said the Aztecs 'could fly like birds'. The similarity with the Frenchman's quote about the Incas caught my attention.

Had ancient American cultures managed to construct a crude form of hang-glider? Surely it wasn't so impossible for a mountain people to have designed a basic flying canopy? I wondered why such an obvious question was ranked as being on the lunatic fringe. Looking over at Deiches, his face pressed into the tattered file, I began to remember why. But even so, I found it strange that no mainstream scientists had considered the idea of gliding in ancient times.

'I know how they made flying carpets,' winced Deiches, eager to regain his audience.

'How?'

'The designs of Persian carpets ... they hold the secret blueprints,' he lisped. 'Decode the patterns, and you can make a carpet fly.'

Deiches smiled the smile of a man who had solved this, and many other riddles.

'Your Incas flew all right,' he said. 'How d'you think they built the gigantic lines in Peru's Nazca Desert? Beware of the crackpots – like the ones who say the symbols were landing strips for aliens. That's nonsense! They were no such thing ... they were landing strips for gliders, Incan gliders.'

With a deep sigh, I looked over at William Isadore Deiches, as he bobbed back and forth in his chair. Condemning him as a psychopath would have been too easy. Most of his expertise was beyond me, but he was the one man prepared to accept the idea of American flight in ancient times.

I drained my tea and thanked Mr Deiches for his time.

'You can't go yet,' he said. 'I've got to show you this...'

The retired cash register repairman, turned aviation specialist, ripped a fragment of paper from his file. He passed it over. My head jerked back as I focused on the sketch. It depicted a glowering figure with outstretched wings, taloned feet, and a crown covering his scalp. Writhing sea-snakes and trophy heads decorated the motif, which was labelled at the bottom. The label read 'Peruvian Birdman'.

Deiches squinted, and wiped his nose with a grubby handkerchief.

'Thought you'd like it,' he said.

'Is it an Inca? Is there a link between the Birdmen and trophy heads?'

'I'm not going to give you all the answers,' he riposted. 'If you're so keen, why don't you go and do your own research?'

'Where would I go?' I asked. 'I've already been to the British Library and the Aeronautical Society.'

Deiches wasn't impressed.

'You can't do research sitting here in England,' he said.

'But what would I look for?'

The flying carpet expert took another gulp of his tea.

'You have to look for the Birdmen, of course.'

*

A few days after my encounter with Deiches, I took the train down to Purley to visit Sir Wilfred Thesiger, who was living in a residential home nearby. I would always try to meet the veteran explorer before setting off on a journey. He is a master when it comes to advice on planning an expedition.

While on the train, I scribbled what I knew on the back of an envelope: *(1) Feather dipped in blood. (2) Spanish monk who may have thought the Incas could fly. (3) Many references to flight in ancient times. (4) Mystery of the Nazca Lines in Peru. (5) Picture of Birdman, decorated with trophy heads*. It wasn't much to go on but, as I stared at the notes, I felt a surge of adrenaline. The puzzle was without doubt cryptic, but I was sure there was a trail leading to an answer, a trail leading to a journey.

The late-Georgian building, set in acres of lush grounds, was a far cry from Kenya's Samburuland, where I had first met Thesiger a decade earlier. Even though in his ninetieth year, Sir Wilfred was still hard as nails, bursting with strength. Bounding up the stairs to the second floor, he led the way to his room. Knick-knacks from Africa and Arabia were dotted about: a curved *jambiyah* dagger from Yemen, an Abyssinian talisman, a Zulu shield and *assagai*.

'So, tell me,' Thesiger said, once installed in his favourite chair, 'where are you off to?'

'I've decided to go to Peru.'

'Never been to the Americas myself,' he replied. 'Peru ... was that the Aztecs?'

'Incas.'

'Ah, yes, the Incas,' said Thesiger, staring into space, 'and what's taking you down there?'

Previous discussions with the great explorer had established his aversion to air travel. Most of his journeys had begun with a sea voyage. So it was with unease that I mentioned my interest in Incan gliders.

'I've heard that the Incas could fly,' I said casually.

Thesiger drew in a sharp breath.

'*Aeroplanes*! Can't stand the things,' he said. 'That infernal combustion engine.'

'I don't think they were actual planes with engines,' I said weakly, 'probably more like gliders.'

Sir Wilfred cocked his head back.

'You're going to need some good equipment,' he replied. 'What're you taking?'

Until that moment, sitting as I was in Sir Wilfred's study, I hadn't given much thought to the technicalities of the trip. A trailblazer of the old school, Thesiger judged expeditions on the quality and amount of equipment taken along. He was a man who'd never been hampered by the stringent luggage restrictions of modern air travel.

'I'll be taking all the usual stuff,' I said, motioning sideways with my arms.

Thesiger scratched his cheek. He was waiting for an inventory.

'Ropes,' I mumbled, 'lots of rope ... and some mosquito repellent, a good water-bottle, and of course some tins of corned beef.'

'Rations ... very important,' wheezed Sir Wilfred. 'But what about transport once you're there?'

In line with his dislike of aircraft, I was aware of Thesiger's hatred of all motor vehicles. Stretching in my chair, I announced: 'Llamas, I'll be using llamas.'

'Ah,' he said, slapping his hands together with relish, 'animal transport. Can't beat it. Never used llamas myself.'

'They're basically camels,' I said knowledgeably, 'just with smaller humps.'

'A camel could take you to the ends of the Earth,' he replied dreamily. As someone who had twice crossed *Rub' al-Khali*, the Empty Quarter of the Arabian Desert, barefoot, Thesiger was a man who knew his camels.

Satisfied with my transport arrangements, he swivelled in his chair. Another pressing question was concerning him.

'What if the rations run out, and you're starving?' he asked darkly.

My eyes widened at the thought.

Sir Wilfred leaned forward, the shadow of his towering frame looming over me like a storm-cloud.

'You may have to turn the transport into food,' he said.

*

A large-scale map of Peru was unfurled at Extreme Journey Supplies, a trekking shop in north London. The salesman cast an eye across it and shook his head.

'Peru,' he said with loathing, 'it's a hard one.'

'*Hard?*'

'There's mountains,' he mumbled, running a thumbnail down the Andes. 'Then you got desert over 'ere, jungles down 'ere, and coastline ... *lots* of coastline.'

'Diverse little country, isn't it?' I said.

'Gonna cost 'ya,' he replied, fishing a check-list from a draw. 'What d'you want first?'

'I think I'd better start with a knife.'

'What sorta knife?'

'I'm going to need one with a sharp blade.'

'How sharp?'

'Sharp enough to skin a llama,' I said.

An hour later I found myself inspecting a mass of gear. The shop's manager had come to attend to me himself. A major journey called for the best equipment money could buy. I surveyed my purchases and grinned, Thesiger would be proud. Like him, I was becoming preoccupied by inventories.

Realising that I was every salesman's dream customer, the manager went over the check-list. A team of assistants scrambled to pack the gear into bags.

'Water purifying pump, Force Ten high altitude tent,' he began in a baritone voice, 'Omega Synergy sleeping bag, mosquito net, two litres of Deet, jungle hammock, trekking pole with built-in compass, thermometer, signalling mirror and distress whistle, titanium Primus stove with extra fuel, six carabiners, two hundred feet of caving rope, a four-cell Maglite, self-inflating mattress, wire saw, hypothermia blanket, folding spade with combined entrenching tool, fire-lighting flint, lightweight mess tin, more rope, emergency surgery unit with brain drip, mentholated foot powder, ergonomic water bottle with in-built drinking straw, and twenty-two family-sized sachets of Lancashire Hot Pot.'

'What about the knife?'

The manager tapped the sheet with the end of his pen.

'And last but not least,' he declared grandly, 'a sixteen-inch, nickel-coated Alaskan moose knife, with a blade sharp enough to ...' the manager paused to look at me. 'Sharp enough to skin a llama,' he said.

3

Inca Trail Warriors

It was well below freezing as I stumbled out of my tent into the blackness, a torch in one hand, a soggy roll of loo paper in the other. With the night to cloak me, I went in search of a patch of field in which to purge my faltering digestive tract. Within a week I'd ripened from headstrong adventurer with a quest, to incontinent wreck.

I had arrived in Lima with the intention of picking up the trail to the elusive Birdmen, whoever they might be. I had no idea where the path might lead, or the hazards which might line its route. My *modus operandi* was to forge ahead, quizzing anyone and everyone for scraps of information. Looking back, I can only marvel that I embarked on such a long journey with so little in the way of concrete data. But, in hindsight, this lack of research may have been my greatest asset.

Weighted down instead with equipment, I made a beeline to the ancient city of Cusco. From there I signed up for the Inca Trail, the trek across the mountains to Machu Picchu. The Incas' most sacred city seemed the obvious place to pick up the trail in search for the Birdmen of Peru.

The four-day hike was described by my guide-book as 'ten times harsher than Everest'. Waving it off as no more than a piffling stroll, I had thrust my trekking pole into the dirt. A man with as much gear as me, I mused, was surely unstoppable.

Since my rendezvous with Deiches, I'd read what little I could find regarding flight in antiquarian times. The line between myth and fact was clouded in uncertainty. Cold hard facts were few and far between. I scrutinised the more reputable ancient texts, hunting for clues.

I read of a man named Ki-Kung-Shi who supposedly built a chariot with wings in the reign of Chinese Emperor Ch'eng T'ang, eighteen centuries before the birth of Christ. The chariot looked rather like a paddle steamer. Another source recorded that two thousand years ago, in the Chinese kingdom of Ki-Kuang, (its people, supposedly, had one arm and three eyes each) flying machines were common. And, in Ancient Greece, Archytas of Tarentum, a friend of Plato, had constructed a wooden dove. When it flew it became one of the wonders of the ancient world.

Dig deep in folklore and you start unearthing examples of primitive flight. Most test the boundaries of belief. Danish legends tell of flying sun chariots over Trundholm two millennia ago; the Indian epics Ramayana and Mahabharata contain references to flight – the most famous being the zeppelin-like *Vimana* aircraft. Zimbabwe had 'towers of the flight'; the Maoris had a tradition of flying-men, as did the English, beginning with King Bladud.

For some reason the notion of Incan flight shone more brightly for me than all the rest. Perhaps because the empire of the Incas rose at a time when a few scientists and free-thinkers in Europe were working on the idea of flight. Roger Bacon, Leonardo Da Vinci and others, gave serious thought to the problem of sustaining a man's weight in air. But they were lampooned for using hammers and nails rather than magic, alchemy, and other accepted tools of the time.

*

On the third night on the Inca Trail, after a suspect bowl of stewed *cuy*, which we know as guinea pig, I asked the guide, Patricia, if she had heard whether the Incas flew. A sensitive woman with deep-set eyes and an infectious smile, she'd laughed at my question. Only when I declared that I wasn't joking, did she become more serious. Like many Peruvians I quizzed, she was capable of extraordinary perception in esoteric matters. And, as with many others, she had a nugget of information to pass on.

'When my grandfather was a young man in Urubamba,' she said, stirring her guinea pig goulash to cool it, 'he was walking in the woods near his home. At the foot of a tall tree he came across a young condor. Its wing had been broken. Taking pity on it, my grandfather gave the bird a little meat. He took it home, where he cared for it through the winter. After many weeks, when it had recovered, he let it go free.'

Patricia slurped her stew and stared into the camp-fire.

'From that day on he had wild, vivid dreams,' she said. 'He dreamt he was an Inca flying, gliding through the empty sky ... he dreamt he was part condor, part man, a man from ancient times.'

*

By the time I had struggled back to my tent from the lavatory field, Patricia was ready to leave. It was just before three a.m. She supervised the porters, two of whom had been assigned to haul my luggage across the passes to Machu Picchu.

Laden down with non-essential knick-knacks, I limped forward on bleeding feet. I cursed myself for giving in to the salesman's tempting merchandise; and I damned Deiches. If it hadn't been for him, I would have been tucked up at home dreaming of adventure. The porters scuttled ahead under the weight of survival gear, their sandals biting into the granite-paved path. All around us the jungle slept.

Patricia told me to keep a look out for *Cuscomys ashaninka*, a new genus of mammal, the size of a domestic cat, which had been discovered in the hills for the first time a few days before. But I was in no mood for nature. I inched forward through the darkness, my hand on Patricia's shoulder, like a gas victim from a forgotten war.

Four hours later the undergrowth appeared to know that dawn was near. The food chain had woken and was hungry. After breakfasting, one creature would become an early meal for another with wider jaws. A thousand birds nudged about in the foliage, restless to take flight. Each nest sheltered a clutch of mouths waiting to be fed. Darkness lifted by gradual degrees, although there was still no real light. At last the first shades of cypress and olive green came to life.

The track had levelled out, and was now clearly visible. I responded by moving faster, bounding across the neatly-fitting flagstones. A thermometer, distress whistle, and signalling mirror clattered from my jacket, like tools hanging from an astronaut's suit.

Turning a sharp bend, I was struck dumb by the view. Stretching out ahead was a valley. At its centre lay the ruins of a city. The valley was like none other I have ever witnessed, just as the city itself has no equal. The colours, the shadows and the sense of secrecy, were bewitching.

I rested there at *Intipunku*, the Gate of the Sun, before starting the short walk down into the ruins. The air, which had shed its nocturnal blanket, smelled of fennel, although I could not see that aromatic herb growing among the smooth-edged granite stones. As I descended, the first fragment of dawn rose out over the dark peaks, giving them colour. No more than a glow of light at first but, as the moments passed, the glow transformed into a bolt of gold. I watched transfixed and, as I did so, it struck the ancient ruins of Machu Picchu.

The Spanish ravaged the Incan kingdom, stripping away its riches. But they missed this, the greatest jewel of all. Before walking the Inca Trail I had wondered how the sacred city could have eluded the Conquistadors. Far too steep for their horses, the trail – supposedly the original route of pilgrimage – appears to lead nowhere. Only after four days of hiking across mountain passes, do you reach the city itself. The elusive path had kept the Incas' secret safe.

Current thinking says that Machu Picchu was probably deserted before the Conquistadors arrived. Some experts say it was abandoned after a plague; others that the religious centre may have moved elsewhere.

The American scholar Hiram Bingham is credited with redis-covering Machu Picchu. Leading a Yale University team to the site in July 1911, he claimed to have found the Incan stronghold of Vil-cabamba. A historian rather than an archaeologist, Bingham knew how to put together an expedition and his team was remarkably well-equipped. When I read his book *Inca Land*, I wondered if he'd visited the same mountaineering shop as me. The inventory of his equipment suggested that superior salesmen had been at work.

Bingham's gear included: a mummery tent with pegs and poles, a hypsometer, a mountain-mercurial barometer, two Watkins aneroid barometers, a pair of Zeiss glasses, two 3A Kodak camera, six films, a sling psychrometer, a prismatic compass and clinometer, a Stanley pocket level, an eighty-foot red-strand mountain rope, three ice axes, a seven-foot flagpole with an American flag and a Yale University flag, four Silver's self-heating cans of Irish Stew, a cake of chocolate, eight hardtack biscuits, as well as raisins, sugar cubes and mock-turtle soup.

Gazing down across the valley, it was hard to imagine that until Bingham's arrival Machu Picchu was lost in jungle. The canopy of trees which had hidden and protected the sacred city for centuries has long since been hacked down. Modern times have brought mod cons in abundance, paving the way for the tourist bandwagon. The most notable additions were an exclusive hotel and the railway, which runs from the nearby town of Aguas Calientes down to Cusco. Each year brings newer and more costly comforts. The latest idea is to build a cable-car which will ferry even more tourists up to the sacred city from the valley floor.

But for two hours each morning, Machu Picchu belongs to the weary, stomach-clutching legion of Inca Trail warriors. The ruins are deserted and lie silent. For those who have staggered over the passes, the reward is like slipping into Disneyland before the gates open. You have a chance to breathe deeply, to soak up the textures, and to absorb the lack of human sound. But then, on the dot of nine, as if some invisible gong has been struck, the first of a thousand tourist coaches winds its way up the hairpin bends to Machu Picchu. Within moments, the turnstiles are spinning, the flush toilets are churning, and soft drinks fizzing, as the seething mass of Banana Republic explorers descends.

Tour groups, speaking every language in the world, criss-cross the place like spiders weaving a giant web. Stubbing out their duty-free cigarettes underfoot, rubbing sun-cream into their wrinkles, troupe after troupe of khaki-clothed tourists hustles forward, desperate to get their money's worth in this, the greatest archaeological theme park on earth.

*

On the western edge of Machu Picchu, we came across a group of seven East Europeans, clustered around a curiously-shaped granite block. The tourists, dressed in matching lilac robes, were barefoot, except for one woman who was wearing purple moonboots. They were chanting some kind of invocation. Patricia frowned, then shook her head woefully.

'They are always doing this,' she said.

'Who?'

'Those purple people. They come from Poland and think they are Incas. They come to take power from the *Intihuatana*, the Sacred Stone.'

We watched as the Poles, their palms pressed against the granite surface and their eyes tightly closed, sapped the rock's energy.

'What's so sacred about that stone?'

'The Incas used to tie the sun to it,' said Patricia. 'It proved their power over nature. When the Spanish found those special stones, they broke them up. I wish this one could be broken,' she said, her voice rasping with anger, 'then maybe the Polish people would go away.'

Soon after, Patricia's wish was granted. The sacred stone was crushed to bits during the filming of a beer commercial.

Without wasting time Patricia led me from the holy rock, down through the terraced ruins, pointing out the principal buildings along the way.

Since Bingham, every generation has dreamed up new theories to explain the ruined city. Experts have claimed it was a fortress, a private hacienda, a nunnery, centre of learning or religion, even an observatory.

'Look at this place,' Patricia said, sweeping her arm in an arc over a bluff of rocks, 'this is called the Temple of the Condor.'

I entered the shrine.

'To me it does look like a temple dedicated to birds,' said Patricia. 'See here, how the wings of the condor are represented by the rock. And here, how the image of a condor has been carved from a piece of granite.'

The guide wiped her neck with her hand. 'But has it got anything to do with birds at all?'

'What do you mean?'

'Bingham thought it was the prison, where convicts were chained up or killed,' she said. 'Others have said it's a princess's tomb, a kitchen, or a place where maize was stored.'

I stepped out of the way as a river of retired Israelis flooded in. Before we knew it they were upon us. We held our ground. The Israeli leader, waving a pink flag – embroidered with the legend *Moses Basket Tours* – was a force to be reckoned with. He spewed out a couple of lines about the temple, clapped his hands signalling for photography to begin; glared at the Bengalis; clapped again, and led the way to the Temple of the Rainbow.

Every three minutes another wave of white-skinned, blue-rinsed retirees splashed in, and swirled around us. Between the waves, I made a hurried inspection of the sanctuary. The form of the condor was blatantly obvious, lying outstretched on the floor, its wings writhing behind, and its beak lurching ahead. This was no prison block or princess's tomb, but quite obviously a shrine dedicated to flight.

Patricia pointed out the groove in the bird's ruff, where sacrificial llama blood might once have run. A rush of energy gripped me as the next swell of Israelis surged into the cove. Surely this, the Temple of the Condor, was connected to the Birdmen?

Patricia noticed my particular interest in this shrine.

'Why are you so interested in birds?' she asked, scrunching her cheeks into a smile.

'I have heard that the Incas glided over the jungles,' I said.

'They may have done so,' Patricia said. 'But you don't understand.'

'Understand, what?'

'You are thinking of the flight itself, which is meaningless,' she said. 'And, you're missing the real question.'

I paused, as another wave of tourists hurled themselves into the temple. A moment later they were gone.

'What is the *real* meaning, the *real* question?'

Patricia ran her fingers across the stylised stone wing of the condor.

'Whether the Incas flew or not is irrelevant,' she said. 'Instead, you must ask why they wanted to fly.'

Reflecting on Patricia's words, I recalled that, on a trip to Mexico, I had once come across a *fiesta* in the small Yucatan town of Ticul. The highlight of the festival was a ceremony, called *Volador*. It's said to have been started by the Aztecs. Three men, guised as birds, with papier-maché beaks and feathered robes, leapt off a miniature platform at the top of a towering pole. Each had a cord tied to his ankles, which had been wound around the pole. As the men vaulted from the platform, they swung round and round, unwinding as they flew.

A Mexican friend told me that *Volador* represented freedom, and the devotion of man to God. For years I had puzzled over this. But it helped me to understand why the Incas might have wanted to fly. It wasn't about getting from A to B. It was about something far more fundamental, far more spectacular.

The Incas could have had no need to use flight as a means of transport. Such a thing would surely have trivialised what they considered to be a sacred medium. Yet they must have had good reason for yearning to glide, to soar free in the air. Perhaps, like the condor, the Incan Birdmen were messengers to the Gods.

*

Two hours later I was perched up on the summit of Huayna Picchu, the sugar loaf peak which overlooks the ancient city. The climb is strenuous, especially when you have a bout of the runs. Crawling on my hands and knees up the sheer faces of stone, I began to wish that I'd stayed with Patricia. I had left her in the café down below, with a plate of roasted guinea pig.

Staring out across the valley, down to the Urubamba River, was invigorating beyond words. The light was now a syrupy yellow, bright yet not harsh. A chill wind ripped through my hair, whistling between the crags. I yelled at the top of my voice. But no one heard me. Then, like a cat stuck in a tree, I peeped down at the ruins. The lack of safety devices was unnerving, but at the same time exhilarating. One slip of the heel and Huayna Picchu would have embraced another victim.

The rush of the wind was telling me to thrust away from the rock and jump.

'You will fly! You will fly!' it called.

'But I have no wings. It'll be suicide.'

'Make a canopy,' urged the wind. 'With a sail streaming above you, you'll glide down to Earth.'

I closed my eyes and sensed the current of air on my face. Then I breathed in deeply.

'Trust me, and I will protect you ... I will hold you as you fly.'

I opened my eyes a crack, and began to understand the significance of Machu Picchu. Stretching out in symmetrical flanks, on east and west, the ruins were arranged as wings. Once I saw them, I couldn't get them out of my mind. They gleamed up at me, glinting in the yellow light.

Machu Picchu was laid out in the shape of a condor.

I would have slithered my way back down to the café much sooner. But a refined-looking Peruvian man was watching me.

'It's a condor!' I shouted. 'Machu Picchu's a gigantic condor!'

The man was dressed in a sheepskin jacket, with the flaps of a woollen hat pulled down snugly over his ears. His nose was streaming, and his cheeks were scarlet. In his hands was a tin, and in it were coca leaves.

'The condor is the messenger,' he said in English, offering me some of the leaves.

'Whose messenger?'

Resting the tin on his knee, the man washed his hands over his face.

'The condor links us to heaven,' he said. 'Just as it did the Incas. It is the bridge, the bridge between man and God.'

'Could the Incas glide like condors?'

The man twisted the corners of his mouth into a smile.

'We can all fly,' he said.

'*All* of us?'

The man nodded.

'*Sí*, all of us.'

He paused, to regard me sideways on.

'*Todos tenemos alas*, we all have wings,' he said, 'but we have forgotten how to use them.'

4

Cusco

Long ago, when the Incan empire was no more than a twinkle in the Creator's eye, the land was dim and untamed. Manco Capac, the son of the sun, and Mama Ocllo, the moon's daughter, set off to dispel the darkness. Emerging from the still waters of Lake Titicaca, the couple roamed the Andean wilderness in search of a place in which to construct a great capital. When they arrived where Cusco now stands, Manco Capac thrust his staff into the soil to test its fertility. The rod sank deep, verifying the land's richness. So he told Mama Ocllo to bury a magic pip in the earth. From that seed, Cusco grew ...

Some say the city was built in the shape of a puma, others that it was designed to match the harmony of the Milky Way. As with Machu Picchu, we may never know the real secrets of its past. The Conquistadors reported to Madrid that they had set eyes on the most magnificent treasure in the New World. They were not speaking of the fine buildings, but of the gold which lay within them.

Every ounce of that intoxicating metal was turned into ingots for the voyage back to Spain. Sacrificial urns, idols and plates, crowns, exquisite brooches, buckles, and *tumi*, sacrificial daggers, were melted down and shipped away. Ironically, Peru has once again become the centre of a world gold rush. Multinationals have flooded in, hiring local labourers for a pittance, in the dangerous business of extracting the ore. Hundreds of mines have sprouted up across the Peruvian Andes. But little has changed in the five hundred years since the first Conquistadors arrived in search of El Dorado. The gold mines are still being worked by *garimpeiros*, local miners, for foreign masters, their precious bounty being shipped abroad as before.

Recently scholars have begun to realise that, while popular with the Incas, gold was never given pride of place. The Incas regarded textiles as far more important. When they first arrived in Peru, the Spanish were presented by the Incas with spans of lavish llama-fibre cloth. Considering the gesture to be nothing short of raillery, the Spaniards began a full-scale invasion, fuelled by insatiable greed.

After carving their way across Peru, the Conquistadors found themselves face to face with the Inca, Atahualpa. Covered by sheets of gold, and robed in blue livery, he was borne forward on a litter carried by eighty men. The young Emperor's head was weighted down by a golden crown; a collar of enormous emeralds choked his neck; his face was shrouded by a long fringe of wool, his ears hidden by disks of virgin gold.

Atahualpa was wrenched from the litter and thrown into a cell, and the slaughter went on. Like his people, he couldn't understand the conquerors' fixation. The Incas assumed the Spanish either ate gold or used it in some bizarre medicinal preparation. According to the popular tale, Atahualpa marked a line high on his cell's wall, offering to fill the room to that mark with gold in exchange for his freedom. The chamber, eighty-eight cubic meters in size, would be filled once with gold, and twice with silver.

The entire empire was mobilised to ferry llama-loads of gold from all corners of the realm. While his people sacrificed their assets to free their sovereign, Atahualpa remained locked up. The prison guards were said to be amazed by the richness of his costume, which included macaw-feathered robes, and an unusual bat-hair cape.

At last almost six thousand kilos of gold and twice that of silver were accumulated and handed over. The Inca braced himself for freedom, but the Spanish general, Francisco Pizzaro, had other ideas. Perhaps sensing an Incan uprising, Pizzaro accused Atahualpa of treason, the penalty of which was to be burned at the stake. The sentence was later changed to strangulation. When he was garrotted outside his prison cell in Cajamarca, many of the Inca's wives and sisters were said to have hanged themselves so as to accompany his spirit into the afterlife.

*

Plaza de Armas, Cusco's central square, was once the point at which over twenty-five thousand miles of Incan roads converged. Before the arrival of the Conquistadors, it was known as *Tahuantinsuyu*, The

Four Quarters of the Earth, and was laid with soil from the distant reaches of the empire. It has borne witness to battles, executions, mutinies and plagues, to great banquets, coronations and sacrificial rites. These days, virtually every central plaza in Peru is known as Plaza de Armas, in honour of those who died in the 1879 war with Chile.

From the moment I set eyes on that great square, something stirred inside me. Along with the incessant stream of travellers, I realised at once that Cusco was different. Like them, I stopped dead in my tracks, put a hand to my mouth, and held my breath. It was as if I had been let into an extraordinary secret.

Long shadows of the winter afternoon veiled the maze of terracotta-roofs. Cobbled passageways with sheer stone sides led off to the east and the west. Arched doorways hinted at the courtyards which lay behind. Whitewashed walls trimmed in bougainvillaea dazzled me as I explored the back-streets of what must be the most enchanting city on the Latin continent.

At almost eleven thousand feet, the vanilla-scented air was frosty with cold. A gang of street-vendors bustled forward, wrapped up in their winter woollies, tilted bowlers pulled down tight. Every Cusqueñian seemed to be clutching a shallow basket of goods; hand-woven Alpaca gloves, ponchos and raspy woollen socks; *quenas*, pan-pipes, under-ripe lemons, jars of honey and Inca brand cigarettes. For every tray of merchandise there were ten newly-arrived tourists with a little money to spend.

Cusco is a city of bargains. The South American equivalent of Kathmandu, it's saturated with impoverished adventurers who refuse to leave. Like me, they know that such precious destinations are hard to come by. Stroll down narrow alleys off the main square, and you find rows of shops, selling the effects of the desperate. Half-empty bottles of pink Pepto Bismol, goose-down sleeping bags, waterproof matches, limp loo paper and tubs of Nivea sun-cream.

It was at the back of one such shop, which doubled as a café, beneath a rousing portrait of Ché Guevara, that I met Sven.

He watched me carefully as I poked about in a display barrel of pawned accessories. I examined the blade of an Opinel pocket-knife, checked the sell-by-date on a slab of Kendal mint cake, flicked through a dog-eared, damaged copy of *West with the Night*.

'Do you play chess?' he asked with a lisp.

'Badly.'

Before I could stop him, the hunched figure had pulled a board and pieces from his grubby satchel and laid them out. Male pattern baldness had robbed his head of hair, except for a long tuft at the front. His complexion was fair, his eyes an imperial blue, and his forehead was severed by lines. A much-darned grey pullover rolled up to his chin like an orthopaedic neck-brace.

He thrust out a square hand.

'Sven,' he said, 'from Bratislava.'

I took a seat in the window alcove, adjacent.

'What shall we play for?' he asked.

'I have no chance of winning, I'm hopeless at chess.'

He pulled a yellow Sony Walkman from his satchel and placed it beside the board.

'You can have it if you win,' he said.

My eyes widened with greed.

'What happens if I lose?'

Sven stretched over and tugged at my scarf.

'Wool?'

'*Alpaca*,' I replied.

The game lasted six moves. As my king fell on his sword, the Slovak reached over, unwound my scarf, and twirled it around his own neck.

'It's quite nice,' he said.

'I should hope so, it was a birthday present from my mother.

Sven swept back the tuft of liquorice hair.

'I have the advantage,' he said softly. 'I assume you've never been banged up in a Slovak prison.'

The chess-player wouldn't say why he had done seven years in a high-security jail. But he did reveal, over a cup of *coca de maté*, that his friends called him Walkman. He was walking around the world in the name of peace and poetry.

'The countries which pass beneath my feet,' he mumbled, staring out the window. 'They are the future. Forget Europe, it's finished.'

'Which is your favourite place?'

The Slovak bent down to loosen his bootlaces.

'How can a father choose between his children?' he asked. 'Macedonia was rough like the surface of the moon; Jordan was tender as a baby's cry; Egypt smelled of jasmine, and the Sudan ...' Sven paused to sip his maté. 'The Sudan,' he said, 'was silent as a prophet's grave.'

*

Round the corner from the pawn-shop, Señor Pedro Valentine was holding up a pair of my underpants, stretched out between his arthritic thumbs. Indicating the superior quality of the cloth, to a shop full of female customers, he pouted like a Milanese gigolo.

'That's the finest cotton I've seen in thirty years of laundering,' he said. 'I bet they hold your *merchandise* just right.'

Half a dozen crones cackled. I confirmed that the underpants had served me well, especially during the hazardous days on the Inca Trail.

Once the elderly women had left, Señor Valentine made me a business proposition. He said that if, on my return, I exported him a container of English underpants he'd sell them in Cusco. He could muster a sales force of schoolboys. We'd be sure to make a fortune. The men of Cusco, he said, were sick to the back teeth of abrasive local underwear.

Señor Valentine handed me a stack of laundered clothes. Then he picked out a pair of barberry-red knickers and pressed them to his nostrils as if they were a rose.

'*Huele*, have a sniff,' he said conspiratorially, 'a German girl just brought them in, she was *muy bonito, very* pretty.'

The old launderer jiggled his hands over his chest suggesting large cleavage.

'My wife shouts at me,' he said, 'she asks why we don't have a tourist shop like everyone else. She may be angry, but every man in Cusco is jealous of Pedro Valentine. After all,' he continued, 'who else can sniff the fragrance of fresh knickers all day long?'

*

Night falls fast in the Andes, and with it comes bitter cold. A boy of five or six waylaid me as I ascended the cobblestone slope towards my hotel, in Plaza Nazarene. His nose was running, his hair matted with dirt, and his cheeks the colour of oxblood; their capillaries ruptured by the daily cycle of fire and frost. He tugged at my trouser-leg, bringing me to a halt. Breaking into a tap-dance, he displayed a box of battered postcards. As I scanned them one by one, the boy advertised the extra-low price, one *sol* for ten. Cusco's tourist shops peddle a fine selection of cards, all of them promoting the beauties of Peru. But the young salesman's were from a different stock.

The cards portrayed a lesser-known side of the nation. The first six showed an assortment of hideous mummified bodies. The next was of an Andean medicinal stall, replete with llama-foetuses; then there were a series of ferocious-looking men in ponchos, balancing guinea pigs on their heads. But it was the last card which gripped me. It was a highlight from a textile. I looked at the image closely. It showed a crazed sub-human figure, with a leering expression, claws, crude wings, and a string of decapitated heads running down its back. The picture resembled the one Deiches had shown me. Its caption read *Alado Hombre del Paracas*: the Birdman of Paracas.

I slipped the child a handful of coins and put the cards in my jacket pocket. This last might be the clue I'd been waiting for, for the trail to the Birdmen was growing cold. But for now it was time to rest.

*

Sven had had a productive morning. Piled high on an empty café chair were an assortment of his winnings. A bottle of Jack Daniel's, a green mohair sweater, six paperbacks, two Frisbees, a canvas rucksack, and a cluster of juggling balls. His expensive Walkman was positioned prominently beside the chessboard – like an unobtainable prize at a fairground stall.

'What about a cup of coffee for a poor Slovak?'

Sven had made an art form out of attracting charity. He considered himself to be above using money. The Queen, the Pope and he had one thing in common – none of them carried cash.

I pulled out the postcards I had bought the night before.

'Wonderful,' he said, 'mummies and dried llama foetuses.'

'What about this one?' I pointed to the Birdman.

'*Alado Hombre del Paracas*,' he read, rubbing the tip of his nose with a bishop. 'Mummified bodies are one thing,' he replied, 'but never make light of the winged-men.'

'Who are they?'

The Slovak glanced through me with his gaze.

'Look at that picture,' he said. 'What do you see?'

I studied the image: 'A wild creature, half-man, half-bird, adorned with severed heads.'

'Is that *really* what you see?' asked the Slovak. 'Look again. Look beyond the obvious.'

Again, I scrutinised the figure, taking in its wide psychotic eyes, its spewing tongue, the individual stitches of embroidery.

'They flew,' I said under my breath. 'I'm sure of it . . .'

Sven splayed his fingers on the table like the legs of a starfish.

'They glided, they soared,' he said, 'like flying squirrels.'

'Were the Incas the first to make a gliding wing?'

'We have a saying in Bratislava,' he said: 'The wings of an eagle are the arms of a man.' The Slovak twisted his fingers faster and faster until they blurred. 'If you believe they flew, then they did.'

At that moment a tall, spindly woman entered the café. A mane of jet-black hair peaked into a crest above her forehead, before cascading down her back. Silver hoops dangled from her ears, reflecting the light as she walked.

As soon as Sven spotted her, he covered his face with his hand and let out a groan.

'Who's she?'

'It's Ariadne,' he said.

On his journey through Eastern Europe, across Africa and the New World, the Walkman had encountered all kinds of obstacles. In Cairo he had been accused of dousing a shopkeeper with petrol and setting him alight. Outside Maputo, in Mozambique, he'd been attacked by a pack of wild dogs and in the back-streets of Santiago he had been accosted by a glue-sniffer with a razorblade. Yet, no scourge, it seemed, had been as great as Ariadne.

'God knows why she fell for me,' he said as she sidled over. 'She's followed me for close to a thousand miles. I don't know how to get rid of her.'

Without a word, Ariadne put her coffee cup on the table and pressed her hand into mine. She must have been in her early forties, about Sven's age. The dark rings which circled her eyes suggested insomnia. Her long fingernails dug into my wrist.

'Enchanté,' she said in a Parisian voice. 'Sven didn't tell me he had a friend.'

'We played chess,' I said, faltering.

Ariadne scrunched up her eyes to focus on the postcard. Then she ran her tongue precisely across her upper lip, as if licking an envelope.

'The mystery of the Winged Ones . . .' she said.

'Do you know about them?'

Ariadne's face twitched, implying that she did.

'That fabric is from the necropolis at Paracas,' she said. 'For two thousand years it covered the dead.'

'A dead Birdman?'

'Perhaps.'

Draping her shale-black sheepskin coat over a chair, Ariadne lit a clove cigarette. Sven nudged the ashtray over. Soon the café was thick with pungent smoke.

'I'm looking for traces of the Birdmen,' I said.

Ariadne inhaled deeply.

'Have you been to Taquile?'

'Where's that?'

'The sacred island in Lake Titicaca.'

Again, she inhaled, holding the smoke in her lungs until her eyes watered with unease. 'They say the cloth which is woven there can fly.'

5

A Sacrifice

Clutching to folklore and fragments of fact, I made for Cusco's railway station and I clambered aboard the train bound for Puno, on the western edge of Lake Titicaca. With my bags stowed on the luggage rack, I took my seat in Inca Class carriage, and stared out at the platform.

A young Quechuan woman was crouched in the shade, a scarlet blanket spread before her like a toreador's cape. Spread upon it was a pile of dried coca leaves. She adjusted the torn brow of her hat, stroked a hand across her cheek, and waited. All around the island of her shawl, feet were criss-crossing: porters' dusty lace-ups, backpackers' thongs, an official's brogues, a contingent of matching Japanese Reeboks. With an abrupt jolt the train was alive. It came again, jerking me forward and back, as the wheels gnawed into the tracks.

We rolled through the shanty-towns at walking pace. A line of women were selling guinea-pigs, carrots and fruit; their husbands gambling at cards, their children running slipshod through the dirt, like lambs before the dogs. A barber was clipping at a *mestizo's* proud moustache; beside him, a tarot reader was deciding someone's future. An army of peddlers offered pink plastic combs, dusters and brooms. A pair of fighting cocks lurched at each other in the dust, and a class of school children stood to attention, singing.

Soon we had left Cusco behind. The train pushed its way southeast through the green Vilcanota valley, before climbing steeply towards the 14,000 foot La Raya Pass. The air and vegetation were thin and getting thinner.

In the Inca Class carriage a general state of pandemonium prevailed. The guard was trying to revive an old lady who had passed out. A waitress, wearing an ultra-short mini-skirt, was doing her best to deflect the advances of a rowdy Italian. The little girl sitting opposite me spewed her half-digested lunch onto the table between us. Before her mother had a chance to wipe it up, the girl's younger brother drew a face in the mess. A group of kids pelted the carriage with stones. I buried my face in a guidebook and prayed for Puno to arrive.

As pebbles continued to ricochet off the windows like hailstones, I felt a tap on my shoulder. I looked up. A figure in a black Afghan coat was looming over me.

It was Ariadne.

'Going to Puno?'

I grunted.

Ariadne thrust her duffle bag onto the rack.

'Then we shall be companions,' she said.

Six hours later I had heard every event of Ariadne's life. She had overlooked no detail. Right from the start, hers had been a troubled tale. Her father had abused her, and her mother had pushed her pram down a flight of stairs for no apparent reason. As a teenager she'd taken up with the drummer of an underground rock group called *Retch!*, before joining an order of Scottish Rosicrucians. For the last five years she had roamed the world, in search of herself, and in search of a suitable man to father her children.

Unable to bear another word of autobiography, I asked her about the Winged Ones and about the flying textiles of Taquile island. Ariadne pulled a stick of raven-coloured mascara from her purse and applied an even coat to her long lashes.

'Be patient and you will discover the answers you are seeking,' she said.

*

As the Inca Class carriage jarred its way across the *Altiplano* – the high Andean plateau – where only the hardiest men and beasts survive, I watched the sun dip down behind a copse of polylepis trees. We had stopped a dozen times at inconsequential stations. At each, a crowd had been waiting with their goods. All sorts of dishes were held up to the windows – roast mutton served in a twist of newspaper, stuffed peppers, *charqui* (beef stew), llama jerky, soft cheeses, and thick fermented *chicha*. Each village had its own speciality. Some sold alpaca gloves, statuettes of Santa Rosa, *quenas* or llama-hide drums.

Just north of Juliaca, at Pucara, thirty women leapt from the sidings. They were selling unglazed ceramic bulls painted with symbols – a sign of virility and fortitude, brought to the Americas by the Spanish.

As the train pulled into Puno, a great commotion began. Wild dogs charged headlong at the iron wheels, howling like demons. Old *mestizos* clapped their hands; their womenfolk whistling through broken teeth. Their sons hurled stones. In any other city, or any other country, the train's arrival might not have excited the raising of a single eyebrow. But, for some inexplicable reason, the locomotive's entrance into Puno was an event to be celebrated.

On the platform six llamas, adorned with ponchos and rich brocades, had been positioned as a grand guard of honour. Managers from a hundred small hotels mobbed the mass of backpackers, duelling for their custom. Muttering that his name was Ricardo, a fawning hunchbacked man pulled my luggage onto his shoulders, and led me away. I had no idea who he was, or what his hotel was like. I didn't even know if he had a hotel. I was sure of the one certainty – that back in Cusco, Sven would be toasting his success in ridding himself of Ariadne.

Puno melts into the oatmeal horseshoe of hills like a North African town. Its square-shaped buildings, pocked with dents from stone-throwing boys, couldn't have changed much since a Spanish count settled it as an outpost more than three centuries ago. Glinting before it, like a step-cut sapphire, hushed and brooding, lies Titicaca. The massive body of iridescent water keeps its secrets safe. One tale says that the Incas tossed an immense gold chain – weighing two thousand kilos – into the waves, to prevent the Spanish from taking it. Another legend says that only he who has seen his likeness reflected in the waters will know true happiness.

I hurried down to the Titicaca's edge and peered over the side of the long jetty. A swathe of parrot-green algae masked my reflection. Nearby, an armada of leaking boats bobbed about on the water, ready to take tourists to the islands. A short distance off, a traditional canoe made from *totora*, a kind of reed, was heading shore-ward. The craft, a scaled-down version of Heyerdahl's *Kon-Tiki*, was being punted through the algae by a boatman.

I had spent the night at Ricardo's house, which doubled as a 'tourist dormitory'. It had just one bed. When no one was staying at his home,

Ricardo slept in the bed. Even though I agreed to pay the going rate, I felt bad about turfing the old man out. The floor was better for his back, he said, blowing his nose on his hand.

Ariadne, who'd shunned the lodgings, had gone off to find a youth hostel. She suggested I was mad to stay in a place lacking a mattress, blankets, running water and heat. The absence of such luxuries certainly did lead to a cold and unpleasant night. But I was more than happy to endure a little discomfort, for it warded Ariadne away.

*

To the right of the jetty, beside a vibrant orange boathouse, stood a great example of brutish Victorian achievement. Her name was *Yavari*, and she was the oldest ship afloat on Lake Titicaca. Restored in her original livery of green, black and white, she was cushioned in algae. I climbed her narrow gangplank and learned of her remarkable voyage.

Yavari was built in 1862 in Birmingham by the James Watt shipyard. Together with her sister ship, *Yapura* (now used as a hospital launch by the Peruvian Navy), she was packed into crates in pieces and sent to South America. Once the 1,383 pieces had got as far as the Peruvian coast, they were strapped to mules and lugged over the western Andes. Each mule could carry no more than four hundred pounds; and *Yavari* weighed two hundred tons. Not surprisingly, the journey took more than six years.

Unperturbed by the lack of available coal in the Andes, Watt had designed a steam engine which would run on llama dung. The iron-hulled queen of Titicaca plied the lake's dark waters for a century. The only drawback was the enormous quantity of llama excrement needed to power the vessel at such an altitude. Every time she docked, the entire crew had to scurry out to the fields with baskets to scoop up handfuls of llama dung.

On my return, Ricardo asked if I'd seen my reflection in the lake. When I replied that I had not, he stretched an arm above his head, and poked about in the rafters. The sound of bottle being pulled through a nest of rats followed. A moment later he was blowing the dust from a demijohn. Wrenching out the cork with his teeth, he poured a few drops of the *chicha* over the stone threshold of the house.

'*Para los espiritus*, for the spirits,' he said.

I told Ricardo that my fortune had been read by a tarot-reader in Cusco.

'*Una bruja*, a witch, no doubt,' he declared, rubbing his eyes with his thumbs.

'She said that good luck would follow me like the sun.'

Ricardo pulled up a stool and sat. His head tilted towards me, a result of his crooked spine.

'You have no idea,' he said contritely. 'This is a very unlucky place indeed. There are bad spirits in my home.'

Ricardo nudged at the sitting-room.

'Why do you think I have so many amulets?' he said.

Now that he mentioned it, there were a great deal of good luck charms, even by Peruvian standards. The windowsill and man-telpiece, the bookshelf, door-frame, and a dozen niches around the room, were cluttered with the trinkets.

'As a young man I was athletic,' he said. 'Local girls fought over me, and my friends called me *el suertudo*, the lucky one.'

Holding the demijohn to his lips, Ricardo took a swig.

'I was married to the most beautiful woman in Puno,' he said. 'Her eyes shone like black diamonds, her skin was tinted like the dawn. We moved into this house, had a pair of sons, good health, and all the luck in the world.'

Ricardo swigged at the bottle a second time. He craned his neck up to look me in the eye. He swigged again.

'What went wrong?' I asked.

'The fortune drained away,' said the hunchback. 'Like water swir-ling from a bath. My wife drowned in the lake, then my boys gave in to fever. Then this!'

Ricardo thumped his back with his fist.

'All of us cursed ... cursed by the spirits hidden in these walls.'

'Why don't you pack up and leave?'

Again, Ricardo swigged at *chicha*.

'Hah!' he roared. 'The spirits ... they would hunt me down, just as they hunt any man who steps across the threshold. No one can ever escape them!'

I'm not naturally superstitious, but the prospect of being pursued by my host's spirits was unsavoury. Given the circumstances, I wondered why he invited strangers to stay.

Ricardo crossed the room and foraged in a niche beside the wardrobe. He removed a hand-sized ceramic figurine: it was of a short man, his mouth open with laughter, his colourful costume dangling with belongings.

'Ekeko,' he said, passing it to me. 'The god of fortune.'

I had read about Ekeko. Long ago he had been an Ayamara deity, carved from stone, celebrated for bringing good harvests. With the colonial influence, he became white-skinned and moustachioed, and was eventually made from clay. Ekeko must never be sold. But when he's given by one to another, the receiver is blessed with immeasurable fortune.

Ricardo drained the demijohn of *chicha*, and burped.

'*Amigo*,' he said gently, 'you seem like a good man. You have kind eyes.'

I began to thank him, but he raised a finger to stop me.

'Take this Ekeko,' he said. 'Keep him warm and dry, and,' Ricardo paused to burp again, '... and he'll bring you more happiness than you have ever known.'

*

Next morning, after a second night in Ricardo's bed, I plucked the bare necessities from my bags and headed down to the jetty. The time had come to search for the flying textiles of Taquile. I strolled through the market en route to the lake.

A little girl was hopping between the crates of guinea pigs; her younger sister dancing after on tiptoes. The rows of Ayamara women were preening their stalls, dusting off the merchandise. Chinese-made Barbie dolls and chewing-gum from Vietnam, cakes of prune-coloured laundry soap and caps for toy guns, make-up mirrors, light-bulbs, batteries and chain. But the pride of place on every groundsheet stall was reserved for fuchsia-coloured fizzy drinks. Peruvians old and young have a great fondness for *gaseouse*, drinks with so much synthetic dye and carbonation that one sip and your mouth goes numb. I later heard of a street-side dentist who used the beverage as a local anaesthetic when he was pulling out teeth.

On the jetty I made out the familiar outline of Ariadne. She was standing against the railing in her trademark Afghan sheepskin coat. I smiled, but secretly I wished she would leave me alone. She handed me a turquoise slip of paper, and pointed to a clinker-built launch.

The craft was low in the water, skulking down like an Alsatian on all fours. Its captain had taken the cowling away from the engine and was huddled at the stern. First he threatened the delicate machinery with a claw hammer, then struck it six times. The blows were accompanied by a string of Quechua swear-words. Miraculously, the engine was running three minutes later, urging us into the cloisonné-blue waters of Titicaca.

As we pushed away from the shore, towards the centre of the lake, I threw back my head. Cumulus clouds hung above us like floating islands. Huddling in the bow of the boat, a family from Taquile were getting a free ride home. The father was holding a baby llama to his chest furled in a blanket.

Ariadne lit a clove cigarette, pushed her sunglasses onto her head, and foraged in a buckram holdall by her feet.

'I went shopping,' she said, through the corner of her mouth.

'Souvenirs?'

She squinted until her eyes disappeared.

'Love potions,' she sniffed, pulling out a tatty plastic bag. It contained an indistinct object, wrapped in bandages like an Egyptian mummy. As Ariadne held the object between her knees, unwinding the cloth, I caught a whiff of what smelled like rotting meat. It reminded me of a Pakistani morgue in which I had once had breakfast. I gagged into the collar of my shirt.

It was a dried llama foetus. Ariadne cupped the trophy in her hands, bent her head down, and touched her lips to it in a kiss.

'Isn't she beautiful?' she asked.

The father from Taquile looked over, and clutched his llama foal closer.

'What's it for?'

'An aphrodisiac, of course.'

'How do you prepare it?'

The Frenchwoman turned to give me a poisoned stare.

'Are you knowing anything?' she said. 'You make *un potage*, a soup.'

I wondered silently why humans feel it necessary to do such strange things with their time. All over the world people are at it: eating fish intestines, mealy grubs and monkey brains, dissecting tarantulas and breeding worms, bungee-jumping, bear-baiting and extracting healthy, unborn llamas from unsuspecting wombs.

I explained to Ariadne that, to most of us, the very idea of swilling down a dried llama bisque was deplorable.

She wrapped up her aphrodisiac, ensuring the legs weren't poking out.

'What's wrong with eating foetus?' she said.

I squirmed.

'Surely you have heard of Shenzhen?'

'Shen...?'

'In China,' she said, puffing at her cigarette, 'across from Hong Kong.'

The family from Taquile and I exchanged a troubled glance.

'Soup made from aborted foetuses ... it's an ancient remedy.'

I squirmed again.

'It's delicious,' said Ariadne.

'You've tried it ... you've actually drunk foetus soup?'

'Oh, so many times,' she said whimsically, 'when I lived in Hong Kong. It's good for the liver and the kidneys,' she said, tucking the dried llama foetus back in her bag. 'And of course,' she added, 'there's nothing like it for a hangover.'

*

The villagers of Taquile cluster around when they spot a launch arriving. Few tourists journey out to their island. Those that do are offered reed toys and whistles, alpaca tooth charms, and gaudy blankets embroidered with local scenes. Some locals invite the travellers to watch traditional dances, to go fishing, or to stay in their homes. Keeping change at bay, Taquile has resisted the temptation of building hotels or proper restaurants.

Once he had stepped ashore, I asked the man with the llama foal if he knew of any weavers. At first he was wary, something to do with Ariadne's fixation for dried foetuses, no doubt. I lied, saying she was a vet, with an interest in medical specimens. Then I explained my own interest – Taquile's textiles.

The man passed the foal to his wife. I looked at his face closely, taking in the ridge of his nose, his chapped lips and the trace of whiskers at the corners of his mouth.

'Are you a believer?' he asked, cryptically.

I nodded.

'Then you can come with me,' he said. 'Hector, my grandfather, will be waiting.'

We tramped a mile or two inland, breaching low stone walls and jumping ditches, cutting a path across the burnt sienna farmland. Before I knew it, we had almost crossed the island, which only measures four kilometres by two.

A few tourists might have found Taquile, but very little has changed there in the last three hundred years. The island is still divided into six agricultural sections, called *suyos*; each of which has been administered by the same family for centuries. The crops grown on Taquile would have been familiar to the Incas – a long potato called *oca*, broad beans, maize, wheat and *quinua*, a staple grain rich in protein.

The Spanish treated the island as a great *hacienda*, where guests could feast on the lake's inimitable supply of trout. In the years after Peru's independence in 1821, Taquile served as a penal colony. Now that they are again left to their own devices, the islanders spend their time tilling the dusty fields, weaving, and preparing for the calendar of festivals.

In the shadow of a doorway, propped up against a low wall, or sitting on a clump of rocks, every man and woman is busy making cloth, or precious fragments of regalia. Most of the islanders have three or four separate costumes – for working, festivities, weddings and daily life. Cloth is a sacred material on Taquile, as it was to the Incas, and the civilisations which preceded them. The colours are blazing: reds and scarlets, peacock greens and brilliant blues.

As I took in the array of women's attire, flowing skirts dyed with cochineal, and jet-black shawls, I was struck by the similarity with the Kalash tribal dress of Northern Pakistan. The costumes of Taquile and of the Kalash – former inhabitants of Nuristan – were both born of a fierce rugged landscape.

Hector was sitting on a rounded step outside his ancestral home. From the condition of his fine clothing I could tell that he was a man of status. His white muslin shirt, black trousers and two-tone waistcoat were impeccably kept. But then, the sleeves of the shirt were neatly rolled up, exposing his dark, muscular forearms. Around his abundant waist was tied a *chumpi*, a woven belt, not unlike a Japanese *obi*. On Taquile Island belts have been important for centuries, embroidered with information about the agricultural and social calendar for the year to come. And on his head, Hector wore a tomato-red *pinta-chullo* hat, its point flopped down like a jester's crown, the sign of a married man.

Spread before him was a *wak'a* loom, upon it a half-finished poncho. The old man stood up when he heard us approaching. He kicked on his rubber-tyre sandals, wiped his nose with the side of his hand, and ducked his head low in respect.

'*Que camine con fuerza y derecho todo su vida* – may you walk tall and be strong your whole life,' he said, pressing his hand into mine. 'You must sit on my right.'

As I thanked him, I studied Hector's face. It was a sea of elephant skin, wrinkled and heavy, with a crag of a nose running down the centre like an outcrop of granite. His lips were plum-red, his cheeks scattered with grey stubble. Both eyes were frosted with cataracts. Hector was blind.

Ariadne stepped up to be introduced. The old man drew the lids across his opaque eyes, and held his breath. His expression seemed to sour.

'This is an acquaintance from France,' I said.

'*Mal de ojo*,' whispered the ancient. 'Please tell her to leave us. She has *mal de ojo*, the Evil Eye.'

Ariadne began to laugh.

'He can't even see me,' she said. 'Poor old man!'

Hector's grandson stepped in.

'Grandfather, she has come from so far.'

The old man stared at Ariadne, his blind gaze unflinching.

'Her eyes are dangerous,' he said.

Unable to take the humiliation, Ariadne grabbed her holdall, and set off towards the dock. I didn't try to stop her. But as I watched her stomp back through the fields, I reflected on Hector's comment. The Evil Eye was brought to the New World by the Spanish, who had adopted the custom from the Arabs centuries before. In an ultra-superstitious society like Peru, it fits in very well. Across much of the Latin continent, I've seen people warding it away. No one remembers that like smallpox, influenza or measles, it's not native to the continent. As in any North African village or Middle Eastern town, Peruvian children are given amulets to protect them. Everyone is on the lookout for misfortune, ill-health – the signs that *mal de ojo* is watching them.

Hector told his grandson to put away the weaving.

'Now the sun has passed the highest point,' he said, 'we must not work, but drink.'

A bottle of *chicha* was brought out by Hector's daughter, a woman with a soft, innocent face.

'Respected Señor,' I said, as Hector downed his third glass of the cloudy liquid. 'I have come to your island, drawn by my fascination for *los textilos antiguos*.'

The old man put down his glass and sniffed the air.

'The ancient textiles ... *all* handmade textiles, have strength,' he said.

Hector leaned back, slapped my knee with his hand, and urged me to drink some *chicha*.

'This will make you strong,' he said. 'Strong like the condor.'

I declined the offer.

'Now, we make the fabric for the wrong reasons,' he mumbled. 'These ponchos which we weave are made to be sold.' Hector paused to sip his glass. 'To be sold to people like you,' he said. 'But when I was a child we understood that this cloth was sacred. We used to sacrifice it to the spirits.'

'Did you burn it ... like the Incas did?'

'Yes, yes! We would light a sacred fire,' said the old man, 'and throw upon it our most valued work.'

The Spanish invaders documented well how the Inca himself would wear new robes each day. The previous day's costume would be committed to the flames. I gave thought to the Incas and their ancestors, for whom cloth was a cornerstone of culture. The link between ancient flight and textiles was as unlikely a link as I could imagine. But then, in my travels, I have found that the true answer often lies behind the most improbable door.

Hector tugged at my arm.

'We no longer make such sacrifices,' he said. 'That is why we are so poor.'

'*Estimado Señor*,' I said, 'could I buy a piece of cloth for us to sacrifice?'

The old man's blind eyes seemed to light up for a moment.

'A sacrifice,' he said gently. 'To rid us of *mal de ojo*.'

An hour later Hector was weighing a fine, hand-woven *chumpi*, a traditional belt, in his hands. Made from llama hair, dyed claret-red, and about six inches in width, it was embroidered with vertical stripes. A central band of hexagonal motifs ran down the length of the belt. I had paid one of Hector's neighbours an exorbitant sum for the item, and was beginning to regret the decision to burn it.

'It's a fine one,' remarked Hector, kindling a fire with some dry leaves and a knob of butter. 'The sacrifice will bring us good fortune.'

Once the flames were licking the sticks like serpents' tongues, Hector began to sing. It was a solemn song. His daughter opened the windows of the two-room shack, perhaps so that his words could waft into the home. The neighbour's children watched from a distance as Hector, still singing, laid the *chumpi* on the flames.

Harsh, asphyxiating smoke rose from the fire.

'Breathe it,' said Hector, inhaling.

I took a deep breath, and coughed violently, until I tasted blood at the back of my throat. The colours of the *chumpi* were washed by the flames – golden yellows and aurora reds.

'The textiles from Taquile have special strength,' said Hector. 'They can make a man invisible.'

'What do you mean?'

'Breathe it ... taste what is secret.'

Again I breathed in, filling my chest with the llama hair smoke.

'Once more ... breathe it once more ...'

I was soon reeling, light-headed, my mind floating.

Hector poured a few drops of *chicha* on the flames. More smoke spiralled upward, choking us.

'*Nuestros antepasados podían volar* – our ancestors flew,' he said.

I turned sharply to look at Hector.

'They flew?'

'They used the magic of the textiles to fly.'

'*How?*'

'They wove wings, covered in stork feathers ... then they flew to the gods – they were messengers.'

As we sat in the cloud of llama hair smoke, the *chumpi* still burning ferociously, I tried to make sense of the old man's words. I thought of the Volador ceremony: of men striving to be airborne, to be in the realm of their gods. I thought, too, of the man I'd met at the top of Huayna Picchu. He had also spoken of messengers. Then I thought of William Deiches with his blueprints for a flying carpet, and about the bloodied feather with its triangular notches.

The smoke seemed to be getting denser.

'Did your ancestors run out of their houses and simply flap their wings to fly? Can you tell me about the Birdmen, Señor?'

Hector poured a little more *chicha* onto the fire, before wetting his lips with the bottle's rim. He shook his head from side to side.

'No, no, they never flew here,' he said. 'Isla Taquile is too sacred a place. It was here that mankind was born.'

'Then where did they fly?'

'They journeyed onto the mainland,' he replied.

'At Puno, did they fly at Puno?'

Again, Hector shook his head.

'From the towers, they flew from the towers.'

'Which towers? Where?'

The old man stirred the flames with his cane.

'They flew from the towers at Sillustani,' he said.

6

Tower-Jumpers

Ariadne regarded me with eyes fired by fury on the journey back across Titicaca to Puno. She felt certain that Hector and I had dreamed up a scheme to keep secret knowledge from her. Gathering the bulk of her hair in her wiry hands, she teaselled it through her long ebony nails. I ignored her, hoping that she would latch onto another unsuspecting traveller.

I trawled my hand through the water and thought about the meeting with Hector. What had he meant when he said that the textiles from Taquile could make one invisible? Perhaps flight and invisibility were the same experience to the Inca. The boatman jerked me back to the present. He was docking at the jetty and expected payment.

'Señor Hector is an old fool,' he said as I gave him the fare.

I was taken aback by his remark.

'How do you know that I met Hector?'

The boatman tied the tether to the jetty in a bowline.

'I am from Isla Taquile,' he said, as if answering my question. 'I remember when the Señor was not blind, when he could dance and drink all night.'

He handed me my change.

'His feet no longer dance,' he went on, 'but Hector likes his *chicha*. It makes his tongue wag like a dog's tail.'

To step ashore at Puno once again, was to leave the mysteries of the great lake to another boat load of travellers. I wondered whether I would ever stand on its shores again. A stray nerve nudged me in the spine. Somehow I felt certain that I'd never return to Titicaca. I left the boatman with a common phrase, *'Hasta la vista'*, until we see each other again. As he passed my canvas bag up to me he winked.

'You will not come back,' he said.

Over a dinner of *ceviche de truche*, raw trout marinated in lemon juice, I explained to Ariadne that henceforth I would be travelling alone. I did not say it was because she was driving me mad, just as she had done to Sven. Nor did I tell her that I was heading for Sillustani, or that I had already hired a llamateer.

Picking a bone from her mouth, the Frenchwoman said nothing. Perhaps she was thinking of her turbulent childhood, or of the invented pain which encircled her life. When she had finished eating, she removed something from her oversized handbag and placed it on the table. I recognised the tatty plastic wrapping.

'I wish you luck to find the Winged Ones,' she said tenderly. 'I'm sure that you will.'

I thanked her. It was an awkward moment.

'You will need strength,' she said. 'Make a broth with this and drink it at dawn.'

As Ariadne slid over the dried llama foetus, I felt a jab of pity in my ribs. What a tragedy, I thought, that such a proud person should believe in such nonsense.

*

Manuel arrived, as planned, before the first rays of almond light had broken the horizon injecting life into the *Altiplano*. His shadowy face was locked in a frown, even when he was laughing. He owned three llamas. They seemed uninterested in the twenty-mile walk north-west to Sillustani. Woken early by their master, they were ready to start grazing. Whipping the largest of the beasts with the back of his hand Manuel demonstrated their sturdiness.

'They're strong as oxen,' he said, smirking.

'How long to the towers of Sillustani?'

The llamateer cleared his throat and spat at the dust.

'Four hours,' he said, 'perhaps less.'

Taking the reigns of Julia, the smaller female, I walked at the rear.

I had left the dried llama foetus with Ricardo, as an extra amulet to bring good fortune to his home. He had put it on the mantelpiece, beside a figurine of Christ.

Most visitors to Sillustani take a taxi or tourist bus. I wanted to slow the pace, to deviate from the beaten track. I had much to think about along the way. Rather than arriving at any solid answers, my journey so far had been a string of irresolvable questions. Stumbling along with llamas would, I hoped, put me in the right frame of mind to notice a breakthrough when it came.

A fog of llama dung smoke hung over Puno. We were soon out of the town, climbing up the escarpment. Higher and higher, above the silent waters of Lake Titicaca, onto the *Altiplano* itself. Pancake flat and the colour of Brazil nuts, it extended forever like East Africa's Great Rift. The first blend of clouds was stirring, brewed afresh in the limitless sky. Llamas were grazing in small groups, their petulant faces searching for food. Thesiger would have been proud of me, I thought, for making the most of animal transport.

Manuel tugged at the male's reins. Despite his pretence of machismo he was a kind-hearted man. He told me that his grandfather or great-grandfather, he wasn't sure which, had worked for Hiram Bingham. He'd been a muleteer in the 1911 season when Machu Picchu was rediscovered.

'Señor Bingham was a good man,' explained Manuel, as we trudged along. 'He gave his men good food ... *American* food. And the mules were not beaten. But ...' he said, pausing to pec, 'Señor Bingham claimed he *found* Machu Picchu.'

Manuel scratched his head with a broken fingernail. 'I don't understand it,' he said. 'You see, the local people – they had never *lost* Machu Picchu.'

As we walked along, Julia dragging her feet beside me, I began to understand the fascination for the llama. Camels and men have a mutual loathing for one another, but llamas are different. I put the peculiar bond down to shared height. A llama, which usually stands as tall as a man, will swivel its head and peer at you on the level – psychopathically. I got the feeling that if she had arms, Julia might throw them around me one minute, but stab me in the back the next.

I bragged to Manuel that I had a sixteen-inch, nickel-coated Alaskan moose knife, brought along in case one of the team went lame and hunger set in. He was unimpressed, and used the opportunity to harangue me.

He said that llamas are man's greatest friend. They keep the people of the Andes alive. Their coats are used for wool, for rugs and for ropes; their meat is eaten, their fat is used to make candles, and their dung is burned on stoves. Slipping me a sideways glance, the old llamateer added that some deranged people even dried their foetuses and made soup.

Eventually, I spied a lake stretching out to the north, its surface shining like watered steel. Known as *Lago Umayo*, it's unconnected with Titicaca. On a high promontory in the western quarter were dotted a number of strange cylindrical towers, built from smooth-sided blocks of stone.

'*Bienvenido*, welcome to Sillustani,' said Manuel.

The *chullpas*, round-sided towers, are thought to have been con-structed by the Ayamara-speaking Colla tribe, between the 14th and 16th centuries. Shortly before the Conquistador invasion, the Collas were overthrown by the Incas. Their most celebrated families had been buried in communal tombs, in funereal towers. Some rise up as high as fifty feet, overlooking the pristine waters of Lake Umayo.

Leaving Manuel to tend the llamas, I made my way up to the tallest of the *chullpas*. The ground was rocky, the grass long and flaxen. The tower's stone blocks were flush together like mosaics, its funerary contents ransacked by *huaqueros*, grave robbers, centuries before. It was here, from these great towers, that Hector said the Birdmen had flown. With the right wind, and a wide canopy of textile as a wing, I could see no reason why a man might not have glided from the greatest *chullpa*, safely down to the margin of the lake. He might have sacrificed some cloth, breathed its smoke to make him bold, thrust his arms sideways, and jumped. As a messenger he would have been in the air, aloft, if only for a few seconds, to deliver a message to the gods. Perhaps death would await him on landing; maybe that was the point – a suicide flight.

Despite Hector's certainty, I have found no written sources to connect Sillustani to the Birdmen. To the experts, the *chullpas* were merely towers where an ancient people interred their dead. But then again, I pondered, rubbing a hand over the curious masonry, perhaps the Birdmen never existed at all.

History is abundant with tower-jumping episodes. Medieval Europe saw hundreds of respectable young men with home-made wings, or billowing robes, hurl themselves from towers, in their desperation to fly. No one is sure why, but tower-jumping was to medieval man as great a craze as bungee-jumping has been in recent years.

In his *History of Britain*, Milton records the fate of Oliver of Malmesbury who fixed wings to his hands and feet in about 1070 AD and leapt from a tower. He's said to have flown for more than a furlong before crashing to the ground. He lived but was maimed. Another famous jumper was the Marquis of Bacqueville. He announced that he would fly from his riverside mansion in Paris's rue des Saints Pères, and land in the Tuileries Gardens. A great crowd gathered. The Marquis jumped with wings attached to his arms and legs. He didn't make it as far as the gardens. But, fortunately for him, he landed on a washerwoman's barge and only broke a leg.

Giovanni Battista Danti, a contemporary of Leonardo da Vinci, jumped from a tower too. He's said to have glided over Lake Trasimeno in 1490. A few years later, in 1501, another Italian adventurer called John Damian was taken in as a physician to the royal household of Scottish King James IV. While at the castle he practised alchemy and made a celebrated flight. Bishop Lesley, in his *History of Scotland* (published in 1578), wrote: 'He causet make ane pair of wings of fedderis ... he flew of the castell wall of Striveling, but shortlie he fell to the ground and brak his thee bare.'

The early 16th century saw dozens of tower-jumping episodes. It was a time not long after the *chullpas* of Sillustani were built. For all we know, the Birdmen were jumping at Sillustani at the same time as their tower-jumping cousins in Europe were plunging to their deaths.

While the llamas grazed, I paced around the ruins. Manuel pulled a few coca leaves from a pouch and started to chew them. He was lying on a great slab of trachyte, gazing up at the turbulent mass of clouds.

'What do you think?' I asked.

'About what?'

'Do you think once, long ago, men jumped from these towers and flew?'

I had expected Manuel to laugh at the question. Instead, he put a coca leaf on his tongue and closed his eyes.

'They may have jumped, and they may have flown,' he said. 'But why did they wish to fly?'

'As messengers from one world to the next?'

'Of course,' he replied. 'They wanted to reach the real world, to leave the illusion.'

'This is an illusion?'

Manuel sucked at the quid of coca in his cheek.

'Look around you,' he said, his eyes still closed. 'None of it exists at all.'

'That's a question of philosophy.'

'To reach the *real* world you must die first,' said the llamateer.

'Jump from the *chullpa* and even with the best wings you're likely to die,' I added.

'There are other ways to die, other ways to fly.'

'How?'

'In your head, in your thoughts,' said Manuel.

'You mean by taking coca?'

'No, not coca.' Manuel let out a breathless chuckle. 'Stronger stuff than coca.'

'What about by inhaling the smoke of llama wool?'

'No, *mucho más fuerte*, much stronger.'

'What could be stronger than llama-wool smoke?'

Manuel opened his eyes. 'Search and you may find it,' he said.

7

Festival of Blood

The Israeli couple sitting opposite me on the bus from Puno to Arequipa were locked in a passionate embrace. Their bodies were contorted around each other in a double helix, the sound of their mouths sucking, like Japanese blowfish. The Andean ladies with pigtails and multiple skirts did their best, like me, to avert their gaze. They slurped at cups of orange jelly, soaked up the blaring salsa music, and giggled spontaneously at bumps in the road. And there were many bumps, for the dirt road from Puno to Arequipa is one of the roughest on the continent.

Every twenty minutes the bus driver would slow his vehicle, sound the Klaxon, and grind to an uneasy halt. The entire contingent of old women with bundles on their backs, students and dancers, theologians and salesmen in threadbare suits, would troupe out. All were searching for the same thing – pots of orange jelly. Their demand for it was seemingly insatiable. The man sitting beside me asked whether I might keep an eye on his cardboard box, full of live guinea pigs. As he scrambled for the door, desperate for jelly, he twisted his nose towards the Israeli sweethearts. In the unwritten lore of the Andes, such people were not to be trusted.

Peruvian bus journeys are always eventful. Whereas in other countries a long ride in a disintegrating bus is a vile prospect, in Peru it's something to relish. Like children ecstatic for a fairground ride, customers fight each other to be the first aboard. They clutch their tickets with anticipation, thrilled at the idea of a jolting, dust-choking, twelve-hour trip.

Part of the hysteria was due to the date. It was the 27th of July –

the day before Peru's day of independence. Everyone was hurrying back to their villages in time for the *fiesta*.

Digging a white plastic spoon into his sixth tub of phosphorescent jelly, the man thanked me for looking after his *cuy* so ably. The cunning Israeli guinea pig thieves, he hinted, had been thwarted.

He slapped his hand in mine.

'My name is Manolo,' he said. 'We are brothers. Come with me to my village, come to celebrate!'

I explained that I was en route to Arequipa, where I had heard a man was building a glider of traditional Incan design. A throwaway remark, made by a backpacker in Cusco, was gnawing away at my mind. After Arequipa, I was heading up the coast to Nazca, to inspect the desert lines. I was searching for Birdmen, I said.

Manolo seemed displeased by my choice of destination.

'Come to my village,' he urged again. 'Come and see *Yawar* ... we have caught the condor!'

At first I didn't understand what the man was going on about. I feared that the excitement of the bus ride, and so much jelly, had taken a heavy toll on his sanity. But then, as he told me more about the planned celebrations, I realised my good fortune. *Yawar* was something not to be missed at any price. No other festival in the Americas is as significant to the folklore of flight.

Thanking Manolo for his invitation, I accepted. When he leapt from the bus at the small town of Pati, with his box of *cuy* cradled in his arms, I too descended.

The village itself was reached after hours of hitching rides. Manolo helped me into the back of a lorry carrying melons. As we fishtailed our way north, up a narrow track, he told me about his guinea pigs.

'They're the finest *cuy* in all Peru,' he said. 'I bought them from a *campesino*, a farm worker, near Puno. We'll snap their necks, marinate them overnight, and fry them on a hot griddle,' Manolo rubbed his palms together indicating great heat. '*Cuy chactado*,' he said. 'It's my family's favourite.'

The melon truck dropped us on the outskirts of a small mining community. We must have made an incongruous couple: Manolo with his guinea pigs, and me staggering under so much luggage.

Festivities were well under way. The main street was criss-crossed with banners. An inexhaustible supply of old men lounged on their verandas swigging *chicha*, in honour of their ancestors. Their wives were snapping the fragile necks of *cuy*, slicing potatoes and preparing *estofado*, a thick chicken stew. The early evening air was live with music: the sound of flutes, trumpets, drums and, of course, the sound of *quenas*.

Manolo took me to his house and introduced his family. His wife, four children, two aunts and grandmother shared the modest three-room shack. No one appeared surprised that a stranger had been invited at the last minute. The best chair was dusted down and placed in the shade for my comfort. Refreshments were brought out. Then Manolo quizzed his wife about the *Yawar*. When she had reported the details, he touched a hand to his heart and thanked God.

'*Te lo dije*, I told you!' he exclaimed. 'A magnificent condor has been lured by the fresh horse meat. We haven't caught one for three years, and so there was great anticipation.'

Manolo gulped his drink. Like everyone in the village, he could hardly contain his excitement.

Yawar Fiesta, 'Festival of Blood', has been practised for at least four hundred years in southern Peru. The festival is as popular now as ever, an indication that political correctness hasn't yet reached the Andes. A celebration, held in small towns and villages on the *Altiplano*, it honours the condor, the king of all birds.

Each year the ritual is the same. First a team of hunters go high into the hills in search of a condor. They abstain from cigarettes and drink as the great birds have a keen sense of smell. When they have come to a spot frequented by condors, they slaughter a pony by strangling it. Offerings are sprinkled around its body. The hunters pray to God to send down a condor. Then they hide among the surrounding rocks, and wait. Sometimes, days pass before a condor lands to feast on the pony's flesh. All the while the hunters chant prayers and fill their minds with pure thoughts. Some years no condor descends, and the hunters return to their village with their egos bruised. In a good year, if the condor lands, it gorges itself on the fresh horse meat. With a full gizzard, the bird attempts to fly. But having eaten too much it's unable to take off. Choosing their moment, the hunters strike. Throwing a poncho over the bird, they trap it, and tie its feet together. They would never harm it, for to do so would be an act of sacrilege. Overwhelmed with joy, the hunters embrace their quarry, and toast its health with *chicha*. They return homeward, with the bird wrapped tight in a blanket.

As the party returns to the village, trumpets resound, celebrating
the capture of the condor. It's taken away and plied with more food
and *chicha*. By the day of independence it's ready for the extraordinary
festival.

Manolo drank all evening and by midnight he was very drunk
indeed. He had made sure the *cuy* were marinated in his secret sauce,
and that his wife had pressed his best clothes for the next day. I
suggested we go to sleep. Fighting to stand upright, he smacked his
hands together.

'How can a man sleep,' he roared, 'when there is still *chicha* to be
drunk?'

*

The central square was packed with people even before the band
arrived. No one wanted to miss out on the best seating or, worse still,
to miss the main spectacle. They all knew that the *Yawar Fiesta*
comes at most only once a year. I heard the crackle of maize roasting
on low charcoal stalls, and saw hawkers with barrows of pastries, ripe
oranges, and skewers of beef heart ready to be sold. On every wall
children were in position, their short legs dangling down, gob-stoppers
rattling in their mouths. The old women, dressed in their finery, were
fanning themselves with their bowlers. Laughter rang through the
plaza like the click of castanets.

Manolo wasn't going to let the temperature or a hangover spoil his
fun. It was a baking afternoon, in the high 80s, but he wanted everyone
to see him in his best clothes. The flaps of his collar stuck out over a
green mohair sweater, on top of which he wore a woollen peacoat.
Beads of perspiration merged into droplets on his forehead, before
cascading down his face. He greeted old friends, bragged about the
cuy he'd brought from Puno, and drank toasts to the Festival of Blood.

From the distance came the piercing sound of a piccolo. Then the
thunder of a bass drum, trumpets, and cymbals cracking like gunfire.
The bandsmen in their tight woollen caps and matching ponchos
swaggered towards the plaza. A hundred feet kicked the dust as they
danced, hips hula-hooping and hands clapping, as they heralded the
arrival of the show.

Following behind the musicians were a mass of revellers, coaxed
into hysteria by a cocktail of adrenaline and drink. Among them, its
immense ten-foot wings held outstretched, its beak bound with

twine, was the condor. Black in colour, with an ivory ruff and blush pink head, the bird was guest of honour. With the horde pressed into the far corner of the plaza, the serious business of *Yawar* could commence.

A young bull, unable to move in its tiny pen, was readied for *el corrida de toros*, the fight. A sackcloth saddle was fixed to its back as hands taunted it through the bars. When the saddle was tight, the condor was harnessed to the bull's back. Facing forwards, its feet were sewn into the cloth.

Only then, as the band's cacophony ranted around us, did the free-for-all begin. The gate to the pen was hauled aside and the bucking-bronco ran wild. On its back, writhing like a phantom from the limits of Hell, was the condor. As the bull lunged through the plaza, the bird's tremendous wings heaved up and down, desperate for flight, its beak tearing into the beast's back. Would-be matadors, their courage bolstered by drink, stumbled into the square, only to be stampeded one by one. In the frenzy of wings and hooves, bovine and bird blended into a single creature from Greek mythology. Neither seemed to cherish the performance, a fusion of two traditions. The bull symbolises the power of the Conquistadors, and the condor the might of a proud native people.

When the fantasy was at an end, the animals were cut apart. A bowl of *chicha* was placed at the condor's beak, and the bull was pushed back into its enclosure. A group of mauled matadors swapped tales of their bravery, and tight-fitting shoes danced once again in the plaza's dust. Then, with the band romping triumphantly through the streets, the bird was dragged to the edge of the village. Twisting its neck back in horror as it glimpsed the crowd, the condor thrust its mighty wings and soared up into the steel-blue sky.

*

Another cramped long distance bus whirred west towards Arequipa. Up on the roof a herd of sheep were balancing alongside the bags, their feet trussed, their faces rapt with alarm. They bleated, but no one was listening. Below, in the cabin, a demonic figure with gritted teeth crooned over the controls. Like a schoolboy piloting a make-believe Zero fighter, he mimicked the clatter of gunfire. The bus swerved left, then right and left again, the driver spinning the wheel recklessly through his muscular hands.

In the belly of the bus a little girl had spewed orange jelly down the aisle. The man beside me, a clone of Manolo, slapped his knee. Was he angry at the pools of amber vomit? With the glint of a gold tooth, he laughed at my question. A child is *el fruto de la innocencia*, the fruit of innocence, he said.

As we jerked about, I found myself thinking about *Yawar Fiesta*. If the root of the festival was a love for the great bird, why expose it to such torture? The only parallel I could think of was *lomante*, the Ainu Bear Festival. The Ainu, the original people of Japan, loved bears beyond all other creatures. They considered them to be mothers of the Earth, venerating them just as the Andeans do the condor. In the early spring a male bear cub would be caught in the mountains. It was taken to the village, kept in a small cage, and fed on delicious morsels. If it was too young for solid food, an Ainu woman would suckle it. The little bear was given as much as he could eat, to fatten him up. When mid-winter arrived, and his pelt was thick, he was taken from the cage.

The villagers declared their love for the little bear, praising him as a god. They placed him beside their altar and worshipped him. Then, one at a time, they would shoot blunt arrows at him with their bows, wounding him. Death was agonising and slow to come. Once dead, the bear cub was the focus of a midnight ceremony. Its brain, tongue and eyeballs were hacked from the skull and adorned with flowers. And, as they celebrated the bear's beauty, the Ainu feasted on its meat.

Back on the bus, the driving was getting worse. We veered to the left, round a hairpin. I joked to the man beside me that the driver must have been a *kamikaze* pilot in a former life. Another retch of jelly came and went. Then, as we strained to sit upright, the driver aimed the vehicle at an upcoming slope and banged in the clutch. Never before have I experienced such propulsion. On the roof the sheep must have been fumbling to escape. Inside, the rows of passengers blurred together. I snapped for air, my diaphragm distending, my cheeks pushed back by gravitational force.

A drop of three thousand feet sheered away to the right. We might have sailed over the edge, but the road and the bus swerved left in the nick of time. Gradually, the bus came to a halt and the driver stood up. Removing his Fedora, he passed it back, mumbling. The starched hat was handed from one to the next. As it made its way round the bus, even the poorest passengers tossed something in. I was unsure what the levy was for, but even so I threw in a few *centimos*. It was given back to the driver. He climbed down from the cab. Facing the precipice, he crossed himself, kissed his knuckle, and hurled the contents of his Fedora over the cliff.

Unfamiliar with the tradition, I quizzed the man beside me.

'*Es para los mártires*, it's for the martyrs,' he said.

*

The White City, as Arequipa is known, nestles at the foot of the snow-capped volcano, El Misti. The peak reminded me more than a little of Mount Fuji, and a year I spent starving on the streets of the Japanese capital: the bad old days, kept alive by a diet of ornamental cabbages, stolen from Ueno Park. But Peru's second city couldn't have been more different from Tokyo except, that is, for its fear of earthquakes. Its low buildings were constructed from sillar, a local pumice the colour of bleached whale bones.

Arequipeñas had the time to be sophisticated. They sat in cafés off Plaza de Armas, discussing politics, reading the papers, having their shoes shined. Gone was the scruffy, honest clothing of the Andes. Gone, too, were the dark, furrowed foreheads, born of worry and overwork.

The manager of Hotel El Conquistador offered me a room for a third of the normal price. In many countries I would think twice about turning up at a deluxe hotel and offering a pittance for the best quarters. But in Peru, where wheeler-dealing dies hard, ruthless bargaining is expected. I asked the manager if he'd heard of a local man who was building a glider. He nodded earnestly.

'*Sí, sí Señor!*' he clamoured. 'Everyone knows Carlos. I will telephone him for you.'

Once my bags had been dragged to the room by the manager's son, I inspected the bathroom for spiders. I never quite understood why, but Peruvian bathrooms were awash with them. In one hotel, a cleaner told me they came up from the sewers.

For an hour I waited for the telephone to ring. It did not. There was a delicate tap at the door. I opened it. In its frame was standing a lanky young man with pale skin, sullen eyes, and a mole on his cheek. He looked Russian. He said that his name was Fernando and that Señor Carlos had sent him to collect me. His master was, he confirmed, building a traditional glider. But, he went on in a gravelly voice, his real passion was bringing Juanita back.

'Who's Juanita?'

Fernando smiled nervously at my lack of knowledge.

'Juanita, the ice woman,' he said.

Once aboard his dilapidated red Lada, Fernando insisted on telling me all he knew about Juanita and the campaign to save her. The story began in 1995 when the mummified body of a young Incan girl was discovered on Mount Ampato, not far from Arequipa. The girl, who was entombed in a block of ice, was thought to have been sacrificed to the mountain spirits, some five centuries before. But no sooner had her mantle of ice been chipped away than Juanita, as she became known, became a political hot potato. Like a rock star hurled into the big league at a tender age, Juanita began her world tour. For three years she criss-crossed the United States, shuttled about in a giant deep freeze. At an engagement in Connecticut she was even presented to President Clinton. She was currently appearing at venues across Japan.

'Arequipeñas have had no opportunity to enjoy their mummy,' said Fernando dolefully. 'We don't understand why she's in Japan ... we want her back!'

The scarlet Lada rumbled east from Arequipa, towards El Misti. The fields, terraced by the Incas centuries before, were thick with garlic. Crooked *viejitas*, old women, were busy with bringing in the crop, wide hats shielding them from the winter sun. Fernando explained how the soil was suited well to the cochineal cacti as well as garlic. The female cochineal beetles, he said, are brushed from the cacti and pulverised. It takes seventy thousand of them to make a pound of the red dye.

Ten minutes later we were pulling into the drive of a spacious wooden house, encircled by a fence of tall cacti. Before I could get out of the car, an elderly man came out to greet me. It was Carlos.

A pair of bifocals balanced on his nose, magnifying his teal-coloured eyes. He must have been over seventy, but had a youthful energy. His face was refined, edged by unwrinkled cheeks and an angular jaw. A bald patch at his crown was expertly concealed by a wave of oyster-grey hair. Like Fernando, whom he appeared to treat as an adopted son, Carlos spoke good English.

He led me into the house. The panelled walls of the sitting-room were adorned with images of Juanita, the local girl turned ice maiden. They showed her in all her finery, wrapped in a funeral cloak, a mouthful of jumbled teeth leering from her noseless face. But Juanita was just one of so many distractions. The walls and bookshelves, tabletops and bureaux were cluttered with mementos. There were framed letters and leather-bound books, a Confederate flag on a stand, a pair of duelling pistols, and six Samurai swords on a rack. One entire wall was taken up with an 18th-century map of Paris, and on another, were a dozen etchings of West African warriors in towering Dogon masks.

Over the fireplace was hung a large section of scarlet textile. The size of a pillowcase, it depicted the now-familiar forms of pre-Incan Birdmen.

'It's from the necropolis near Nazca,' said Carlos, noticing my interest.

I said that I had come to Peru in search of the Birdmen, but was doubting whether they existed at all.

'Mankind understood the principles of gliding centuries ago,' he replied. 'But, incredibly, it took him so long to design a flying wing.'

'They say it began in the 19th century ... Otto Lilienthal, the Wright brothers and all that.'

Carlos rubbed his hands together.

'Do you believe that?' he said. 'Do you really believe that man was so slow to master something so simple?'

Fernando went out to wash his car.

'What do you know about kites?' Carlos asked me.

'That they've been used in China for three thousand years,' I said.

'Exactly,' said Carlos. 'They show that man has understood aerial dynamics for centuries. A general in Han Dynasty China flew a flock of musical kites over an enemy encampment the night before a great battle,' he said. 'Attached to each kite was a whistle. Thinking the sounds were the voices of angels warning them to run for their lives, the enemy fled.'

'But a kite is just a kite,' I said. 'It's far too flimsy to carry a man.'

'That's where you're wrong,' Carlos declared. 'What about Alexander Graham Bell's manned kite, *Cygnet*?'

I hunched my shoulders.

'It was forty feet long,' he said. 'Piloted by an army soldier, it flew for seven minutes ... that was in 1907.'

Carlos tugged off his bifocals and dabbed his eyes with the corner of his shirt.

'Since my wife died,' he said, leading me to a shed behind the house, 'I've been tinkering.'

The workshop was in a dreadful state. Wood-shavings, newspapers and tools were scattered about. Carlos flicked on the light. Taking up most of the floor was a wooden framework. I looked it over carefully, making out the single broad wing, and the substructure.

It reminded me of the boy at my boarding school who built an aeroplane in the woodwork shop. He used to taxi around the grounds in it in his spare time. Everyone was so used to him trundling about the perimeter of the playing fields that they hardly took any notice. One Saturday afternoon, during a rugby match with another school, a freak gust of wind thrust the fragile craft skyward. The first fifteen watched as it ascended, higher and higher. At five hundred feet it levelled off. Then it nose-dived to Earth. The boy was rushed to hospital, and survived, but his plane disintegrated on impact.

'There's another six months to go,' said Carlos, 'but you get the general idea.'

'A hang-glider?'

'Exactly, or if you like, it's a kite without strings. I've based the project on the Colditz principle.'

'What's that?'

Carlos ran his hand over the balsa frame.

'You probably know of the glider built at Colditz during the War.'

I said that I did.

'Then you must know that its designers used the simplest materials – cloth and wood, nothing fancy.' Carlos led me back to the house. 'I'm not saying this is what the Incas glided with,' he mused. 'But I *am* saying they were advanced enough to have worked it out.'

Like the boy at my school who'd built a plane, Carlos was charged with great enthusiasm for the project. But he had not yet been injured. He was sure that the Incas had a basic knowledge of gliding, citing the existence of the Nazca Lines as certain proof.

'Go to Nazca and walk on the *pampa*,' he said. 'As you walk, look at the ground, and look at the air. Understand the feebleness of man, and sense the spirit which keeps the birds above you aloft.'

8

Susto

Nazca is a one-horse town set on the edge of the Pan-American Highway. It is encircled by the Atacama, one of the Earth's driest deserts. The ground is pancake flat, the dust so fine that it burns your throat and blinds your eyes. You might expect tumbleweed to blow down the main street, or a gunfight at the local bar, because this is Peru's Wild West.

The men are rough and tough. They talk big, drink hard, and walk as if they're wearing spurs – every man in Nazca is a Marlboro Man. As they swagger about, leaning back into their boots, you get the feeling that the locals realise their luck. And it is luck, the kind which wins lotteries. Every man, woman and child in town is touched by it – a miraculous stroke of fortune.

Imagine that for centuries your ancestors cursed God for a land so parched that crops wouldn't grow. One generation after the next choked on the dust, and yearned to escape. They lived in a place where travellers never stopped; where there were no proper buildings or money for schools. But then, quite by chance, a discovery was made, which flipped fortune's coin from bad luck to bonanza. Busloads of tourists started to arrive day and night. They wanted hotels and bars, restaurants, internet cafés and guides. Best of all, they were willing to pay.

The Nazca Lines are one of the world's great unexplained phenomena. The only certainty is that they're out there: a series of immense figures and geometric shapes etched into the desert's delicate face. They are so immense that they can only be seen from the air. Some are outlandish geometric shapes, deciphered as animals – among them a monkey, a whale, a dog, and a spider. But the most

sensational figures at Nazca are the birds. More detailed and numerous than the others, they include an albatross, a parrot, a condor and
a hummingbird.

The pilot who first noticed them as he flew over Nazca in the '30s,
had no idea what he'd discovered. Within years, a barrage of crackpot
scientists, mathematicians and free-thinking hippies arrived. For
every visitor, there was a new theory. Virtually everything you hear
about Nazca is speculation.

The first theorists were remarkably controlled. They said it must
have taken a thousand years for the Lines to be etched into the dust;
that the procedure had begun four centuries before the birth of Christ.
But as time passed, imaginations ran wild. The Lines, they now said,
were ancient running tracks, a map of the heavens, a calendar of the
seasons, a code to fertility rites, irrigation channels, or patterns for
weaving yarn. Those in the theory business know full well that the
wackier their idea, the more publicity they'll get. Perhaps that's what
inspired the young German, Erich von Daniken, who appeared on the
scene in 1968. His idea was that the Nazca Lines were high-tech'
landing strips, left by extraterrestrials.

*

An eager lady with sallow cheeks and a walnut-whip of grey hair,
greeted me to Hotel Hummingbird, located just off Calle Lima. She
pranced up and down the reception area, a stout body on nimble feet.
Her name was Florence. What good luck it was, she said, that I'd not
been trapped by one of the town's many touts.

'They eat you alive, like piranhas!' she exclaimed, gnashing her
dentures.

Before I could protest, Florence had signed me up for the Hummingbird Package. Squaring a stack of vouchers in her hands, she
leant over the counter and ran a sharp fingernail down my shirt-front.

'The Hummingbird is for lovers,' she said.

'But I'm alone,' I replied, realising the impropriety of the remark.

Florence coughed with enthusiasm, and pressed her teeth back into
position with her thumb.

'Maybe I'll see you later,' she said, handing me the key.

'What are all these vouchers for?'

Florence flicked through them like a croupier shuffling cards.

'For the Hummingbird suite, a meal in Hummingbird restaurant, a cocktail in the Hummingbird bar, use of Hummingbird's internet, the Hummingbird city tour, the Hummingbird laundry and discotheque and swimming pool, access to the Hummingbird museum and tourist kiosk, the Hummingbird viewpoint, the Hummingbird bus service, and,' Florence waved the last coupon, 'for the flight over the Nazca Lines on Hummingbird Airlines.'

I handed over an obscene amount of foreign currency to cover the deluxe Hummingbird Package. Despite my bitterness, I couldn't fault the hotel owner's talent for business. He was cleaning up nicely. It was hard to imagine what he'd think of next. Florence twisted a nail round a long grey curl at the edge of her face.

'Next week we open Hummingbird karaoke,' she said.

*

The Hummingbird bus dropped me at a small airport, not far from the town centre. Wherever I looked, I saw smooth young men. They all had the same denim jackets, Italian sunglasses and wetted-down hair. Some were selling souvenirs and baseball caps; others were too cool to work.

As he took my voucher for the Hummingbird flight, a, teenage Marlboro Man clicked his fingers at my chest and pointed to the righthand seat of a single-prop' Cessna 172. I scrambled up into the cockpit. The pilot handed me a photocopied map of the Lines. In a single movement, he slipped on a pair of Ray Bans, slicked back his hair, and pushed in the throttle.

At seventeen, I'd somehow managed to talk my parents into sending me to flight school. A pilot's training, I had assured them, would surely come in useful in years to come. An ultra-relaxed Norwegian had taught me to fly small, high-wing Cessnas. Scanning the controls brought back distinct memories. I'd been an unaccomplished pilot, and had spent most of the time out of control over Florida's Panhandle.

Soon we were lifting steeply into the sky, flying north-west towards the *pampa*. The late morning air was choppy, churning with thermals. Down below, the brilliant sunlight played on the sands, accentuating every ditch, every furrow. The black basalt crust of stones, which so reminded me of Iraq's western desert, stretched from one horizon to the other. Ancient dried riverbeds were quite clear, following the undulations, giving chaos to what was otherwise uniform.

The first image we saw was a whale. The pilot banked into a steep turn. Then on the left were trapezoids, and on the right the 'astronaut'. Another turn, and a giant pair of human hands, a dog, and a tree. Every few seconds the pilot would wrench back the column and roll the small plane into another turn. I shouted against the thunderous noise of the engine, asking him to go easy. Banking hard to the right, he pointed out of the window. On the flattened desert floor, its beak pointing south, was the image of a condor. And, a moment later, *el colibri*, the hummingbird.

Engraved into the basalt surface, the hummingbird was poised at the edge of a low plateau. Its wings, tail and elongated beak were unmistakable. As I gazed down at the figure, the aircraft surging from side to side, my mind ran free. How and why could such an exquisite symbol have ever been drawn?

Not long after Von Daniken had been to Nazca, an American called Jim Woodman arrived. The year was 1973. Having studied ritual smoke balloons, which are still flown in Guatemala, Woodman began to put together his own theory. The Quechua language, he noted, has a word for a 'balloon-maker'. He had discovered fragments of local pottery, too, which showed the crude image of what he said was a balloon. Woodman saw textiles taken from graves at the village of Cahuachi, not far from Nazca. The weave was impressive (185 × 95 threads per square inch): surprisingly tight considering they were 1500 years old. Woodman felt certain the ancient man had flown at Nazca. A lighter-than-air method was the only way, he said, that would explain the Lines. He asserted that by flying high above the *pampa*, the designers could have mapped out the shapes to scale before etching them.

Like so many before him, Woodman set out to prove his theory.

He put together a team of engineers and aviation specialists. They designed and built *Condor I*, an enormous tetrahedron balloon. The gondola was made from *totora* reeds from Lake Titicaca; the woven envelope had a capacity of 80,000 cubic feet. But instead of air, it was filled with smoke. Dotted on the *pampa*, Woodman's team had found the remnants of what they thought were burning pits. These, they said, were used to fill the ancient balloons with smoke. (I saw no such pits, but did find large amounts of charcoal on the Nazca plains.)

On a clear spring day in 1975, *Condor I* confounded its critics and lifted up into the desert sky. It flew for several minutes, reaching a thousand feet above the Nazca Lines.

For my money, Jim Woodman is more from the Thor Heyerdahl school of science, than from the Von Daniken stable of pseudo-science. He with his balloon and Carlos with his hang-glider were convinced that only a flying man, a Birdman, could have drawn the Nazca Lines. But it seemed as if some fragment of understanding was missing. Surely the theorists were off track: forcing pegs into holes they didn't fit.

As we braced ourselves for landing, I was still thinking about *el colibri*, the hummingbird. I didn't doubt that the technology existed a thousand years ago to have drawn it, but my thinking had begun to change. None of the theories had taken into account *why* ancient man would have wanted such gigantic symbols around him.

The more I pondered it, the more obvious it seemed that the Lines weren't designed to be seen by the eyes of men at all. They must have been intended for the gods, and the gods alone. Why else would they have been so vast? Maybe that was the whole point. They were drawn so large as to be invisible to mortals. It reminded me of a famous Guy de Maupassant anecdote. The author ate lunch every day in the restaurant halfway up the Eiffel Tower, although he was well-known for despising it. When asked why he did so, he replied that it was the only place in Paris where he could not see the damned *Tour d'Eiffel*.

Perhaps the sheer enormity of the Nazca figures obliterated them from sight in the same way. As for a method of drawing accurately an image which is more than a hundred metres in width, I didn't see how being above the *pampa* would help the designers in the least. Surely a basic form of *Sketch-a-graph*, or a string and a stick, would be the only tool necessary to map out the cryptic Lines.

*

The best thing about Nazca was the hardware shops. As dusk fell over the town I stumbled on a row of them, tucked away near the bus station. Not since East Africa had I seen such a varied stock of Chinese-made goods: hand-grinders for mincing beef, liquorice and loo seats; sticks of school chalk, and coal tar soap, nail clippers, fountain pens, and cheap rubber bands. The owner of one such shop was called Pepé. He was a great bear of a man with a pot-belly, a grease-stained shirt, and a week's worth of stubble on his cheeks. His face was dominated by a pair of drooping eyes. When I entered, he was squinting at a newspaper in the faint light of a low-watt bulb. As soon as he saw me he jumped up, dusted off a stool and beckoned me to sit.

'*Es usted muy bienvenido*, you are very welcome, Señor,' he said, clapping his hands together. 'It is wonderful to have you here!'

I thanked him for his reception.

'*¡Qué alegria!*' he called, 'your arrival calls for celebration!'

Pepé bent down behind the counter and pulled out a scruffy shoebox. He withdrew the lid, the tip of his tongue clamped between his lips. I leaned forward to see what was in the box. It was a light-bulb. The shopkeeper unscrewed the low-watt bulb and replaced it with the one from the box. The room was filled with an abundance of creamy yellow light.

'I keep it for special occasions,' lisped Pepé.

In the bright light I scanned the shelves.

'This is nothing but rubbish,' he huffed. 'It's a terrible shop. I forbid you to buy anything. How could such a fine man be expected to buy such rubbish?'

He handed me a mug of tea.

'Hungry, are you?'

I said that I was not.

'Go on,' Pepé replied. 'I always have a snack around this time.'

He called loudly for his son.

The child's feet could be heard behind the counter. He appeared a moment later with a plate of crackers.

I took one of the biscuits. Pepé pointed to a small glass bottle filled with what looked like salt.

'Gone on, have some,' he said. 'It's magic.'

The boy sprinkled a few grains of the mysterious powder onto my biscuit. I took a bite. It tasted savoury.

'We put it on everything,' said the shopkeeper grandly.

'What *is* it?'

'*Ajinomoto* – it's monosodium glutimate.'

With three of the crackers inside me, I was converted. It was great stuff. You just had to think of roast beef, meat loaf or a nice rack of lamb, and it was as if you were tasting it. Despite Pepé's protestations I bought two bottles of the food enhancer, certain that they'd come in useful somewhere down the line.

The shopkeeper asked me what I thought of Nazca. I said how lucky the people were to have the Lines.

'You're right,' he replied. 'Everyone for miles around is jealous.'
'You couldn't wish for a better tourist trap,' I said.
The shopkeeper scratched his stubble again.
'Are you mad?' he said. 'There's much better stuff than the Lines.'
'What could be more popular with tourists than the Nazca Lines?'
'*Las momias*, mummies,' said Pepé. 'Got thousands of them. We've hardly even started with them yet.'

One of the highlights of the Hummingbird Package was a quick stop at the infamous *Cementerio de Chauchilla*, not far from Nazca. A guide whistled for the driver to stop. He beckoned us to follow him to the graves. This pre-Incan burial ground, marooned in the middle of the desert, is marked by a tattered tin sign. It's a bleak attempt at tourism. Along with a dozen Germans – retired workers from a ball-bearing factory in Dusseldorf – I tramped from grave to grave. Forty or fifty funeral pits had been excavated, looted long ago by *huaqueros*, grave-robbers. All valuables had been expertly stripped away: jewellery and trinkets, pottery, seashells and funerary shawls. The remains were gruesome by any standards.

Propped up in each pit were a couple of mummified figures, huddled against a wall, knees pushed up against their chins; ragged clothing bundled around them, half-peeled away. Their skin had been seared off by the sun, hanging in patches off the bleached bones. Lower jaws were drooping, eye sockets empty, teeth knocked out, hair matted, and facial features awry, like cadavers from a low-budget horror film.

The German cameras clicked, as the guide pointed out the details.
'Look at that one,' he said. 'See how its skull is deformed.'
We peered down into the grave. He was right. The head was unusually long, like comic book sketches of a 'small grey' alien. Cranial deformations were once popular with the ancient Nazca and Paracas civilisations. They're so strange that you find a smile creeping over your lips, as if someone's having you on. The brow is high, leading back to an elongated swathe of skull. Some scholars say the crania were deformed in childhood, in the name of beauty. Others contend that the technique relieved migraines, cured insanity, or may even have been used as a punishment. A pair of boards would be bound tightly to either side of the head, pressing it out of shape.

Working in the 1920s, the celebrated Peruvian archaeologist Julio C Tello made a special study of the deformed skulls. His work led to a 1929 law, making grave-robbing a national crime. Credited with the first major archaeological finds near Nazca, he claimed to have found babies which still had the deforming boards bound to their heads.

When the Hummingbird bus had screeched back into town, I dropped in to Pepé's shop before dinner. The room was dim, lit again by the low-watt bulb. The shopkeeper was hunched over the counter, struggling with a ledger. He seemed depressed.

'Is everything all right?'

Pepé looked up. His bloodhound eyes drooping behind a pair of plastic frames.

'I can't sleep,' he said. 'And my head aches as if a great stone's pressing down. Worst of all is that the numbers never add up.'

The shopkeeper pointed to the page of sums.

'For twenty years,' he went on, 'Nazca has boomed. Anything which opens here succeeds. The town's got more rich people than I can count. Look at that Señor Rodriguez with his dammed Hummingbird Tours. He must be in league with the Devil.'

I vouched for the Hummingbird experience.

'Why am I the only man in Nazca whose business does so badly?' moaned Pepé.

I peered once again at the shelves of his shop. They were crammed with useful stuff, and the prices were reasonable.

'I'll tell you why things are so bad,' he winced.

'Why?'

The old shopkeeper ran a Biro across the furrows of his brow.

'*Susto*,' he said.

I'd come across *susto* in Latin America before. Part curse and part superstition, it's a regional obsession, which translates literally as 'fright'. Thousands put their misfortune down to it. *Susto* has all the hallmarks of an eastern superstition. I often used to wonder if, like the Evil Eye, it had been brought from North Africa via medieval Spain.

An unexpected bang, a loud noise, or a jerk to the head are all that's needed. Some say it's the reason why Peruvian babies are swaddled tightly for so long. The imagined effect of *susto* is thought to prise the spirit and the body apart.

'How did the *susto* find you?' I queried.

The shopkeeper glanced down at the floor.

'I don't know,' he said. 'I spend all my time sitting here trying to remember; and the more I think about it, the more the *susto* bites.'

Most conversations with Pepé involved talk of *susto*, and invariably ended in the same subject – mummies. He saw the preserved bodies as the real future of Nazca. The Lines, he said, were a mere distraction. Mummies were different. They held answers to all the questions. If only he could rid himself of the *susto*, he was sure that the mummies would bring him fame and fortune.

'Out there,' he said, 'the *pampa* is littered with graves. Most of them are undisturbed. Why bother with the desert symbols when you've got the actual people who drew the Nazca Lines? I don't know why those stupid scientists keep coming up with new theories, when they could study the mummies.'

Pepé had a point. He leant back in his chair, his mind momentarily drawn away from *susto*. I told him about my Hummingbird trip to the burial ground at Chauchilla. The Germans and I, I said, had been impressed. Propelling his fist down on the counter like a hammer, he scoffed.

'That's nothing! Chauchilla's a child's playground. Wait till you see Majuelo!'

'Where's that?'

'Across the *pampa*, far from Nazca.'

'Can I go there?'

The old shopkeeper hugged his arms around his chest.

'*Es un lugar peligroso*, it's a dangerous place,' he said firmly. '*Mucho susto*, many frights.'

9

The Trophy Head

Were it not for the occasional swoop of a Cessna in the sky above, Nazca's desert would have been silent. Sightseeing tours, a recent disturbance in a sea of tranquillity, come and go as the Nazca mystery is touted to another coachload of foreign tourists. I found it ironic that most Nazcans had never seen the Lines from the air; few could have afforded the flight. But most had no interest anyway in what they considered merely to be tourist bait. In Nazca, everyone was praying for the same thing: that the tourists would keep coming, and that it didn't rain. One man told me that if it rained for more than two hours the Lines would be washed away.

I set off early in the morning to cross the *pampa*. At the wheel of the tired old hatchback was Pepé's eldest son, José-Luis. A Marlboro Man in the making, he had the greased back mop of hair, the fake Ray Bans, and had already mastered the wink. José-Luis agreed to take me to the vast burial ground at Majuelo if I'd tell him all I knew about English girls. He had heard, he said, that they favoured white handbags, which they danced around at the discotheque.

We veered left, off the Pan-American Highway, down the only route which crosses the Nazca Lines. The even sound of rubber on tarmac was replaced by a grating noise, as the tyres cut into the basalt. The car filled with dust. On either side of the track the level planes stretched out like contours of the moon.

As the hatchback jarred along, I thought about Pepé's obsession with mummies. Although morbid, it wasn't an unknown pre-occupation. The shopkeeper had been right – you can learn a great deal from preserved bodies. But there's more to mummies than meets the eye. Pepé was probably unaware of the West's own fixation with mummies. We have all but forgotten their historical role in European medicine. For centuries nothing was regarded as more powerful a physic than powdered mummy. It was credited with curing all kinds of ailments, including rashes and migraine, palpitations, epilepsy and plague. Throughout the Middle Ages, European aristocrats would tuck a sachet of mummy powder into their sleeve. Any sign of malady, they'd guzzle the contents down. Even as recently as 1908, the German drugs company E. Merck were advertising 'Genuine Egyptian Mummy, as long as supplies last, 17 Marks per kilogram'.

Forty minutes after turning off the desert highway, we descended onto what looked like a parched riverbed. The banks were caked in dry compressed mud, as if the river had raged there only days before. But water couldn't have run in that channel for centuries. We ploughed ahead, José-Luis driving at high speed like a getaway driver. He told me of his big plans – his dream was to open a hotel and bar. He'd buy a fleet of planes, he said, and give Señor Rodriguez some competition. Then the English girls with white handbags would be all over him.

He guided the hatchback down an embankment and through a copse of warango trees. Beyond them was a farmstead. We left the car at a distance, and walked towards the low adobe buildings. A dog voiced our arrival from the shade. The *campesino* and his wife didn't need the dog's alarm. They had spotted our trail of dust long before. Emerging gingerly from behind a fence made from the branches of a thorn tree, they came to greet their visitors.

The harsh desert existence had taken a dreadful toll. The man's face was chapped like rawhide, its skin blistered from a life spent working in the open. The woman, too, was wizened long before her time. I learnt later that she was forty-eight. She looked more like eighty. A decade of pregnancy had stolen her youth. She had given birth to twelve children, five of whom were dead.

José-Luis called out his name.

'*¡Amigo!*' cried the farmer. 'My friend! *¿Cómo está su padre?* How's your father?'

Pepé was well, he said, despite his bad luck.

'*¿Susto?*' asked the farmer.

José-Luis nodded.

We were ushered inside, out of the sun.

The farmer, Juan, pulled a plastic sheet away from the best chair. Wiping away a residue of dust, he motioned me to sit. The heat made conversation almost too much work. I admired a poster of Princess Diana, pinned up on the cracked mud wall.

'Ah, she was beautiful,' said the farmer softly.

'God takes what He loves most,' whispered his wife.

In the background I made out the atmospheric buzz of a radio. The woman, known to all as *Tia*, aunt, had switched it on full volume. Like the best chair, the radio was saved for the rare arrival of guests.

José-Luis said I was interested in the ancient people of the Atacama. He explained that I'd come across the ocean, from the 'Land of Diana'. When he thought I wasn't listening, he added that my heart was strong; I could not be frightened.

Juan went over to the corner and delved his hands into a cardboard box. He returned a moment later with a parcel, wrapped in brown paper.

'We found this seven years ago,' he said, as he handed it to me.

Gripping the package between my knees, I pulled apart the sheets of paper. Had I been a believer in *susto*, it would have got me right then. I jerked backwards. On my lap was a mummified human head.

Juan said that since they had found the trophy head in a grave behind the house, they had been blessed with good fortune.

'We honour it at Christmas, at Easter and festival times,' he said. 'It's a part of our family, as much as anyone else.'

The head had all the classic hallmarks of the ancient Nazcan techniques. The skin was intact, although preserved with a clay-like preparation. The eyes were sealed shut, the lips pinned together with thorns; and a carrying string had been threaded through a hole, trepanned through the brow. My interest in *tsantsas*, shrunken heads, had introduced me to all kinds of trophy heads.

Ethnologists have long debated whether human trophy heads were those of dead relatives, slain warriors, or even of people sacrificed at the graveside. Whatever the truth, one thing is certain – the trophy heads found at Nazca are expertly mummified. The general consensus is that the skin was peeled away, before the heads were boiled. Then, when the brain had been cleaned out, the skin was reapplied and layered with preservatives.

I was struck by the likeness of the trophy to the *tsantsas* for which I had such a fondness. Shrunken heads, like Juan's trophy, were typically suspended from a string, and had the lips skewered with splinters of chonta palm. This prevented them from calling out to members of their own tribe. (Similar, too, are the trophy heads from Nagaland, in India's North-east, which have buffalo horns fixed to the ears, to stop the head from hearing its rescuers.)

Juan was pleased at my praise for his trophy. No house, he said, should be without such a possession, an honour to the ancestors.

'I'll get you one,' he beamed.

'Where from?'

Juan's face erupted in laughter.

'*Sígame*, follow me,' he said.

We trouped out of the house, past the sleeping guard dog, and on through the warango trees. The noon sun rained down, scalding our backs. Juan led the way across a flat expanse of dust.

Waving the flies from his face with his hat, he pointed to a steep bulwark.

'Up there . . .'

The farmer, José-Luis and I staggered up the bank. The sand was so fine that a footprint disappeared as soon as it was made. It was littered with bottles, plastic bags and tin cans. A handful of thorn trees clung to the soft sand, providing some leverage as we clambered up.

Climbing over the top of the hill was like emerging from the trenches into no man's land. The scene was one of unimaginable devastation. Not even a Calcutta body dump could compare. There were human remains everywhere. Mummified bodies, recently hacked from their graves, their skin leathery, yet preserved. The plateau was pitted with thousands of tombs; their sides fallen in, the contents either stolen or strewn about. The bleached-white bones were too numerous to count. They shone in the sunlight, the last remains of an ancient people, forsaken by their ancestors. I saw ribs poking up out of the sand, femurs and jaws, the mummified spine of a child, and skulls – thousands of them, many with their hair still attached. Dozens had been deformed; others were trepanned.

As well as bones there were baskets made from cotton and fibre. For each mummy there had been a basket, in which it had sat cupped upright in the foetal position on a wad of cloth. Leading mummy experts say the burial position, the layers of cloth, and the baskets, are all for a reason. They were, they say, part of an elaborate drainage system. Liquids exuded in the years after death would naturally drain through the body, seeping down, and out through lower orifices, into the basket's pad.

Juan led me across the immense burial ground. I watched my step, fearful of falling into one of the pits, or of treading on the mummified remains. Every few feet the farmer would stop to tug a fragment of cloth from the dust, waggling it to shake off the sand. He handed the scraps to Tia, who had caught up with us.

Juan stopped at a deep crater.

'This was a big tomb,' he said. 'An important one was buried here.'

Tia and he helped me into the hole. They swished away the sand. First they dug out the resident mummy. He looked rudely awakened, ripped from his cocoon. His hair was long and soft, his skin the colour of honey, the individual pores quite distinct. The line of his ribs was clearly visible. The stench was rank as the smell of a Masai encampment. But it was nothing like the vile, chaotic smell of rotting human flesh.

The body was bound in textiles. Juan peeled a grand mantle away from the mummy's back. He shook off the sand. Along the border of the blanket was a row of images. I looked at them closely. They were Birdmen.

Tia was still digging. She excavated a second figure.

'It's a woman,' said Juan. 'See *sus pechos*, her breasts.'

As he fumbled about, showing me the mummified bust, the woman's right leg fell off.

'They're very fragile,' he muttered, handing me a head.

'This is for you,' he said. 'It's just like the one in the house. It will bring you good luck.'

Thanking the farmer, I rejected his offer. 'It belongs here,' I said. 'I won't be taking anything away with me.'

Juan couldn't understand why anyone would turn down a fine trophy head.

'¿*Esta seguro*? Are you sure?' he trilled. 'It's got a very nice face.'

The business of human remains is an unpleasant one. Our society dislikes the subject of corpses and death. Much has changed since ancient times. The Incas would bring out their mummified leaders during festivals. One 17th-century etching in Guaman Poma's chronicle shows the grinning cadaver of an Inca being paraded through the streets. The practice appalled the Spanish. But, as I squatted in the burial crater, surrounded by mummies and trophy heads, I felt none of the fear which so often accompanies death in our own world. The mummies were not skeletons but people, with faces, fingernails and hair.

I couldn't blame Juan and his family for robbing graves. The drought had killed their pigs and their meagre crops had shrivelled. How else were they to support themselves? Juan played down the extent of his part in what is a massive local operation. But, as I went back to the car, he asked respectfully if I'd like to buy some blankets, ornaments, pottery or beads. The burial ground on their doorstep was like a blessing from God. It must have contained more than 30,000 graves, only a fraction of which had been touched.

Ninety-five per cent of the antiquities in Peruvian museums are said to have been dug up by *huaqueros*. They have little or no scientific provenance as a result. Nazca's street corners are loaded with an army of agents, eager to sell the robbers' bounty. But the best loot bypasses Nazca, heading straight for the auction houses in the West.

José-Luis threw the hatchback into gear and aimed it at the embankment, as if it were a tank out on manoeuvres.

'Tonight's a full moon,' he said, as we gathered speed. 'Juan and his family will be busy digging.'

'Robbing graves?'

Pepé's son jerked his head in reply.

'It's time for the sleeping to be woken.'

*

Back at the Hummingbird Hotel, a man in an embroidered *kurta pyjama*, Indian costume, was propping up the bar, quaffing Pisco sours. The drink, a local speciality, is made from whipped egg white and Pisco, a grape brandy. His name was Freddie, and he told me that he'd just come from India, where he had spent seven years searching for a guru. It's a line that is usually enough to send me running for the door. As far as he was concerned, he went on, mind-altering substances were the real attraction of Nazca. I would have left right then, but I was reminded of the llamateer, Manuel, who'd led me to Sillustani. He had spoken cryptically of drug-induced flight.

I told Freddie about my feather with three notches, the message, and of the Birdmen, whose images I'd seen on funeral blankets. I asked for his thoughts. Did he think man had flown in ancient Peru?

Or was it flight of a different kind – allegorical rather than actual?
Freddie listened to the questions, and to my description of the
mummies at Majuelo.

Knocking back another Pisco sour, he dragged his fingers through
his beard.

'You won't understand those mummies,' he said, 'unless you think
about the drugs they were taking when they were alive.'

'Drugs?'

'Of course,' said Freddie. 'I'm not talking of LSD or tabs of ecstasy,
but natural drugs ... psychotropic plants, like the San Pedro cactus.'

I remembered seeing it growing on the Inca Trail.

'The Nazcans were taking San Pedro,' he said. 'If you look at the
pots, the textiles, and the other things they made, you'll see it.
Sometimes they're holding it during rituals; other times you find it
as a star-shaped cross section. San Pedro's still an important tool in
any Andean shaman's arsenal.'

'But does San Pedro give the sensation of flight?'

Freddie said that usually it didn't.

'For that there was a tea made from a vine,' he said. 'It gave the
feeling of growing wings and flying. It used to be common around
here. Your Birdmen from the mummy blankets were probably taking
it. Why else do you think they're reeling like that, like dope fiends?'

'What's this tea called?'

Draining his fifth Pisco sour, Freddie breathed into his fist.

'*Ayahuasca*,' he said. 'The Vine of the Dead.'

10

Vampires

The Paracas peninsula is named after the harsh wind which tears in from the ocean and flays the desert coast. Like the Mistral of southern France, it's a merciless force of nature endured by generations, but never welcome. For more than 3,000 years man has braved the treacherous shores of Paracas. The shacks may have tin roofs now, and there's a wrecked Dodge truck outside every one, but little else seems to have changed since ancient times.

At dawn, fathers and sons head out to sea in frail skiffs, bobbing on the Humboldt Current like toy ducks in a bath. Left at home, their wives and mothers nurse the babies, clean the home and scrub the porch. Their work is never done, but their laughter rings through the backstreets with the howl of the wind.

Freddie had passed on to me the basics of *ayahuasca*, the hallucinogen once used by the coastal peoples of Peru. The potion was, he had said, made from a stew of plants. It opened a door into another world. I had posed many questions, but Freddie was hesitant to reveal more. He told me that he wasn't qualified to discuss *ayahuasca*.

'Then who is qualified?'

Freddie scribbled down a name.

'Professor Cabieses, that is if he's still alive.'

'Where does he live?'

'Have a look in Lima,' he said.

*

An opal-green Ford Zephyr Six with bald tyres and a windscreen webbed with cracks, purred up the highway and into Paracas. Its owner was a precise man from the old school, when taxi driving was an art. He wore leather gloves, and shifted the gears with meticulous care. I complimented him on his vehicle. Of course, he said, the chrome was no longer as shiny as it should be, and the upholstery was stained where a passenger had spilt glue. They were a pair of old workhorses, he laughed. Since 1958 they'd done the *collectivo* run from Nazca to Paracas ten thousand times. But now they were tired.

The Zephyr cruised to a halt at the neck of the peninsula and I got down with my bags. Travelling with so much baggage was a cross to bear. I was beginning to wonder if I would ever use all this precious equipment. Was I ever going to need the carabiners or the caving rope, the folding spade, the Lancashire Hot Pot or, for that matter, the moose knife?

Late in the afternoon, before the sun had set, a golden ball over the Pacific, I paid a visit to the Paracas Museum. The clerk was busy swatting flies in the pool of light on his desk. He was surprised to have a visitor, and fumbled in a drawer for the visitor's book.

Paracas is the name of the wind, but also the name given to the pre-Incan culture which once existed on the coast. It's thought to have thrived between 1300 BC and 200 AD. The Peruvian archaeologist Julio C Tello first brought fame to the region, when he noticed that the undulations in the sand were actually burial mounds. Above ground little remains of the culture. But dig down and you reach the treasure. The Paracas civilisation was an advanced one, producing some of the finest artefacts ever made in Latin America. Without doubt, the most wonderful and possibly the most sacred of all, were the Birdmen textiles.

One display in the museum showed how the mummies were cocooned well below the surface, wrapped in multiple layers of fabric. The funeral blankets, ponchos and shawls were made exclusively to be worn in death. They were not made to fit the cadaver, but to cover the actual bundle which surrounded the corpse. Unlike ancient Egypt, where only dignitaries were mummified, the Paracas and Nazcan people preserved all their dead. Important members of society were buried with masses of loot. Bows and arrows, pipes, sling-shots and pottery are commonly found in the graves. Mummified animals have also been unearthed, including dogs, cats, birds and foxes. Some preserved bodies were wrapped in no less than eighteen cloaks and mantles, with as many as thirty garments.

The *huaqueros* who ravage the burial grounds on a daily basis, have been smitten by gold fever. Hacking their way through the layers of cloth, they prise open the mummies' mouths in their quest for gold. They tear fingers off hands to get at jewellery. Laden with treasure they hurry away into the night.

Thousands of rare textiles have been unearthed in Peru, spanning as far back as 3000 BC. These days they are regarded as more precious than gold, just as they were to the people who made them. No other region on Earth can boast a longer textile history. The work must have called for a communal effort, bringing llama wool from the mountains, dyeing it, designing patterns, spinning, weaving and embroidering. Centuries before the first lump of Latin American clay was worked into a pot, Paracas was a centre for textile production.

With allegorical flight in mind, I studied the textiles, searching for clues. Woven into the fabric were a wild assortment of images, including hundreds of Birdmen. The main figures were comprised of sub-images. In the wings of the Birdmen were rows of trophy heads, serpents and daggers. They had streamers spewing from their mouths and ornamental crowns. All were awash with colour, as if inspired by a psychedelic dream.

The flight of these Birdmen wasn't forced and cumbersome like *real* flight. It was graceful and easy, like an angel wafting through a dream. A few of the mantles bore rows of 'falling' shamans, plunging Earthward with glazed expressions. Perhaps these were clues that the Birdmen flew, at least within the limits of their minds.

*

Not far from Paracas is the town of Pisco. It is inextricably linked with vampires. Cast an eye across its Plaza de Armas, and you will see members of the vampire cult. They come to the town in their hundreds. Dressed in black coats and matching boots, with lines of kohl circling their eyes, punky hair pushed up in quiffs, they sit on the benches, waiting for the night.

I wasn't really interested in vampires, but a chewing-gum seller said I'd regret it if I didn't look into the town's fiendish tradition. So I hailed an Indian-made auto-rickshaw and told the driver to head for the cemetery on Calle San Francisco.

Standing outside the graveyard was a man selling enormous blooms of chrysanthemums. He asked if I wanted to buy flowers; I replied that I wasn't sure who I'd come to see.

A few steps further and a guide offered his services.

'Come to see Sarah Ellen?' he asked.

'Um, yes, I think so.'

'She's over here.'

As he led the way down to the other end of the graveyard, he told me the legend.

'She was a young English girl,' he said. 'She died and was buried here in 1913. No one knows much about her ... but a few years ago your vampire friends started arriving.'

'But I'm not a vampire.'

The guide looked me in the eye.

'Are you sure?'

I nodded earnestly.

He pointed to a grave set into a wall.

'Perhaps you are telling the truth,' he said. 'It's women who come mostly, from all over the world. From France and Germany, Australia and Japan. They bribe the police, so that they can spend the night here.'

'Do they lay flowers?' I asked.

'Hah!' came the reply. 'No, they don't leave flowers, but they leave *other* things.'

'What?'

'Bits of meat, strange amulets and dead cats with their heads cut off. Some of them have tried to open the grave,' he said. 'I think they want to take *un recuerdo*, a souvenir.'

'A souvenir?'

The guardian wiped a hand over the plaque.

'A finger, a hand, something like that, something to take away and show to their friends.'

*

The Ormeño bus from Pisco to the Peruvian capital was so plush that the backpacker sitting beside me took off his shoes and socks and nuzzled his toes into the thick-pile carpet. We glided up the coast road, the triple-glazed windows tinting the light, and muting the sound of the wheels. I stared out at the desert, which stretched to the east like a silvery-grey bedspread of sand. In the few places where it had been irrigated, maize and bananas thrived. Dousing the dust with a little water is like touching it with a magic wand.

The backpacker fished out a crumpled guide to Peru and thumbed through it. From the state of the book, I could see he'd been on the road for months. He seemed on edge, eager to share his enthusiasm for this rare luxury. I knew he was English even before he opened his mouth, because an Englishman abroad is always reluctant to be the first to break the ice. He wriggled his toes and thumbed harder through the book.

'D'you see the deformed skulls in Paracas?' he blurted, 'the ones which look like alien heads?'

I replied that I had.

'I've just bought one,' he said, pointing to a dented steel box on the luggage rack.

'What are you going to do with a deformed skull?'

'It's for my museum.'

For the rest of the journey, the shoeless backpacker informed me of his lifelong passion – a museum of curiosities. The collection, built up over twenty years, already boasted a number of important objects: a pickled tumour from a dead woman's groin, an Eskimo's seal-intestine coat, death masks from China, and a selection of trepanned skulls. He even had an 'exotic mermaid' – half-baboon, half-fish – faked in Victorian England. The man claimed to have turned his Merseyside house into a shrine, devoted to freakery. Modern museums, he said, were fearful places, packed with dreary objects. Building on the foundations of the past, his collection was full of spirit.

His aim was to match the museum of Peter the Great. The Russian Czar's storehouse had been packed floor to ceiling with oddities. Many of the exhibits were still breathing. There were live children with two heads, sheep with five feet, and a variety of deformed babies. The caretaker was a dwarf with two fingers on each hand and a pair of toes on each foot. When the dwarf died, he was stuffed and plonked on the shelves with the other exhibits.

The coach trundled through *los barriadas*, Lima's shanty-towns. Veiled behind high municipal walls, they hid a world of burden, very different from the luxurious bubble that was the Ormeño bus. The interlocking maze of wooden shacks stand testimony to those who've come in search of a better life. Lured by the prospect of magnificent wealth, theirs is a life of unimaginable hardship. They survive on less than nothing. Once they have tasted the drug of the metropolis they can never return home.

Lima's traffic stop-starts its way down the choked highways, jolting forward a few inches at a time. No one questions the lack of speed, they're used to it. Unwinding their windows, they make the most of the ride. Weaving between the cars are thousands of *ambulantes*, street-sellers. Whatever you want to buy, they have it stuffed into their sacks. Bubble gum and baseball caps, playing cards and fluffy dice, posters of Marilyn Monroe and maps of France, light-bulbs and eyelash curlers, ball-point pens and sellotape. In a city where wages are so spectacularly low, even respectable professionals can be found on the streets supplementing their income after work.

I don't know what manner of lunacy came over me, but I checked in to Lima's Hotel Gran Bolivar. The old lady of Lima society, built in 1924, the Bolivar was once *the* place to be seen. It's a colossus of a building, haughty and proud, with birch-white walls and a formidable entrance on Plaza San Martin. An hour of bargaining secured a grand suite on the third floor, at the knock-down price of $25. The manager appeared anxious for custom, as the place was virtually empty.

The bellboy led the way down a palatial corridor. He stopped at a tremendous doorway, flanked by fluted columns. As he slipped the solid brass key into the lock, my conscience beckoned me. How could I stay in such luxury after seeing shanty-towns minutes before? I was racked with guilt, and was about to deliberate on my fortune. But the tour of the suite had begun.

The hardwood doors were dark with lacquer, their knobs moulded with the hotel's monogram. A study led from the dining-room which overlooked the Plaza. The curtains, which were double-lined, reeked of a time when curtains were a detail of luxury rather than merely an accessory to keep out the light. Like the others, the drawing-room was tiled in herringbone parquet. The veneer of its cocktail bar was chipped, where generations of shakers had been forced down a little too hard. The bellboy pointed out anterooms and cubby-holes, a writing desk with secret drawers, and a vast walk-in closet with an automatic light. Then he rocked on his heels waiting for a tip.

When he had gone, I telephoned an old family friend, living in the exclusive Miraflores district of Lima. She burst into tears when I told her where I was staying.

'Leave at once!' she said. 'It's so dangerous there. Everyone knows the Bolivar's haunted by the woman with the butcher's cleaver.'

'But my door is locked.'

'She can enter any room by passing through the walls,' said my friend. 'She'll hack off your head and drink your blood.'

I told her about the monogrammed door handles, the parquet floors, the lagoon-like bath, and the lack of other guests.

'Why do you think the place is empty?' she said. '*Everyone* knows of *la señora que carga una hacha de cocina*, the woman with the meat cleaver.'

'But I've paid in advance.'

'I don't care what you've paid,' she said coldly. 'But spend a night in that hotel and you'll be dead before morning.'

11

Conspiracy

The round bar at Hotel Gran Bolivar was once known as the 'Snake Pit', because every socialite tongue could be found there, hissing gossip. These days it's hardly patronised at all. Bartenders are positioned at strategic points around the salon, waiting for the bustle of clientele which never comes. Their bow-ties are tight, their hair groomed back with brilliantine, and their eyes alert. Each evening, the small dancefloor at the centre of the room is swept and polished with beeswax. But years have passed since feet last swanned over its parquet.

Despite my friend's fretting, I survived the night at Gran Bolivar. I'd seen no ghosts, but had woken with an excruciating headache. It felt as if I'd been clubbed with a baseball bat, but the woman with the cleaver had left me alone.

After breakfast, I set out into the river of honking traffic in search of Professor Cabieses. The street corners were jam-packed with money-changers, clutching rolls of dollar bills. They vied for space with a swarm of hawkers, selling potted plastic flowers and hurricane lamps, frying pans, Zippos and chicks dyed pink. One man ran into the road with his stock of squirming puppies. Anywhere else motorists might be uninterested in snapping up a dog. But in Lima, where there's a deep mistrust of retail stores, the street is the only place to shop.

The Peruvian capital gets a bad rap from tourists. They say it's rundown and dangerous, that the sewers stink and that everyone you meet is out to either rob or kill you. It is partly true. I've never known another city where a waiter chains your bag to the table, or where the knifings are more common.

At its height, Lima was one of the grandest cities on the continent.

It was rated as more beautiful than Paris, as refined as Rome. Stroll in the backstreets off Plaza de Armas and the flamboyant baroque doorways, heavy with crests and friezes glare down. Like the enclosed balconies of the *palacios*, the palaces, they signify the opulence of a colonial power with a point to prove. But the high life came to an abrupt end in 1746 when a great earthquake struck. Most of the resplendent villas and colonnades, the plazas and the *palacios*, were reduced to dust.

In the century which followed, the wars of independence slashed the capital's population, as Limeños were sent to the front lines. With time, their city was rebuilt, but it never regained its majesty.

A few telephone calls tracked Cabieses to a large teaching hospital near Miraflores. An elite suburb, the area is reserved for those who have made it. In Miraflores rich women walk in Italian shoes. With their hair swirled up like candyfloss, they prowl the pavements, flashing off their jewels. The streets are free of *ambulantes*. There's no one touting moss-green lizards or surgical gloves, and the only smell is of espresso brewing on spotless stalls.

Professor Cabieses' secretary mumbled that he had gone to a neuro-surgical conference and would be back in a week. I said that I'd thought the doctor was an authority on drugs. In a secretive voice, the assistant replied that Dr Cabieses was an expert in many things.

Again my journey had been becalmed. With a full week to kill, I cursed myself for conducting a search where any answers proved soon to be further questions. What began as a trail of feathers, was becoming a trial of unfulfilled hope. I went to the concièrge of Hotel Gran Bolivar for words of comfort. He pushed me towards a taxi. *Museo del Oro*, the Gold Museum, was the only thing worth seeing in Lima, he said.

No one was quite certain when Miguel Mujica Gallo founded his remarkable museum, which nestles in the suburb of Monterrico. I cannot think of a greater shrine to the art of collecting. A treasure trove, it's brimming with loot. Even before I'd got into the main body of the building, I found myself wading through Gallo's less important collection – several hundred thousand weapons. He had bought up just about everything one might care to look at, from General Custer's revolver to a set of rare Persian helmets.

The scope of Gallo's museum was impressive, but the size of the collection was almost irrelevant; it was his collecting spirit that mattered. That spirit, I reflected, had kindled my current journey. Everyone ought to be working on a collection of some kind. I would count myself as a collector of *tsantsas*, shrunken heads, even though I have yet to afford one. When I was nine my aunt explained to me that a man without a collection was like a house without a roof. She presented me with a triple-edged Malayan dagger-cane, and advised me to collect sword-sticks, which I have done ever since.

Most of *Museo del Oro* was devoted to artefacts from pre-Incan Peru. There were textiles of Birdmen and funerary dolls, macaw-feather cloaks, Chancay ceramics, ritualistic daggers, mummies, and a dazzling accumulation of gold ornaments. But, for my money, all the rest was eclipsed by four understated objects. Two of them were skulls adorned with yellow and blue feathers. The other two were figurines. About two feet high, they were covered in bright feathers as well, and had crude jeering faces. In their hands were trophy heads.

Back at Gran Bolivar the Snake Pit was still silent. Wringing his hands together, the concièrge told me of the good old days. With a week to get through until the Professor's return, I pulled up a chair and listened.

'Gentlemen used to dress for dinner,' he said. 'And their wives would drift through these rooms in sequinned gowns. It was a wonderful sight, like Hollywood.'

'What of the gossip?'

The concièrge put a hand to his mouth.

'Ah,' he mumbled, 'all those secret rendezvous, all that passion!'

'Affairs?'

'Oh yes, but we never breathed a word,' he said, 'we left the hissing to the snakes.'

'What of *la señora que carga una hacha de cocina*?'

The concièrge's face dropped.

'She has scared away the guests,' he said, sweeping an arm across the foyer in an arc. 'In Peru we are very superstitious . . .'

*

Two blocks behind the Hotel Gran Bolivar, beside a kiosk selling under-ripe bananas, a woman was sitting on a stool. Her shoulders were hunched forward, her greying hair pulled back in a single pigtail.

Her mouth was a blinding smile of white and gold. The seat stood on an oriental prayer rug, beside which there was another stool for customers.

I watched from a distance as people would pause from their hurried lives to hear a tale. They came from many backgrounds: businessmen, secretaries, housewives, even manual workers. The lady would tell them stories. The tradition is one I have known well in the East where everyone can make time for a tale.

Wiping the empty seat with the corner of a rag, the woman invited me to sit. She told me her name was Dolores, and that stories had been in her family for fifteen generations. The tales, which came from the mountains, she said, were magical. They would purify my soul. The charge was three *soles*. I sat down and handed over the coins.

The story was an epic tale of love and honour, compassion and great bravery. Its heroes were Peruvian warriors, caught in a struggle between good and evil. Dolores said the tale had been in her family for three hundred years. Her comment brought a smile to my face. For the story was famous throughout central Asia, and is told in the pages of *The Arabian Nights*.

'The tale has cleaned your head,' Dolores said when she had finished. 'But your mind is still troubled.'

My headache had actually grown worse.

'Tomorrow morning a train will leave Lima for Huancayo,' said Dolores. 'If you want to be rid of your problems, take that train. Go and meet a man called Señor Pedro Oroña Laya. Tell him I sent you. You can find him at *Wali Wasi*,' she said, 'the Sacred House.'

As I still had a few days to spare, I decided to take the story-teller's advice. Next morning I made my way to the station on the southern bank of the Rimac River. The train to Huancayo was about to leave. It carries passengers just once a month, a point of which Dolores must have been aware.

Huancayo is a small commercial town set high in the mountains, in the Mantaro Valley, the bread basket of Peru. Reaching it by railway from Lima was a feat of engineering that only the Victorians would have attempted. Like Kenya's Lunatic Express, which climbs the Great Rift each day, the route was technically impossible. Construction on what became the highest railway line on earth began in

1870. For 23 years the imported Chinese workforce slogged away, boring tunnels and building bridges.

For 11 hours the Huancayo Express ground its way up the rails and into the Andes. The line is famous for its 22 'switch-backs', a system which allows the double-ended train to ascend a steep incline by slaloming forward and back.

Outside, sweeping plateaux gave way to ice-capped mountains and crystal streams. Sometimes the earth was the colour of a doe's hide, and at others it was red as ochre, or grey like slate. There were dark brackish pools of water, like Welsh tarns, and fields which stretched forever. Dogs with savage, bulging eyes ran alongside, desperate to keep up with the carriages. Women paused from their work in the wheat fields to wave, their faces red-brown like polished mahogany.

We passed an open-top hopper waiting on a slip-track. It was filled with large, uniform ingots of silver. The man opposite watched my eyes widen greedily. His face was masked in a clipped white beard, his cheeks high, his eyes like fragments of coal. A long-time resident of Huancayo, he was originally from Denmark.

His wine-red lips spoke cautiously. 'Silver for the *Sendero Luminoso*,' he said, 'for the Shining Path.'

'Surely these are government mines?'

'The government may mine it, but *Luminoso* will take it.'

Peru's recent history has been dominated by the Shining Path. Their brutal, pure form of Marxism is sometimes compared to that of Cambodia's Khmer Rouge. *Sendero Luminoso* may have never got their hands on national power, but all Peruvians have felt their effect. In a campaign dedicated to death, which ran from 1980 until about 1992, they wreaked havoc across the country. More than 25,000 ordinary people were killed by their hand, and a reputed $22 billion worth of property was destroyed. The eventual capture of Abimael Guzman, the Path's leader, put an end to the violence.

'But I thought the days of the Shining Path were over,' I said.

The bearded man grinned.

'Don't believe the propaganda,' he whispered. 'There's a conspiracy going on.'

The carriage swelled from time to time with entertainers hired by the tourist office. A troupe of dancers pranced through, singing folk-songs. A pair of adolescent girls hurried behind them with food. Another followed them, pouring *chicha*, to wash down the plates of

1. Detail from a fabulous embroidered funeral textile, found near Paracas on Peru's desert coast. The llama-wool textile is thought to date from about 50 AD. Its winged figures are adorned with human trophy heads.

2. William Isadore Dieches with a paper model of an Ancient Egyptian glider which, he suggests, was piloted by Tutankhamen and his contemporaries.

3. Funeral tower at Sillustani, near Lake Titicaca, from which,
legend says, Birdmen once flew.

4. The 2,000-year-old remains
of a mummified warrior, buried
with the trophy head of one
of his victims, pulled from
the ground by grave-robbers
near Nazca.

5. Fragments of ancient textiles which cloaked the bodies of the dead at Majuelo's vast burial ground.

6. An ancient mummified trophy head plundered by Juan and his family of grave-robbers. Similar in many ways to Shuar shrunken heads, the lips are sealed and a hole has been made in the brow for a suspension cord.

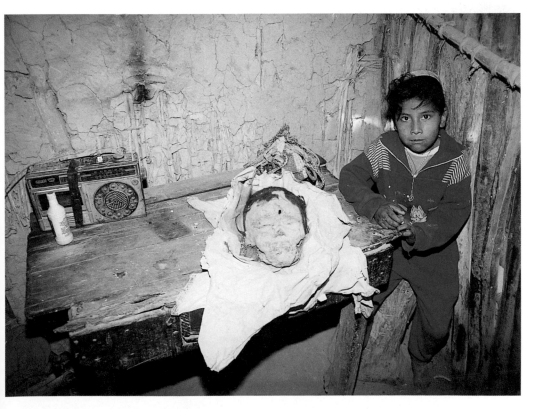

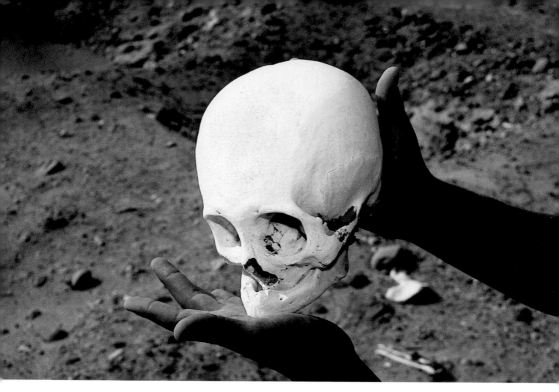

7. The robbed cemetery at Majuelo is littered with deformed skulls such as this. It is thought that heads were deformed in childhood for reasons of beauty.

8. Professor Fernando Cabieses, wearing his prized Shuar shrunken head.

9. The *maestro* Pedro Oroña Laya makes a mask of the author's face in cow dung, near the Andean town of Huancayo.

10. Pedro, who uses guinea-pigs to heal, holds up a cow dung and feather mask. Some of Pedro's followers say that such masks can fly.

11. Anaconda Man posing with an angry anaconda.

12. Striking another pose with a pair of caimans at his jungle hide-out near Iquitos.

13. One of many big bugs being offered for sale on the streets of Iquitos.

carapulcra, a meat and potato stew. After the *chicha* there was bingo, with prizes – raw potatoes and maize. And after the bingo there was an impromptu lecture on llamas.

The Dane rolled his eyes as the occupants of the carriage applauded.

'It's always the same,' he said dolefully. 'The authorities lay on the party, but behind the façade they're scheming.'

'What are you talking about?'

He nudged a thumb towards the llama expert.

'Everyone knows the government is supporting the Path,' said my informant, 'and that guy's in on it.'

'Are you sure he is?'

'Of course!' came the rely. 'Peru's in disarray – forces are colluding.'

'Colluding? Who's colluding with who?'

'I'll tell you,' said the Dane, 'I'll tell you everything.'

A tap-dancer struggled through the carriage against the movement of the train. Then came another round of *chicha*.

'The missionaries are opening up the jungle for the oil companies,' he said. 'The drug barons are being funded by the CIA; the multi-nationals are sabotaging their own factories, and President Fujimori's in bed with MOSSAD.'

'The Israeli Secret Service?'

'Of course!' he exclaimed. 'It's obvious.'

'Is it?'

'My boy,' said the Dane, 'you have much to learn.'

I turned to the aisle, where the next entertainer was on. He was demonstrating how to make a whistling sound, by blowing into his shoe.

The informer scratched his thumb across his chin.

'Peru's teeming with conspiracy,' he said. 'It's been going on for years. How do you think the Nazca Lines got there?'

My eyes left the whistling shoe and focused back on the Danish man.

'What's your theory?'

'It's not theory but fact,' he said. 'Only Maria Reiche and a handful of Nazcans were in on it...'

'In on what?'

'The Lines!' he declared, 'Reiche and the others drew the Lines themselves.'

'But why would they do such a thing?'

'How else do you expect they could have attracted tourists to that hell-hole of a place?'

*

Trawl through the Sunday markets of Latin America and you'll come across some remarkable things. From Tierra del Fuego to Caracas, the selection is very much the same. There are tarantulas staked out in miniature frames, monkey bone aphrodisiacs, and bottles filled with coloured sand; ball-gowns made from magenta nylon and llama skin slippers, sequinned espadrilles and silver poison rings. Like anywhere else on the continent, Huancayo's wares are invariably marked with the name of the town. Peruvian tourists like nothing more than to amaze their friends with the latest stuffed armadillo souvenir, displayed on a plinth, with 'Huancayo' etched neatly underneath.

The town, once crippled by *Sendero Luminoso*, had entered a renaissance. Everyone had tales of the bad old days, when you had to check under your car for bombs. And everyone could tell of a relative or friend who had stepped out after dark and was never seen again. But with Guzman behind bars life was different, they said. One woman, selling scarves at the side of road, pressed her thumb into the air in celebration.

'Our happiness is all the greater,' she declared, '*sabemos lo que es la pena*, because we have tasted sorrow.'

After an earsplitting night at the Hotel Disco, where every room had direct access to the dance floor, I flagged down a taxi and ordered him to *Wali Wasi*. Dolores, the storyteller, had told me to head for the cemetery at Umuto, which I assumed was nearby. I climbed in. The driver's foot lurched down onto the accelerator and we took off at the speed of light. We passed colonial churches and concrete monstrosities, pensioners crooked over walking canes, and a brigade of children with baskets on their backs. The taxi was gathering speed as we approached the countryside. Forty minutes later, we were still racing along, a great plume of dust following our tracks.

Periodically, the driver would swivel round to face me, his maniacal eyes flashing like a *jinn's*, his foot jammed to the magic pedal. He swore that we'd almost arrived. Another hour went by. We careered down a rutted track for a mile or so, and ended up in the middle of a maize field. The driver again turned to face me. The light had disappeared from his eyes. His head ducked with submission. Sinking his teeth into his upper lip, he mumbled an apology, but he had no idea where we were. Could I please settle the bill?

I spotted a child shepherding an alpaca around the edge of the field, and asked him for directions. He pointed to the next field.

'The cemetery is there,' he said. '*El maestro*, the master, lives just beyond it.'

The driver pretended he had been joking. Perhaps, he hinted, my tip could reflect the high level of service.

A few minutes later, I found myself knocking at the mottled door of what looked like a stable block. The mud walls, recently repaired, were decorated with spiral-like symbols.

A little girl opened the door, which led into a courtyard. I glanced around. Hundreds of faces were scrutinising me, their expressions leering like inmates escaped from an asylum. Most of them were made of cow dung. They were painted in gaudy colours, their gaunt features boiling with rage. Each one bore the same impenetrable eyes, and the same disfigured mouth. Some were decorated with odds and ends – old bottles and plastic tubs, bleached bones, contorted roots, twigs and driftwood. The walls of the yard were adorned with yet more art. Dozens of paintings loomed down, each more disturbing than the last. Among them, the skeleton of Death was being crucified, and a woman was being raped by a bull. I wondered what kind of disturbed freak could have come up with such work.

At that moment the *maestro* arrived.

12

Guinea Pig Healer

Pedro Oroña Laya was a cross between Jesus and Chewbaka. He looked like the sort of man who, under more normal circumstances, one might try to avoid. Not since the wilds of the Hindu Kush had I come across such an abundance of facial hair. With his beard and almond eyes the *maestro* could have passed as a Pashtun, from Afghanistan. But, then again, no Pashtun would be seen in sweeping beige robes, with a home-made cross around his neck.

'Welcome to my imagination,' said the *maestro*, gesturing for me to sit down.

I told him that Dolores had sent me, and that my mind was troubled. The master cleared his throat and spat at the dirt.

'I can return the harmony,' he said. '*Estás poseído por el demonio,* you are full of demons. And you are going to need your strength.'

'What for? Why will I need strength?'

The *maestro* didn't answer. Instead, squinting, he cleared his throat for a second time.

'First, I will make *una máscara*, a mask of your face,' he decided.

I followed him out of the courtyard, up the lane to the main road and across into an enclosure. A herd of dairy cows were being milked; the farmer's wife was scrubbing the urns with a wad of straw. The master motioned for me to hold my hands out in front of my chest. I thought he wanted to read my palms. But instead he piled a mass of warm cow dung onto them.

'Take this back to *Wali Wasi*,' he said.

Once sitting on the courtyard floor, the *maestro* pushed his hands through the fresh dung, breathing in the aroma. He then stirred in a dollop of white glue, and kneaded the mixture until it was smooth as jam. I stood in the shade, watching his expert hands moulding my face from the dung. Unlike a conventional sculptor, Pedro didn't look at me once. I presumed he was making a symbolic mask. When the face was completed, it was left in the sun to dry. The *maestro* said he would paint it later, but first he would continue with the treatment, which would make me strong.

He led me under the eaves of a veranda, from which were hanging cobs of dry maize. We stood together beside a miniature shrine. At its base was a human skull, a little the worse for wear. Above it was an assortment of lurid dung masks, including one with red light-bulbs for eyes, a femur for a nose and real human teeth set in its mouth.

The *maestro* told me to wait at the shrine. He disappeared into an anteroom. I heard him poking about, getting the place ready. Clapping his hands, he called me in.

Pedro's was an imagination without limit. As I stepped into the sanctuary, I was hit full force by the extent of his fantasy.

Much of the chamber was taken up by a home-made totem-pole. An anthropologist might have said it was built in reverence to the land; for it was made from maize cobs, dried corn leaves and strands of feathery pampas grass. There were ribbons too wound around its neck, which led to a face so fiendish that it caused me to miss a breath. Its eyebrows and nose were cobs, and its fangs splinters of bone. On the floor around it were clustered a range of offerings – dried herbs and ears of black maize, sunflower heads, and a postal sack tied with a granny knot.

Pedro pointed to a mattress which lay in the shadow of the totem.

'Get undressed and lie down there,' he said.

I wondered why the healing of a troubled mind might require nudity. But this was a clinic without convention. Stripping down to my boxer shorts, I stretched out and pulled the gargoyle-grey army blanket up to my chin. The totem-pole froze me with a grimacing stare. And the *maestro* began his work.

He pulled a handful of coca leaves from a pouch around his neck. Touching them to his brow in respect, he put them on his tongue one at a time. The master's youngest daughter pushed open the door and sat with the offerings. She was given a few coca leaves, and entered the ritual. After the coca there was *chicha* for the girl and the priest. Reclining on the mattress, I questioned what part I would play.

My attention was drawn to the yard. Although I couldn't see what was going on, I didn't need Pedro's strength of imagination to guess. A sow was obviously fighting for its life, desperate to escape a butcher's knife. Its last screams were terrible, high-pitched and frantic, as it sparred with Death. The squeals stopped as suddenly as they had begun. A moment later, the sullen figure of a man swept into the sanctuary. He was barefoot and his apron was drenched in fresh blood. Having honoured the totem with the hog's foot, he slunk way. The *maestro* had paid no attention to the sounds of execution. As I was soon to find out, death was a tool of his trade.

The little girl dragged the postal sack over to her father. He loosened the knot with the tips of his fingers and took something from it. I peered over from the mattress. Pedro was holding a large black guinea-pig. The creature, keenly sniffing the air, was held at arm's length towards the totem-pole. A bottle of *agua de florida*, perfumed water used by Peruvian shamans, was sprinkled over it. After which the master coughed a lungful of tobacco smoke along the length of its body.

Still damp with holy water, the guinea pig was wrapped in a sheet of white wax paper. I was surprised that it didn't wriggle. As with a stage magician's rabbit, it may have been hypnotised in some way. The *maestro* returned to his stool and chewed another handful of coca leaves. His daughter bent over the offerings and lit another candle. As the wick flickered with life, Pedro unwrapped the guinea pig, sprinkled more *agua de florida*, and moved over to the bed.

The shadow of the healer fell over me. He peeled back the coarse grey blanket and went to work. First the *cuy* was pressed to my face, rubbed over my brow, across my eyes, nose and mouth. I felt its warmth, and took in the scent of its soft damp pelt. The sensation was not unpleasant. Pedro held the creature stretched rigid between his hands. He guided it over my body, as if it were some kind of medical instrument. Every inch of skin was touched by the trembling animal. Over my chin and across my neck, up and down my arms, chest and stomach, groin, legs and feet. I turned over and my back was treated.

Anointing with guinea pigs is a common method of Andean healing and divination, known as *Jaca shoqpi*. It's a system of medicine embroiled in secrecy. Despite the influence of Catholicism, *cuy* has remained a central tool in Andean ritual, just as it has a staple food. The strange marriage between New World and Old is represented by a painting which hangs in the Cathedral at Cusco. Painted in about 1670, by Miguel de Santiago, it depicts Christ and his Apostles at the Last Supper. Placed before them is a dish of cooked guinea pig.

When Pedro had finished, I pulled the blanket over my body once again. It was time for the second phase of the operation. The healer dunked the *cuy* in a pot of water, immersing it completely until it squirmed. Then, grabbing it by the scruff of the neck, he held it over a bright-red washing tub. His daughter passed over the blade of a penknife. It had been sharpened many times, its cutting edge eroded by years of abrasion. The *maestro*'s muscular fingers grasped the rodent's back. With great care, he pressed the blade across its lower abdomen in a single incision.

Over the next fifteen minutes he worked away with the knife, separating the pelt from the white membrane beneath. I'm not certain when the animal died; but I am sure it was still alive during the first part of the ordeal. The process of skinning the *cuy* was extremely meticulous; every strand of fur was removed, and not a single drop of blood was shed.

Pedro submerged the skinned guinea-pig in water for a moment. I sensed a draught of cold air across my face. The door had been pushed open a crack. Three or four children from the lane had come to watch their favourite part of the treatment – the dissection. The healer didn't look up, for fear of breaking concentration. An interruption, or *takpa*, is considered to be the meddling of the Devil.

The blade was pressed to the *cuy*'s neck. And, in a long sweeping movement, the master carved the steel down the rodent's body. His hands fumbled to contain the mass of organs and entrails. They glistened, for they had been alive minutes before. I was surprised that during the dissection too there was so little blood, presumably a reflection of the healer's surgical skill.

Pedro caressed his fingers through the jumble of organs. He inspected the *cuy*'s heart and the lungs, its liver and spleen, kidneys and intestines. Then he examined the animal's feet, its head, and the colour of its flesh.

'It is no surprise to me you are troubled,' he said dismally. 'I can see your illness.'

'What's wrong with me?'

The *maestro* rummaged through the guinea pig's intestines like a priest praying with a rosary.

'*Los espiritus malos*, bad spirits,' he said.

'How can you be sure?'

'I see them here in *los entrañas*, the intestines.' He held the entrails up to the candlelight. 'Can you not see where it is scarred?'

Pedro replaced the skin on the guinea pig's body and wrapped it in the sheet of white wax paper. He would dispose of it secretly during the night. I asked whether it could be eaten. The master was disgusted by my question. Not even the most starving wretch of a man, he said, would be tempted by the tainted entrails.

Now that he had reached a diagnosis, Pedro meted out his cure. He moved over to the totem-pole and pulled from it a long cob of dried maize.

'Put this under your pillow when you sleep,' he said. 'The demons will leave you and enter the corn. You will be as strong as a castrated ox, ready for what lies ahead.'

Peering into my eyes, he seemed to see my future, the place where the trail led.

'*En cuarenta noches* ... leave the corn under your pillow for forty nights,' he said. 'You must not shake any man's hand for that time. Then bury the maize in the ground and put a stone on top of it.'

'What happens if I don't do this?'

Pedro stood to his feet and wiped the blade of the knife across his sleeve. His expression soured.

'If you do not do as I tell you,' he said angrily, 'the wicked spirits will multiply. They will fill your head like worms, and will crawl down into your body. Every organ will become infected, your flesh will rot, your bones will crack, and your mind with soften, until...'

He broke off abruptly.

'Until *what*?'

The healer ran a finger round the curve of his ear.

'You would not want to hear,' he said.

13

The Tsantsa's Cheek

The day after my return to Lima from Huancayo, Professor Cabieses' secretary called. The doctor, she said, had just arrived back and would see me at four o'clock.

The neurosurgical hospital's waiting area was a fearful place. Patients hobbled in and out. Some wore bandages wrapped around their heads like clinical turbans; others had retort stands clamped to their spines. The man sitting beside me looked quite normal. But every few seconds he would jerk his head to the left, and wink six times with each eye.

I thumbed through an old issue of *Hola!*, and watched the receptionist file her nails. The procedure reminded me of a blacksmith, re-shoeing a horse. An hour slipped by. The receptionist completed her manicure and started on her hair. More time passed, and she moved onto her lashes. I was about to edge to the door when a short, balding man in an oyster-grey suit marched out of the lift and through reception. The injured and afflicted straightened in respect. The squinting man blinked continuously until tears rolled down his cheeks.

The receptionist slid the tip of an eye-liner across the lid of her eye, inspecting the work in a Gucci compact. She turned to me.

'Dr Cabieses will see you now.'

The professor was rifling through his bookshelves, looking for something. I took a moment to glance round the surgery, which smelled of antiseptic liquid. It was cluttered with potted plants, each labelled with an identification tag. The walls were heavy with framed certificates, the windows hidden by venetian blinds. In one corner was a hatstand on which was slung a sou-wester. To the right of the door stood a San Pedro cactus.

Dr Cabieses removed a slim volume from the shelf and turned to face me.

'I understand you are interested in plants,' he said, in faultless English, extending his arm towards me.

My hand lurched forward instinctively to shake his. Remembering the exorcism in the nick of time, I jerked it back, like a fencer recovering from a lunge. I pressed my hands together in an Indian *namaste*.

The neurosurgeon retracted his hand, and placed a finger on his lips.

'Seen a *cuandero* recently?' he said.

I told him about my visit to *Wali Wasi* and about the exorcism.

'It sounds to me as if you're having sinus trouble,' he said. 'That is, unless you believe in *los espiritus malos*, bad spirits.'

'As a hypochondriac I find myself believing in all sorts of conditions,' I replied. 'I can't help it.'

Dr Cabieses motioned to a chair at the other side of the broad walnut desk.

'The mind is a curious thing,' he said. 'As is the power of belief. Nothing is stronger than a man's faith.'

'What about the effect of *ayahuasca* on belief?'

The professor peered through the venetian blinds, down to the street.

'*Ayahuasca* is a very serious subject,' he said.

I told the doctor of my journey from Machu Picchu to Titicaca, and on to Nazca. I said I was looking for traces of ancient flight, for the Birdmen.

Starting at the left corner of his mouth, a smile swept onto Cabieses' face.

'Your travels have already answered the question,' he said. 'I don't know why you have hunted me down, for you have the answers.'

'What answers?'

Again, the professor peered through the blinds.

'Let us lay the pieces of the puzzle here on the table,' he said, slapping his hand down on the walnut veneer. 'Pizarro's monks talked of Incas flying in the air. Clausijiro, too, said the Aztecs could glide. But,' the doctor continued, 'surely the Spanish opposition for flying men came from how their flight was achieved, rather than from the motion itself.'

'*Ayahuasca?*'

'Precisely,' said the professor. 'It has been used for thousands of years across the region. Monks travelling with the Conquistadors called it the "demonic vine". They persecuted anyone who used it – which explains why *ayahuasca* was forced into hiding.'

Cabieses adjusted his tie.

'You see,' he said, massaging his hands together, '*ayahuasca, Banisteriopsis caapi*, as it's more correctly known, was a pre-Incan device. Of course it could provide a sensation of flight – the sense of travelling to the gods. But the flight is not the content, but the container.'

Professor Cabieses fixed his eyes on mine, ensuring I was following his words.

'The content,' he said, 'the *function* of the tool, that is what solves problems. *Ayahuasca* shows a shaman how to cure an illness, or what the future holds. Other hallucinogens have been used in Native American history,' he went on, 'virola snuff, the San Pedro cactus, peyote, *psilocybe* mushrooms, and all the rest, but none's as important as *ayahuasca*.'

'What of the textiles, the ones which show Birdmen?'

'The winged cloaks, the feathered head-bands, the streams of vomit from their mouths,' declared the professor, 'look at the signs ... they lead to *ayahuasca*.'

Gazing down at the linoleum, I thought back to the burial grounds on the Nazca plain.

'Well,' I said, 'with the death of the Incas, I suppose we shall never know the truth of *ayahuasca*, or the Birdmen.'

Professor Cabieses shook his head in laughter.

'What are you talking about?' he said. 'I told you the Spanish forced your Birdmen into hiding. That's exactly where they've gone.'

'Where?'

'To the jungle!'

The professor explained that *ayahuasca* was still used by various tribes in the forests of the Upper Amazon, in Ecuador, Brazil and Peru. Known by many names – *yagé, pinde, caapi, nape*, among them; its complex chemistry has astounded Western scientists. How, they ask, could such primitive people have happened upon such a sophisticated formula?

The inner bark of the *Banisteriopsis caapi* vine is pounded and

boiled at a certain temperature for a certain time, along with a selection of leaves from other plants. The hallucinatory effects don't come
from the vine, but from the leaves, the admixtures. *Banisteriopsis
caapi* allows the intestines to absorb chemicals they would normally
filter out. As a result, the hallucinogens slip into the bloodstream.

Professor Cabieses leaned back into his chair.

'No tribe in the Western Amazon takes *ayahuasca* as seriously,' he
said, 'as the Shuar. They call it *natema*, and for them it's the key
which gives life meaning. They believe the world around us is an
illusion. The birds in the trees, the worms in the ground, and everything in between – none of it exists at all. Only by taking *ayahuasca*,
they say, can you enter the *real* world.'

'Where are the Shuar?'

'In the Pastaza region,' said Cabieses. 'In the borderlands of Peru
and Ecuador. You may have heard of them before,' he said. 'They used
to shrink heads.'

'I thought that was the Jivaro.'

'*Jivaro*, means "barbarian",' the doctor replied. 'As you can imagine
they don't like being called that. *Shuar* means "men".'

I praised the extinct art of headshrinking.

'Ah yes,' said Cabieses wistfully, '*tsantsas* are wonderful things.
But it's so hard to get good ones these days.'

'Have you ever seen them in the jungle?'

Without breaking eye contact, the professor jerked his thumb to a
cupboard to the right of his desk. Displayed on a pedestal was an
exquisite *tsantsa*.

'Go on,' he said, 'pick it up ...'

Cautiously, I detached the head from the stand and cupped it in my
hands. A plume of thick, clove-brown hair curved down over the
hollow neck. The features had been miniaturised impeccably.

'Look at the ears,' said Professor Cabieses proudly, 'see how they've
been reduced so perfectly.'

I admired them, and checked for nasal hair – the sign of a good
tsantsa.

'Don't worry,' said the doctor, 'it has nose hair.'

The lips were sewn together, sealed like those of the trophy head I
had seen at Majuelo.

Cabieses read my thoughts.

'The trophy heads at Nazca,' he said, 'were prepared in much the

same way. You probably know there's evidence that the]
civilisation once shrunk heads, too.

'Haven't you seen all those heads woven into the funeral te

The professor was right. The wings of the textile Birdmen ar
decorated with trophy heads, just as the graves of the pre-Incas are
littered with them.

'The ancient people of Peru's southern coast and the Shuar of the
jungle,' he said, 'are the same people, with the same culture. If you
want to learn about the Birdmen who once lived at Nazca, go and
meet their descendants – they're alive and well. Go to the Pastaza
and find the Shuar.'

Cabieses ran a knuckle over the *tsantsa*'s cheek.

'They are your Birdmen,' he said.

'Is it dangerous up there?'

'Danger gives life meaning,' retorted the professor.

'Will they cut off my head?'

'There are worse hazards.'

'Like what?'

'*Datura ... La Trompeta de Diablo*, The Trumpet of the Devil,'
said Cabieses. 'Beware of it.'

14

Iquitos

Iquitos is the capital of Loreto, by far the largest department in Peru. It's the only city of any size in a state as big as Germany. The flight north-east from Lima slices across the sierra and the barren highlands of the Cordillera Azul. Peer out of the window again and the mountains are gone, supplanted by a carpet of green. Even from twenty thousand feet you can't help but be struck by its vastness. Millions of trees form a single unbroken canopy. Rivers crawl east and west like colossal serpents, twisting with oxbow lakes. All of it vivid with life, in ten thousand shades of green.

The moment I got out at Iquitos airport, I sensed the jungle around me. The morning air was thick with heat, the sunlight filtered through cloud. Where the runway ended the rain-forest began.

I followed the jumble of passengers across the cracked slabs of concrete towards the arrivals' hall. Like me, they all had good reasons for making the journey. Only wheeler-dealers and the most intrepid tourists bother with Iquitos.

The middle-aged Peruvian who had sat beside me on the flight said he'd come to buy spider monkey bones for a Chinese aphrodisiac dealer. I was surprised he was so open about his line of business. Slip a wad of cash in the right hand, he said, and you could smuggle anything out of Peru. He poked a finger towards a Customs' display case, which featured the skins of animals facing extinction.

'I can get you any of those,' he boasted.

'But aren't they endangered?'

'Hah!' grinned the businessman, 'there are plenty of them left; thank God, as I've got lots of customers in China.'

Long before the first bags had arrived, the luggage carousel came to life. We waited obediently, as the conveyor belt stop-started forward. The baggage did not come. Instead, a bizarre ceremony began.

A procession of thirty figures emerged from a cluster of bamboo shacks at the far end of the hall. They were dressed in fibrous skirts, their faces painted for war. The men led the way, each of them holding a long blowpipe above his head. The women followed close behind, all bare-breasted; and the children were unclothed.

Some of the warriors wore crowns made from the bright feathers of scarlet macaws. They danced around the hall, incorporating the empty luggage carousel into their routine. The warriors would take it in turns to ride the conveyor belt, while pretending to use their blowpipes.

None of the other passengers from the Lima flight showed any interest. I asked the monkey bone smuggler what was going on. Grimacing, he swished his hand at the dancers.

'It's a horrible tragedy,' he said.

'What is?'

'The Bora ... or what's *become* of them.'

'What are they doing here?'

'They live in the airport,' said the trader, 'the government's trying to step up tourism – they thought having a warrior tribe resident in the arrivals' hall would be a good idea.'

'They look quite pacified to me,' I said.

'That's the saddest thing of all,' grunted my confidante. 'The Bora used to be one of the most feared peoples on the Upper Amazon. They used to slaughter anyone they wanted. They loved killing ... *now* look at them.'

A fleet of three-wheel passenger motorbikes, known as *motocarros*, fought to take me into town. The drivers were a rugged breed, their shoulders trimmed with tattoos, bandannas hiding their mouths. The leader of the pack snarled at the others, frightening them away. He wasn't tall, but stocky. Around his neck he wore the skull of a small bird. Spitting a razor-blade from his mouth, he threatened to carve up the rest of the gang. My bags were loaded onto the back of his bike. The driver stashed the blade back in his mouth and pushed away down the patched tarmac towards Iquitos.

The undergrowth loomed up from either side of the road. As someone who's more used to city life, I felt unsettled by the blend of creepers, roots and spiders' webs, which hung in the trees like fishing nets. Unfamiliar sounds echoed from the jungle, over the noise of the engine. I wondered how I'd survive on the long journey into the interior.

I watched in the wing mirror as the driver flipped the razor-blade on his tongue. It was an impressive stunt.

'Don't you cut your mouth?' I shouted.

'It's not as hard as it looks,' he said. 'None of the others can do it, so they're frightened of me. If you don't make a reputation for yourself in Iquitos, *te comerán vivo*, people will eat you alive.'

I thanked the driver for his advice.

'Where are you staying?' he asked.

'I don't have a hotel yet.'

'Iquitos is full of thieves,' he replied. 'I'll take you to my friend's hotel. It's off Plaza de Armas, on Calle Putumayo. Stay anywhere else and you may get your throat slit.'

*

On my travels I've stayed in some extraordinary places. In Rwanda, I once put up at a hotel where the walls were drenched in human blood; in Delhi I stayed in an opium den and, in Varanasi, at a *dhobi*'s, laundryman's, shack. But none of them could compare with Hotel Selva.

The woman at the reception desk asked if her husband could keep his chickens in my bathroom. It was, she said, the only place near the kitchen with direct sunlight. I agreed reluctantly. She pointed down the hall to room 102.

'What about the key?'

The woman shook her head.

'At Hotel Selva we trust each other,' she said obscurely.

The building harked back to a time when Iquitos was one of the most prosperous towns in the world, founded on the rubber business. Its walls and rounded arches were built from solid blocks of stone; the stained glass windows must have been imported from Spain or France. But Hotel Selva had been ravaged by a hundred years of Amazonian wear and tear. The windows had lost most of their glass years before, the guttering leaked, and the roots of a nearby ironwood tree had lifted the flagstones.

The panelled door of room 102 had come away from its hinges. Taking it from the entrance, I propped it up against the wall. With unsure footsteps, I edged forwards into the dim chamber.

I tried the light switch, but there was no electricity. Nor was there any furniture, except for a bare, mildewed mattress. The walls were coated with a veneer of slime. One corner had been used as a *pissoir*. The sounds of female ecstasy flowed from the adjacent room, in time with the creaking of a bed frame. I nudged open the bathroom door. About fifty full-sized chickens were flapping about, agitated by my intrusion. The floor was peppered with excretions and dried blood. A bolt of sunlight lit up the birds. A glance up at the ceiling explained the brightness. There *was* no ceiling.

As I stood there, surrounded by chickens, a second door to the bathroom opened. It led to the kitchen. A hand reached into the sea of birds and grabbed one, as another hand ripped off its head. The chef called back, asking me to keep out of his chicken coop. I had no business to be in the bathroom, he said, as there wasn't any water anyway.

I sat on the flea-infested mattress and took in my surroundings. I would have looked for another place to stay. But, as someone preparing for a journey of certain hardship, I decided that a stay at Hotel Selva would be invaluable experience.

By lunch-time Iquitos was coming to life. *Motocarros* tore down the wide avenues in droves. Shopkeepers wiped down the rich arabesque façades, sheathed in *azulejos*, glazed tiles. A battalion of boot boys slipped from the shadows, and patrolled the streets. Their mothers would be waiting for them to bring money for food.

Glance at a map and you wonder how Iquitos can survive. Like Manaus, its sister city in the Brazilian Amazon, Iquitos is a quirk of 19th-century history. It ought not to exist at all. Nestled on the Amazon's west bank, it's more than two thousand miles from the river's Atlantic mouth. No roads lead to the town; it can only be reached by boat or by aeroplane. Every pot and pan, every tin of tuna fish, outboard motor and drinking-straw has to be shipped in.

I wandered up Calle Putumayo and turned right a block before the waterfront. A hundred years ago the embankment must have been a formidable sight. Overflowing with rococo grandeur, the buildings still had their elaborate Doric columns and lead-lined domes, their cornicing and balustrades. The buildings reflected the men who had erected them: opulent, powerful, arrogant. Men with no fear. They mirrored the might of the great river which they overlooked. But, as with Hotel Selva, time had dealt them a terrible blow. The plasterwork had chipped off, the banisters crumbled, and the Portuguese tiles had fallen like scales from a great fish.

Cast an eye over the palatial buildings, block out the groan of the *motocarros*, and it's not hard to imagine how things must have been a century ago. In a handful of years the rubber barons had transformed themselves from destitute adventurers into some of the richest men on Earth.

One traveller passing up the Amazon in March 1854 afforded Iquitos a single line in his diary: 'A sparse and miserable hamlet,' he wrote, 'consisting of 33 houses, a straw-thatched church.' By 1900, Iquitos was a town of 20,000, of which 4,000 were Europeans. Crates of English banknotes were regularly unloaded at the docks. The rubber barons spent their new-found wealth like water. They bought Italian furniture, satins, silks, the finest porcelain, and entire cellars of vintage Champagne – all of it shipped in direct from London.

For centuries native peoples of the western Amazon have dipped their feet in liquid latex, before curing them over a fire. Columbus reported seeing Indians playing games with strange 'elastic' balls. Rubber had been known of in Europe for a long time, but it was always of limited use. In the winter it became too brittle and hard, and in the summer it grew soft and sticky. But everything changed in 1839, when Charles Goodyear invented vulcanisation.

Paying slave wages, the rubber barons employed thousands of native people as *seringueiros*, tappers. Only they knew where to find the rubber trees, which grew naturally in the jungle. They tapped the latex into cups, coagulated it into thirty-kilo balls called *peles*, and floated them down the river. The latex could only be harvested in the morning and evening – as the sun's heat thickened it. Once he had a bucket of latex, the tapper would cure it a little at a time over the smoke of a fire.

For a period of about thirty years, Iquitos was firing on all cylinders. At the same time that gold was discovered at Klondike's Bonanza Creek, a new élite of millionaires were living it up in the Amazon. But the boom years came to an abrupt end when, in 1912, the first crop of latex was harvested from Oriental trees. A few years before, during the height of the bonanza, Henry Wickham, an Englishman, had smuggled seventy thousand rubber tree seeds to Asia. No one noticed his precious cargo plying its way east towards the Atlantic. With no indigenous diseases to attack them, and arranged in neat plantations, rubber trees thrived in Malaya. Success in the Far East spelled disaster for the Amazon. Its boom was snuffed out overnight.

*

The Amazon River was swollen, its waters much higher than usual. From my vantage point on the embankment I could see dozens of miniature islands – the roofs of submerged shacks. The heaviest rain in living memory had forced thousands of people out of their homes; hundreds more had drowned. I'd heard that high water was good for Amazonian travel. The sandbars which lie beneath the surface – some as large as steam ships – make navigation a constant danger. The higher the water, the faster the current, and the less threat there is of running aground.

As I stood there, the heavens opened and the afternoon rains washed down. I sought refuge in a café called Ari's Burger, on the east side of Plaza de Armas. It was a South American version of Arnold's, the '50s diner from television's *Happy Days*. The floors were chequered, the chrome tables topped in raspberry-coloured vinyl. A jukebox hummed away in one corner. The young waitresses glided about, their feet forced into under-sized plimsolls. They wore a uniform: red skirts, ivory pinafores and matching sun visors. Each of them had the same pouting lips, highlighted with shocking-pink gloss. Spiralling down over the right edge of each sun visor was a tight brown curl.

A teenage waitress hurried over through the tangle of chrome chairs. Puckering her lips as provocatively as she could, she suggested I order a banana split. It was, she said, her favourite. After ordering one, I made the mistake of admiring her curl. She leant down to pick a hair from my shoulder, and puckered a little more.

In Iquitos, casual compliments are taken very seriously. The girl, who said her name was Florita, lamented that she hadn't a date for Gringolandia, the disco. She would wait for me at ten. I choked out a list of excuses, and got back to my plans.

There was still much to do before my search for the Shuar could start. No time for disco dancing. On a paper napkin I made a list: *(1) Guide. (2) Supplies. (3) Boat.*

Florita swanned over with a huge banana split. Its bowl was as big as a geranium's pot. I rooted around with the long spoon, hunting for bananas. There were none. I asked what was going on. Florita said the bananas had been blended up.

Back to the list. Getting a guide was the main worry. I needed a man who knew the Pastaza region, where the Shuar lived. He would have to be adept at diplomacy as well as jungle survival; a knowledge of *ayahuasca* would be useful as well.

Florita told me that I shouldn't look for a guide. If you want something in Iquitos, she said, you wait for it to come to you. Hang around, she pouted, and a guide would turn up.

Exactly thirty seconds later a sleek young man slipped easily onto the chair beside mine. He pulled a Marlboro from a soft pack, slid his tongue down the edge, and lit the end.

'I heard you were looking for a guide,' he said.

'Yes, I am, but how did you know? I haven't told anyone but Florita.'

The man, Xavier, squinted as the smoke furled up into his eyes.

'It's my job to know what's going on,' he said.

If Ari's Burger was Arnold's Diner, then Xavier was its Fonz. His hair was a number one on the sides, sheered with electric clippers, an oily quiff crowned the top. He wore his own self-styled uniform – ripped jeans and a white tee-shirt with the arms torn off. As far as Xavier was concerned, arms were for wimps. Under the shirt, he confided, lay a tattoo of staggering size and imagination: a dragon savaging a mermaid, surrounded by angels. The sting of the needle, he said, had been excruciating.

'Can I see it?'

Xavier swept back his quiff.

'Are you kidding? The girls would go wild.'

Florita tiptoed over and nuzzled a note under my glass. It declared her undying love for me.

'Let's get down to business,' I said. 'Do you know the Pastaza region?'

'No man,' said Xavier, 'I'm not a guide … I'm a fixer.'

'Well can you fix me up with a guide? I need someone who knows the Shuar tribe.'

Xavier's ice-cool expression cracked.

'*Shuar*?' he murmured, miming a round object with his hands.

'Shrunken heads,' I said. 'But they don't do that any more.'

'It's not going to be easy. No one goes up there.'

'Well, I'll have to get another fixer who can find a man brave enough for the job.'

Xavier thumped his breast.

'Give me until this time tomorrow,' he said. 'I'll find you a guide so brave that he could walk through fire.'

*

In the late afternoon I explored the streets leading onto Malecon Tarapaca, the road which runs along the waterfront. Tourism didn't seem to have taken off in Iquitos. Despite this, the backstreets were littered with tourist kiosks. Each one sold the same range of curiosities. There were blowpipes seven feet long, spears and snuff-pipes, feather head-dresses and stuffed piranhas, jaguar teeth necklaces and masks made from caiman skin. Frames panelled the walls of every kiosk. In them giant insects were pinned out.

I sipped a tall blended drink on the porch of a restaurant called Fitzcarraldo. It had once been home to the legendary rubber-tapper and explorer of the same name. Werner Herzog's film *Fitzcarraldo* had made a great impression on me years before. I never thought that one day I might be sitting in the rubber-tapper's headquarters, looking out over the swollen waters of the Amazon.

Fitzcarraldo's story echoes the trailblazer spirit and the wild excesses of the rubber boom years. Born Brian Sweeny Fitzgerald, the eldest son of an immigrant Irishman, he was known in the jungle as Fitzcarraldo. He fled into the Amazon in his early twenties, after being accused of spying during the war between Peru and Chile. Two years later, in about 1877, he had made a fortune as a rubber-tapper, and was one of the richest men in Peru. The money was soon spent.

After watching Enrico Caruso perform at Manaus' £400,000 opera house, Fitzcarraldo swore he'd lure the great tenor to the Peruvian jungle. His dream was to bring opera to the natives. What better way to entice Caruso, he thought, than to build an opera house to match the one in Manaus?

To raise funds, Fitzcarraldo came up with a plan. He would make use of the vast rubber-tree forest on the Ucayali River, where 14 million trees lay untapped. To succeed, he first had to get a boat beyond *Pongo das Mortes*, the Rapids of Death. Everyone said he was mad, which he probably was. He sailed his steamship up a parallel river and forced his labourers – all of them Shuar – to haul it over a hill and down to the Ucayali.

Once the steamer was on the Ucayali, Fitzcarraldo and his companions celebrated with drink. As they did so, Shuar labourers cut the mooring ropes, sending the boat charging towards the rapids. From the start they had planned secretly to sacrifice the vessel, to appease the spirit of the waterfall. The boat plunged over the rapids. Somehow, Fitzcarraldo survived but never lived to build his opera house. He died soon after, in 1889, drowned in the Urubamba River. He was just thirty-five.

Night falls quickly over the jungle. The patina of dusk diffuses into darkness, a signal for the nocturnal world to wake. In Plaza de Armas the street-lights seethed with insect life; mosquitoes, moths and hornets among them, hurling themselves at the orbs of brilliant white glass. The restaurants and bars, bright with neon lighting, were haunted by them. No one but me was in the least bothered.

The only place in Iquitos free from insects was Ari's Burger. Every few minutes one of the bubbly waitresses would float through, spraying poison gas from an aerosol. I sought refuge there, preferring the gas to the bugs outside.

Even before my backside had met the chrome chair, Florita was standing over me. She had missed me during the afternoon, she said, but would miss me even more later in the night. Three other guys had already asked her to the disco, but she'd rejected them in favour of me. She exclaimed that she would never look at another man. Murmuring more excuses, I ordered another banana split.

I closed my eyes as the poison gas rained down. When I opened them, a robust-looking man was sitting across the table. His skin was tanned, his hair expertly cropped and parted at the side. He had an honest face that seemed out of place in Ari's Burger.

'Iquitos is the best kept secret in the world,' he said in a west-Texan drawl, 'but there's a lot of bad people down here. But we're cleaning it up.'

I was on the lookout for conmen, I said.

The Texan tapped his index finger on the raspberry vinyl.

'Don't let down your guard,' he replied. 'The bandits see tourists like you as game ... game to be hunted.'

15

Big Bug Business

An Englishman buttonholed me in the corridor of Hotel Selva. Dark circles lined his eyes; his face was as white as Dover chalk. In a Liverpudlian accent he asked me what I thought of the hotel.

'There's no electricity, running water or glass in the windows,' I said, 'the mattress is rotting, and the bathroom's full of chickens. And there are a pair of nymphomaniacs in the next room.'

'Why don't you find somewhere else?'

Making a fist, I rammed it into my palm.

'I'm going into the jungle,' I said. 'Going to need a lot of toughening up. Even the jungle couldn't be as rough as room 102.'

The Liverpudlian walked down to the reception and asked for a room just like mine, leaving me to wonder what kind of lunatic he was.

Later that day, Xavier strolled into Ari's Burger and winked.

'Got you a guide,' he said.

'Is he brave?'

'Like a *kamikaze* pilot.'

'Bring him over, and we'll have a chat.'

'He won't come to Ari's,' said Xavier, winking again.

César was squatting behind the door of his friend's house, in a shanty town called Punchana. As a successful jungle guide he was, he said, hiding from bad, jealous men – the very same kind of people he'd protect me from were I to hire him.

'If you're going to protect me, you're not going to be able to hide behind doors,' I said.

César paced over to a rocking-chair, made from steel construction poles. He was about thirty, chubby with a big head and a nervous twitch. From time to time his face would erupt in a broad, anxious smile. The more he smiled, the more he twitched. Rocking back and forth nervously on the chair, he told me of his life.

'My brother was killed by *Sendero Luminoso*,' he began in a voice inspired by gloom. 'His body was dumped in the river near Pucallpa, and was eaten by piranhas. Then three months ago my sister died of cancer. My three brothers and I carry on the family name, living however we can.'

'What experience have you as a guide?'

César revived from his fit of melancholy.

'I've been taking tourists into the jungle for twenty years,' he said, 'since I was a child. I speak eighteen languages – German, French, Arabic, Japanese ... and I can navigate by the stars.'

'What about *ayahuasca*?'

He smiled, then blinked as if a bright light were shining in his eyes.

'Taken it hundreds of times,' he said. 'I'm a shaman. I was taught by a *maestro* on the Napo River.'

'When were you last up in the Pastaza region, with the Shuar?'

'*Shuar*?' he mouthed. 'Yes, I know the Shuar. If you look them in the eye they'll slit your throat. If you see their women they'll hack off your head with a machete. And if you show any signs of illness, they'll drown you.'

'Dangerous people, the Shuar,' said Xavier, wincing.

'Only last month a group of missionaries flew up to the Pastaza in a seaplane,' said César. 'They landed on the river. When the Shuar elders came out, the missionaries greeted them. The tribe seemed friendly, so the Christians camped on the river-bank. But in the night the Shuar warriors attacked and killed them all. They chopped off their heads for trophies, and cut up the bodies.'

'Why did they murder them?'

César rocked back and forth tensely.

'No gifts,' he said. 'They came with empty hands.'

Although his nervous disposition worried me, I hired César as a guide. His good English, claimed knowledge of Pastaza, *ayahuasca* and jungle medicine were the credentials I was after. We negotiated a fee and a budget for equipment and gifts. It was a lot of money. Xavier said I could rest assured, for I was hiring the best in the Upper Amazon. César suggested I employ his three younger brothers as porters, for an additional $600. All the money, a total of $3,100, would have to be paid in advance, he said. I handed over a wad of used banknotes.

To save time and fuel, César proposed that we take a river ferry up from Iquitos to San Ramon, at the base of the Pastaza. The journey up the Amazon and its headwater, the Marañon, would take about ten days. We would take food and supplies with us, as well as a small outboard motor and fuel. Upriver we would hire a dugout and fix the engine to it.

César was just about to write me a receipt when there were shouts from the street. Without flinching, he ran out the back door and over a neighbour's fence, taking my money with him.

'What's the problem? That man was shouting ¡Los Policias!'

Xavier lit a cigarette and inhaled.

'Someone must have got robbed,' he said. 'The crime's terrible in Iquitos.'

*

My head was heavy on the fetid pillow that night, under which was the magic cob of maize. I had a dream in which César was laughing demonically. He was about to say something when I woke up, startled by the sound of the bedhead banging on the other side of the wall. I stumbled into the bathroom where the chickens were roosting, and tried to coax a single drop of water from the tap. As usual, it was bone dry.

The cook started slaughtering chickens early the next morning. Over the racket, I heard the manager's wife screaming for me down the corridor. César had sent his brother, Gonzalo, to meet me. I noticed at once the familiar trait of delivering a blink with a smile. He had instructions, he said, to take me to the floating market at Belen.

As we walked the mile or so down Calle Putumayo, Gonzalo told me tales of evil, depraved men, who were hell-bent on destroying his family.

'Iquitos is a dangerous place,' he said. 'People will rest only when you are dead. They use black magic to make you ill, so you die slowly, and with pain.'

'Who are these people?'

Gonzalo blinked, but he was not smiling.

'They are the Mahicaris, the Devil Worshippers,' he said.

Beneath the tranquil veneer of daily life, there lurks an underworld of sorcery and superstition. The entire Latin continent is founded on a bedrock of magical belief. But nowhere else, except perhaps for Manaus, had I come across such a fear of the occult. The Brazilian Amazon has a history of *Macumba*, a religious system blended from West African belief and Catholic iconography. African slaves were never brought to the Upper Amazon, and so *Macumba*, and its sister faith *Santeria*, are unknown in Peru.

Instead, a shamanic tradition has grown up, which touches every member of society. It heals illness when people are sick, and solves problems; for, as I was constantly reminded, everyone in Iquitos had problems.

I asked Gonzalo about the Devil Worshippers. I wanted to meet them.

He bit the corner of his lip and blinked.

'You can't go to the *Mahicaris*,' he said. 'You have to wait for them to find you.'

Belen was buoyant with activity, even though the shops on Calle Putumayo still had their shutters closed. The market area extended down to the sludge-brown water and the floating village. Thousands upon thousands of balsa wood shacks were slotted together. When the water was high, as it was then, the houses simply rose on the tide. Children were splashing, avoiding lumps of raw sewage; their mothers busy washing clothes, and everyone else was doing their ablutions.

In the market, all kinds of products were for sale. We pushed through the crowds, peering at the merchandise, which was offered on makeshift stalls. Meat was being sold at the first area. Fresh caiman legs and jungle pig hooves, chunks of water eel, giant snails, and turtles hacked from their shells, sold along with their eggs. There were other creatures from the river, too, including a *piraruca*, a giant, prehistoric, freshwater fish.

We pushed forwards through the crowds and came to a line of stalls selling live jungle animals. There were three black spider monkeys tied to a pole, $3 each; a young ocelot pacing in a cage ($35); three toucans with yellow bills ($15); a baby anteater ($20), and a curious species of primitive turtle, called a *matamata* ($4).

Gonzalo led me to an area roofed in blue polythene, where *chonta*, the heart of palm, was being shredded into what looked like tagliatelle. No meal in Iquitos is complete without a great pile of it. Beside the *chonta* was a line of tables selling *mapacho*, black tobacco, used in every shamanic ceremony. The leaves are brought from the deepest regions of the jungle, rolled tight into cylindrical batons, like candlesticks at church. The stall keepers, all women, sat on high stools clipping the tobacco and rolling it into oversized cigarettes.

A little further on a teenage girl with red hair and freckles was selling *guajes*. These fruit are best described as looking like rust-coloured hand-grenades. The flesh beneath the carapace, a popular snack, is light orange in colour. It's said to have thirty times more vitamin C than citrus fruit.

Beyond the blue polythene roofs was another market, where medicaments were sold. We always hear in the West how the Amazon is an untapped storehouse of remedies. It's undoubtedly true. But not until you walk through an emporium of raw jungle medicines, can you comprehend the range of plants involved.

Piled high on the tables there were roots, barks, oils and tinctures, each with a specific use. Gonzalo held up a section of *una de gato*, a vine celebrated for its ability to stop cancerous tumours. Beside it was a heap of *coja* bark, used for arthritis; and beside that *siete raices* (seven roots) a bronchial dilator and aphrodisiac in one. At one stall the owner held up a jar. In it was a boa constrictor's head pickled in brine – a remedy against rheumatism. Another table was arranged with dozens of miniature bottles filled with beads – amulets as powerful to the believing as any drug.

Before we left Belen, Gonzalo took me to meet a friend who sold *guajes* at the water's edge. His table was in the shadow of an impressive bandstand, designed and built by Gustave Eiffel, in the good old days. Gonzalo's friend employed a woman whose face was hideously disfigured. She was shy, reluctant to give the usual sales banter. As we looked for a *motocarro* to take us back to Plaza de Armas, I asked Gonzalo if he knew what had happened to her.

'Everyone at Belen knows the story of Rosa,' he said.

'What story?'

Gonzalo wiped his mouth with his hand.

'She used to be the most beautiful girl in Iquitos,' he said. 'Every schoolboy dreamed of having her. Then, when she was about fifteen, a *maestro* said he had seen a vision, in which Rosa was raped by five men. The dream was a premonition.'

'But what happened to her face?'

'Rosa's mother didn't want the dream to come true,' continued Gonzalo. 'The *maestro* said there was only one thing to do – to turn her beauty into ugliness. So one night Rosa's parents dipped her face in acid.'

*

At noon the next day César sent word for me to come to his friend's house in Punchana. As before, I found him crouching behind the door. This time he said he was looking for beetles on the floor. The sitting-room was now filled with equipment and goods. There was enough stuff to kit out an entire shop.

Rocking back and forth on the chair, César publicised what he had bought for the trip: 'Fifty kilos of sugar and two hundred bars of soap,' he said, 'eighty cans of tuna fish, sixty of sardines, thirty tins of butter, three hundred rolls of toilet paper, one hundred kilos of cooking salt, and forty of salt for preserving fish; a sack of rice and another of flour, a box of detergent for washing clothes, two boxes of bleach sachets, twelve dozen eggs, twenty litres of cooking oil, a box of cocoa, coffee and tea, forty fishing hooks, three propeller blades and three sacks of used clothing.'

'Why do we need so much stuff?'

César smiled wide and blinked twice.

'Gifts,' he said. 'Without gifts the Shuar will butcher us.'

When he had finished with the manifest, César asked me for an extra $600. He had overspent on the food and was running short. Cash was still needed to hire a 15-horsepower outboard and to buy fuel. I went into the corner and unzipped my money-belt. Only the emergency money was left.

'Sorry, but I don't have any more dollars,' I said.

César rocked up and down a couple of times.

'Then we won't be going anywhere.'

I handed him the emergency money, and again asked for a receipt. Another excuse was knocked back at me.

In addition to taking clothes, fishing hooks and food, César said the Shuar would expect other things. He hadn't budgeted for these, but advised me to go to the market and get what I could. Gonzalo would accompany me and, afterwards, we could pick up an antidote for snakebites.

'What gifts shall I get?'

'The Shuar like shiny things,' said César. 'Combs, mirrors, beads, that sort of thing.'

Back at Belen, Gonzalo and I trawled through the hardware shops. Like the ones at Nazca, they were piled floor to ceiling with Chinese-made merchandise. I bought a box of plastic combs and another of hand held mirrors, with coloured backs. After hearing César's story of the empty-handed missionaries, one couldn't be too careful.

When the adventurer Lewis Cotlow went into the jungle in the early 1950s, he took lipsticks, mascara, and elaborate cosmetics. Warriors, he said, always needed warpaint for their faces. After Cotlow came a New York socialite, Nicole Maxwell, who spent years in the Peruvian Amazon. She hit upon a novel gift item. Before leaving the United States, she bought dozens of glass eyes in her own eye colour. Indian chiefs were amazed when she brought them out. I thought hard to come up with something as original as glass eyes.

It was then that I remembered the film *The Gods Must be Crazy*, in which a Coca-Cola bottle finds its way into a remote Botswanan village. For the *Khoikhoin* people the bottle was an invaluable tool. They used it as a rolling-pin, a musical instrument, for pounding grain and even as a weapon. Eventually, fights broke out because everyone wanted to use the bottle. The only way to ensure peace was to take not one Coke bottle, but two dozen.

Gonzalo thought it was a ridiculous idea. He said the Shuar would hit us over the heads with the bottles and then slit our throats. It worried me that any story told by Iquiteños, involving the Shuar, ended with everyone getting their heads hacked off. I had a gut feeling that the Coke bottles would go down well. After hunting for more than an hour, we ended up with twenty Fanta bottles. They would have to do.

Gonzalo said it was time to get the antidote for snake bites. But it wasn't sold in the market, he said.

'Where do we get it, then?'

'From Anaconda Man.'

We climbed aboard a dugout canoe near Eiffel's bandstand and headed out through the floating village. Anaconda Man lived a short distance from Belen. Gonzalo said that no one would dream of going deep into the jungle without a remedy for snake bites. A boy of about seven sat at the bows, stabbing his oval-ended paddle into the water. The canoe was precariously low in the water. Gonzalo said this was normal, a result of advanced wood-rot. We ducked every few seconds, to avoid the walkways that bridged the channel. Soon we were out past the maze of houses. With a constant rhythm we jerked forwards through beds of water hyacinth.

A few miles out of Iquitos, the young boatman punted the craft skilfully towards the river-bank. Gonzalo helped me out onto the mud. As I slid up to the grass-roofed shack, its occupant came out to greet us. He was average in height, but had extremely muscular shoulders, stocky thighs, and a maniacal laugh. When he walked, the mud shook. This, Gonzalo whispered ominously, was the Anaconda Man.

We sat on a log and watched as Anaconda Man wrestled a fifteen-foot anaconda. His bravery was fortified by a swig of *chuchuhuasi*, a strange jungle liqueur made from *aguardiente* and the bark of the colossal *chuchuhuasi* tree. It was impressive to see the snake coil around his back and arms, constricting.

When it came to reptiles, Anaconda Man was a show-off. First he posed with his collection of giant snakes. Then he stuffed a baby black caiman in his mouth, and sucked a lizard's head like a lollipop. I told him to stop, but ignoring me, he rammed a larger caiman down his trousers.

Keen to get down to business, I asked him what snakes we might expect on our journey to the Pastaza. Anaconda Man broke into hysterical laughter. There were too many to name, he said, yanking the caiman's tail from under his belt. My tropical medical kit included a list of dangerous Amazonian snakes. It was a long list. The main ones to avoid, it advised, were pit vipers, bushmasters, lanceheads, coppermouths, parrot snakes, as well as boa constrictors and ana-condas. The leaflet went on to say that, without the correct anti-venom, you hadn't got a chance of surviving a snake bite.

Gonzalo slapped his hand on Anaconda Man's back.

'Don't worry,' he said, 'this man has one anti-venom for all snakes.'

It sounded like powerful stuff.

Anaconda Man went into his shack and returned a minute later with a wide-mouthed jar. It contained dull green oil and what looked like anatomical specimens.

'How many do you want?' he asked.

'All of them,' said Gonzalo.

'*Cuarenta soles, 40 soles*,' replied the snake expert.

I dug the money from my pocket. Gonzalo put the jar under his arm and led the way back to the boat. I asked Anaconda Man how to use the remedy.

'When you get a snake bite, rub one of the pieces onto the fang marks. Then swallow it.'

'What are they?' I asked. 'What *is* the medicine?'

Anaconda Man helped me into the boat.

'*Los corazones de serpiente*, they're snake hearts,' he said.

*

Breakfast at Ari's Burger was always a sombre affair. Each face was drawn, reflecting the previous night's debauchery. The scent of Nescafé and cigarettes lingered in the air. Every so often a stray curio-seller would bluster in and tout tarantulas in frames. No one ever bought them. The giant spider market never heated up until at least noon.

One old American was downing his third cup of black coffee. There were four unopened packs of Marlboros stacked up on his table. He had a long day at Ari's ahead of him. Nearby, at the front of the café, a pair of immaculately dressed women were nibbling toast. They were coutured in identical grey and white uniforms, the livery of the Peruvian airline, Tans. They were fresh and alert. And, unlike the rest of the Iquiteños, they were too sophisticated to stare. In Iquitos everyone stares as much as they possibly can. Lecherous old men stare at teenage waitresses with curls, waitresses stare at foreigners, and foreigners stare at busty local women, who stare at the lecherous old men.

Florita served me a cup of Nescafé. She'd been fighting off the advances of an Australian man, she confided. He was very handsome, she said, with a broad chest and dimples in his cheeks. He had asked her to Gringolandia, and he had bought her a bouquet of flowers. Pausing to apply a coat of pink gloss to her lips, Florita pouted harder than I had seen her pout before. All the weary hungover heads turned in slow motion to watch. Even the air hostesses looked over.

'I have two left feet when it comes to dancing,' I said.

'I'll teach you to dance, *me amor*.'

'I go to bed by ten.'

'Then, we'll set off for Gringolandia extra early,' she said.

'But I'm married.'
'So?'

When Xavier turned up I asked him to take Florita aside and set things straight. While I was flattered, there was no way I could go disco dancing with her. I don't know what he said, but later in the day Florita came over to my table. With tears welling in her eyes, she handed me another note.

It read: '*Lo lamentarás*. You will regret your decision.'

Xavier had come to take me to meet César. As we drove towards Punchana, he started bragging again about his tattoo. He went on and on about the pain, and about the size of the dragon. If I were to see the beauty of the mermaid and the angels, he said, I would go mad. I asked if I could see it. As before, he refused. So, without warning, I pulled up his tee-shirt. He thrust his arms across his bare chest.

'I can't see the tattoo,' I said. 'Where is it?'

Xavier pointed to a pair of parallel lines, about a centimetre long.

'*There!*' he said.

'That's not a monster.'

'I haven't got the dragon yet,' he said, squirming, 'but I've got the dragon's fangs.'

Nineteen nylon sacks of loot were blocking the entrance of the Punchana house. They were tied up with yellow string. César was sitting on the concrete floor making calculations. All the food was ready, he said, and an outboard engine had been hired and tested.

César climbed onto the rocking-chair and smiled apprehensively.

'I have to go into the jungle on a quick trip,' he said.

'Can't it wait?'

He shook his head.

'Got an urgent order.'

'An order for what?'

'Insects.'

As well as being a celebrated linguist, healer and navigator, César had a profitable sideline, in the giant insect business.

'I have customers all over the world,' he said, 'they pay hundreds of dollars for the big ones.'

'How big?'

César motioned something the size of a small cat with his hands.

'*Titanus giganticus*, the biggest beetle in the world. They grow up to twenty centimetres.'

'What are they worth?'

'Collectors in the USA or Japan pay $800 for them, dead or alive,' he said. 'I have a friend in Canada who's a very serious collector. His largest specimen is worth $500,000.'

The idea of collecting bugs didn't appeal to me at all. But I remembered how, in Japan, the big department stores would sell live beetles once a year. School children kept them as pets. I even found a vending-machine which sold ten different varieties of live beetle.

Iquitos is a world centre in the big bug business. The Amazon has more than 8,000 species of known insect. Through middlemen like César you can order just about anything you like – from the giant *Morpho hecuba* butterfly to hissing cockroaches, to the Hercules Beetle and even *Titanus giganticus*. In these times of political correctness, where hunting animals is off-limits, insect dealing is still considered acceptable. The bugs are injected with poison, wrapped in tissue paper, and shipped out from Iquitos to insect-lovers everywhere. Thousands more arc packed up as live freight in what's a multi-million dollar business.

As far as César was concerned, big bugs were money for nothing. A couple of nights with a bright light and a giant net and he'd be assured of a valuable catch. As soon as he got back to Iquitos we would leave for the land of the Shuar.

*

When I returned to Hotel Selva the police were searching the place. The manager's wife was answering questions. She looked very frightened indeed. I asked what was going on. One of the police officers said it was to do with a young Englishman who had been staying at the hotel. I remarked that I had met him, although only once, in the corridor. The officer frowned until his forehead buckled. It was a sad case, he said, and not good for Iquitos. The young man had slit his wrists in the night.

16

Vine of the Dead

A long-awaited event was taking place at an electrical shop on the main square. The most eminent members of Iquitos society were present, sipping cool *guaje* milkshakes. They had come to view an exhibition of American food blenders. Across Peru people were passionate about the machines, nowhere more so than in Iquitos.

Along with the other guests, I toured the displays, making appropriate exclamations of awe. But with prices that started at $70, the new stock was out of reach of most Iquiteños. For the climax of the show, a bare-breasted woman, bedecked in feathers, trouped through the shop doing a war dance. I recognised her. She was one of the Boras from the airport.

When the blender show was over, the party moved on to *Casa de Fierro*, the Iron House. Set on the corner of Calles Prospero and Putumayo, it's a solid open-fronted building made from reinforced girders and sheets of steel, painted silver. The building was designed by Gustave Eiffel for the 1889 Paris Exhibition. Like Eiffel's bandstand at Belen, it was brought to the jungle by rubber barons.

On the upper floor of the Iron House was the Regal Bar and Restaurant, run by Bill Wilkins and his Peruvian wife. An Englishman by birth, Wilkins first came to the Amazon to work on a gold mining project. His restaurant was famous for its catfish. As well as serving food, it doubled as the British Consulate.

I told him about my planned trip and where I was staying. When he heard the words *Hotel Selva*, he screwed up his face and took a big gulp of his Bacardi and Coke.

'I've just been dealing with the lad who topped himself there,' he said. 'Nasty business altogether.'

'I heard it was suicide.'

'Slashed wrists,' whispered Bill. 'Had some trouble with the morgue ... They threatened to throw the body out on the street if they didn't get payment up front.'

'Couldn't the British government take care of this one?'

Bill shook his head.

'There's a lot of red tape,' he said. 'We got in touch with the boy's parents in Blighty. They sent a cheque. Had him shipped up to Lima in a box this afternoon. He went by DHL.'

*

With César out searching for *Titanus giganticus*, Gonzalo offered to take me to a healing session. One of the most famous *cuanderos* in the state, an old *ayahuasquero* called Flavio, was going to treat the sick. Some said he had magical powers. He hadn't performed in his native Iquitos for almost a year, as he'd been touring the United States.

Gonzalo said that Flavio had a following across the Americas, and was popular with not just Peruvians. From Vancouver to Tierra del Fuego people knew his work. He had helped the lame to walk, cured the blind simply by touching his thumbs to their eyes, and he'd even brought the dead back to life. When I asked if he believed the stories, Gonzalo seemed confused. Of course he believed them, he said, they were true.

As dusk fell over Belen, we hired a canoe and paddled down the waterways of the floating village. The blue flicker of televisions flooded through the open doorways of some shacks. In others, women were cutting up vegetables or stirring pots of mashed *yuka*, manioc, preparing the evening meal. There was laughter, the sound of bottles clinking together in a toast, and the ubiquitous screaming of babies waiting to be fed.

'There are so many fake shamans,' said Gonzalo, as we continued downstream. 'They pretend to have special powers, telling people lies and taking their money. They say the spells will heal only when they have been paid.'

'What about Flavio: are you sure he's genuine?'

'Of course he is!' exclaimed Gonzalo. 'Not like my neighbour.'

'Who's your neighbour?'

'He's a *maestro*, but a fake. No one goes to him.'

'How do you know he's a fraud?'

Gonzalo ran his fingers through the water.

'We know he's a fake because of his wife,' he said. 'You see, she's got a horrible rash on her face. It's terrible, so ugly.'

'What's that got to do with the shaman?'

'Well, if he was any good, he'd cure his wife first.'

A paraffin lamp guided us to the rendezvous point. The jungle grew right to the water's edge, making disembarking even more difficult than usual. Three or four other canoes were docking nearby. I heard the sound of a *peki-peki*, a motorised canoe, in the distance. Gonzalo said healing sessions were held in the jungle because it made the magic stronger. There was also the small problem of the police. While taking *ayahuasca* isn't against the law in Peru, practising medicine without a licence is.

I paid the boy who'd paddled us downstream, and asked him to stay until we returned. I had no idea how long the healing session would last. We followed the trail of people walking eastwards into the undergrowth. High above, the full moon was bright, illuminating the path through the banana trees. No one carried a torch, and so I refrained from using mine. There was a general sense of expectancy, the participants chatting away as they walked. Like the others, Gonzalo knew the route well.

'Not much further,' he said. 'You can see the fire through the trees.'

He pointed to the glimmer of flames about fifty yards ahead.

'Has it already started?'

Gonzalo made a click with his tongue.

'*Aún no*, not yet,' he said. 'We have to wait until Flavio comes. That may be hours.'

The bonfire was being tended by two boys. They were the only children present. Heaping the pyre with wood, they called for everyone to sit down. The rich blend of smoke and sparks spiralled into the sky. I shielded my face from the fire and scanned the assembly. About forty people had already arrived. Their silhouettes were lit up from time to time, as the breeze punched the flames in their direction. Everyone was in their best clothes, men wearing long-sleeved shirts and their wives in dresses. Some of the women unfurled sheets of plastic to sit on, as the ground was damp.

The air smelled of *mapacho*, jungle tobacco, and of burning banana leaves. No one was very bothered by the foreigner present. They were more concerned about the ailments they had come to have assuaged. Gonzalo told me that Flavio would only heal if the atmosphere was appropriate. Sometimes he had come to the clearing but had not treated anyone at all.

'Flavio's power depends on us,' he said. 'Without the right mood, the *ayahuasca* won't work, and he will tell everyone to go home. Think of pure things.'

'Like what?'

Gonzalo choked as the fire's smoke engulfed us.

'You must think of a bird flying over the trees,' he said, 'or of water running over stones in a stream.'

The ritual began long before Flavio turned up. A trio of women sang hymns. The songs spoke of moral values, of truth and sincerity. When they were over, it was time to pray. The congregation gave thanks to their ancestors, and they prayed for their families. With their hands pressed together in supplication, they urged God to charge Flavio's healing hands with power. May the spirit of Jesus fill him, they said, and may his strength overflow.

'He will be here soon,' said Gonzalo.

'Flavio?'

'Yes ... the atmosphere is almost ready.'

My mind wandered as the sound of the prayers melted into the trees. I tried to focus on pure thoughts, but instead could only think of Sven, the Slovak I'd met in Cusco. I wondered whether Ariadne was still tracking him across the continent. As I thought of him, his face dissolved into the darkness, and was replaced by the haunting, mummified trophy head which Juan the grave-robber had offered me.

Gonzalo nudged me back into the present.

'He is here,' he said. 'Flavio has come.'

Three figures were walking towards us through the undergrowth. The first was carrying a hurricane lamp. As it swung in his hand, it bathed the forest in platinum light. The next man was taller than the first; after him came a woman. She was clutching a bucket and a bag. The man with the lamp greeted the congregation. His cheeks were pocked, his complexion dark. He spoke in a soft, melodic voice. Holding his palms out towards us, he prayed.

'That is Flavio,' Gonzalo said softly, 'he's praying for our souls.'

A series of songs followed, to which one of the women danced. It was less of a dance, and more of a gyrating shuffle. When she had finished, she left the clearing and went off into the forest. She didn't come back.

The hymns subsided, and the *cuandero*'s assistant unfolded a green quilt. He took care to ensure there were no creases in it. As he pegged out the corners with stones, his master addressed the audience. He had come to heal, he said, by the powers which had been given to him. But the true power was not himself, it was not human, but divine. If we respected the invisible forces, he said, they would heal. As mere mortals we could never understand the nature or the method of the healing energy. Anyone who questioned the miraculous cures, he went on, would be afflicted with illness forever. His words took me back to India, where I'd heard godmen give similar warnings.

By the time Flavio started healing, it must have been past midnight. The hurricane lamp was thick with insects long before then. They swarmed over it suicidally, desperate to get to the source of the light.

Gonzalo pointed to the bucket, which had been placed beside the quilt.

'That's the *ayahuasca*,' he said.

He motioned for me to watch. The shaman's assistant went over to the hurricane lamp and turned it off. Flavio swept a white enamel mug into the liquid, and drank its contents. He held out his hands, and the afflicted approached him one by one.

The first person to step forward was a young woman. She couldn't have been more than about twenty. Flavio asked for details of her condition. The man she loved was in love with another, she said. She had come to gain his affection. The healer asked whether she had brought anything which belonged to the man she loved. She handed him a shirt and a few hairs from his brush. Flavio then asked if she had taken *ayahuasca* before. She replied that she had not. The enamel mug was dipped into the bucket and presented half full to the woman. When she had drained the liquid, the shaman told her to sit on the quilt.

Next came an old man. He claimed to be plagued by bad spirits. They had already killed his wife, he said, and his son, and they were now coming for him. When asked about *ayahuasca*, he replied that he had drunk it many times. The mug was filled to the brim and the old man drank. He sat beside the woman on the quilt, and waited.

One after the other, people stepped forward to drink *ayahuasca*. About fifteen came to the *maestro* for his help. Their problems ranged from obscure curses and *susto*, to medical afflictions, such as diabetes and pustules, migraines and malaria. Flavio told three people, all men, that he could not treat them. He didn't say why.

I noticed that each of the patients had brought a trusted friend or relative with them. The reason for this became clear as the *ayahuasca* began to work.

The young woman who was out of love threw up first. Her retching was followed closely by the aged man. One by one, the participants gagged or vomited. Several of them clambered off the quilt to defecate. No one was concerned about embarrassing themselves. They were drunk, their movements unsteady, their expressions delirious. The friends and relatives were at hand to soothe them, and to lead them back to the quilt if necessary. The vomiting lasted only for the first hour or so.

Once he had heard their problems and provided *ayahuasca* to all the afflicted, Flavio took a *chacapa* from his satchel. The tool, a rattle made from dried leaves, is one of the two most important props used by shamans in the Amazon. The other is the tobacco, *mapacho*. Shaking the *chacapa* near the faces of his patients, Flavio began to chant incantations. The endless stream of sound continued for hours. There were no clear words. I was awed by his sheer stamina. The only break was when he lit a wooden pipe, plugged with the *mapacho*. Drawing deeply on it, he inflated his lungs with smoke, blowing it over the patients.

I asked Gonzalo what was happening.

'The *maestro* is leading the sick people through the land of spirits,' he said.

'Are they flying?'

'Yes, some have grown wings.'

'Where are they going?'

'On a journey over the jungle, to search for answers to their problems,' said Gonzalo. 'Flavio is leading them. He might look like a man, but in his mind he's a stork.'

'Doesn't he give them actual medicines?'

Gonzalo grunted.

'*Ayahuasca*'s stronger than any medicine.'

I was startled by a sound in the trees. A sudden shriek as a predator found its prey. The noise disturbed a nest of howler monkeys, which in turn woke up half the jungle. I looked back at Flavio and his patients. They hadn't heard the commotion. The *chacapa* was still shaking, echoing to the rhythm of the chant.

'How could they not have heard that noise?'

'They are flying over the jungle,' said Gonzalo, 'they are far away.'

The session continued for about four hours. By the end of it I was used to the nocturnal jungle sounds and was almost falling asleep. Flavio's patients were regaining their composure. Some of them were still unsteady. Unlike me, their trusted friends were alert, sensitive to the needs of the person in their care. Before they drifted away, back to the river, the *cuandero* counselled each patient in turn.

'What's Flavio saying?'

'He's telling them to drink tobacco water,' said Gonzalo, 'and explaining how they must act from now on. They will only be cured if they do as he says.'

As they filtered off, some of the patients handed the healer's assistant wads of tobacco, a little money, or other gifts. Gonzalo and I made our way back to the canoe, silent like all the others.

The moon was now blanketed by cloud. I was fearful of paddling upstream in pitch-blackness. Dugouts are unstable at the best of times. Gonzalo called out to the young boatman, who was curled up asleep on the bank. In one movement, he leapt up and pushed the stern into the water.

Gonzalo sensed my fear.

'Don't worry,' he said, 'if you drown, you'll go to heaven.'

*

Back in Iquitos, there was no sign of César. I spent my time going back and forth from Ari's Burger to the Regal Restaurant. Everyone in town seemed to know who I was. The old American, who used to sit at Ari's all day, every day, motioned for me to join him at his table. Like most of the other foreigners in town, he was grey-haired, with a pot belly and a taste for nicotine.

'Heard you're going up to Jivaro country,' he said, swigging a *Cusqueña*.

'They don't like being called *Jivaro*,' I said. 'It means "savage".'

'Mighty dangerous up there.'

'Oh?'

He mimed a chicken having its head pulled off.

'A friend of mine went up there back in '73,' he said. 'Took a boat up the Tigre and the Corrientes, right up to the backwaters of the Pastaza.'

He swigged his beer. I waited for the punchline, to hear how the Shuar had gone on a head-hacking spree.

'Did your friend meet any Shuar?'

'Sure he did,' he said. 'And he swapped his Oyster Perpetual for one of those *tsantsa* things.'

'Didn't he get his head chopped off?'

'No way, man,' he said, 'but he did have an AK-47 strapped to his chest.'

Just as I was giving up hope of ever seeing César again, he sent word from the safe-house at Punchana. I was to get there as quickly as I could. Braving the torrential afternoon rain, I rushed over to meet him. The *motocarro* had to drop me at the end of the road, which had become a morass of mud.

César was sitting beside a stack of white Tupperware boxes.

'Did you get any big bugs?' I asked.

He pointed to the boxes.

'Two *Titanus giganticus*,' he said, 'and a load of others, too.'

'Does that mean we can go on the trip now?'

'We'll leave in the morning,' he said.

I ate my last meal at *La Gran Maloca*, literally 'the great hut'. It is generally regarded as the best restaurant in the Peruvian Amazon. From the moment I arrived in Iquitos, I'd heard people going on about it. One man had said that the chef used to work for Fernando Belaunde, the former President of Peru. But after disgracing himself by giving his boss a severe case of food-poisoning, he'd had to escape the presidential palace for the jungle.

A gaunt young waiter with watery eyes showed me into the dining room. He was dressed in a Tuxedo with a black bow-tie. Fine original paintings enlivened the walls, and coy carp moved restlessly in a large tank. The waiter placed a linen napkin squarely on my lap. He spoke English with an unusual accent. He said he was from Hungary. His name was Laslo.

I ordered *Paiche a la Loretana*, a filleted piece of piraruca, served with roasted manioc. Between bites, Laslo would scamper over and check that the fish was satisfactory.

'I must tell you something,' he said, as I praised the chef's skill for the twentieth time. 'I haven't been a waiter for very long. Circumstances have made it necessary for me to take this job.'

'Circumstances?'

Laslo's eyes watered a little more.

'I was working in Dallas,' he said. 'While I was there, a man offered to sell me some land. He said it was in the Amazon. I've always loved the idea of jungle, ever since I was ten years old. So I agreed to buy the land. It's only fifteen hectares ... just a little bit of Amazon.'

'It sounds nice.'

Laslo shook his head.

'I paid far too much,' he said. 'I gave him all my savings. Luckily the Polish millionaire who owns this restaurant, gave me a job. The big problem is that I don't speak any Spanish.'

Laslo invited me to his shack in his little it of the jungle. If I gave him enough notice, he said, he'd cook up a big pot of Hungarian goulash. Early next morning he sent a pair of books to Hotel Selva for me. The first was called *Jivaro: Among the Head-shrinkers of the Amazon*. The other was called *Head Hunters of the Amazon*. Writing of a century ago, its author said: 'Iquitos contained so much human driftwood that there was always some new freak to be met, with a strange tale to tell and a still stranger outlook on life.' Nothing seemed to have changed at all.

I had been worrying that we had too much luggage. As well as my own bags, we now had the gifts and the supplies which César had bought with my money. But in *Jivaro*, I'd read the highlights of the inventory taken by the Frenchman Bertrand Flornoy on his three-man trip into the jungle in the early 1950s. Even by Hiram Bingham's example, it was an impressive one.

Amongst many other things, Flornoy had packed up three-quarters of a mile of blue and white cloth; 10,000 feet of cinemagraphic film; 220 rolls of regular film; 8,000 pills of quinine sulphate; 160 phials for intra-muscular injections; a complete surgical outfit, a selection of dentists' instruments; 400 lbs of *concentrated* bread, 220 lbs of manioc flour, 220 lbs of rice and 900 tins of various foods. The entire lot weighed more than 4,500 lbs. Flornoy even took a taxidermist along.

*

In the good old days of Iquitos's rubber barons, the fine buildings on the water's edge would resound with riotous soirées. Tycoons would out do each other wasting money, to prove their wealth. They held Babylonian parties, with bucket-loads of Sevruga caviar and fountains of vintage Champagne; they lit cigars with £10 notes, and gambled $50,000 on the toss of a coin. If anything, Iquitos's night-life had grown even wilder over the decades. But the fine wines and dinner dress had been replaced by a culture founded on warm beer and watery milkshakes.

The few foreigners living there, had a methodical routine. If the day belonged to Ari's, staring at buxom local women, then the night was the preserve of the Gringo Bar. I had passed it a hundred times, but with a name like that, it had seemed too obvious a place for a gringo to go.

Before going to bed I had buried the maize cob in the dirt behind the hotel, and pulled a flagstone on top of it. Forty nights had passed since I'd been treated by the *maestro* at Wali Wasi. Furling the foam rubber pillow around my head and ears like a bonnet, I tried to sleep. But the sounds of unbridled passion from next door, and the banging of the headboard, kept me awake. I got dressed and went across the main square to the Gringo Bar.

My curiosity was soon satisfied. Dozens of scantily clad local girls were prancing about, jumping in and out of a jacuzzi, into which cascaded a mock waterfall. Most of them had on what the Brazilians call 'dental floss bikinis'. Some were wearing even less. In a town which is said to have eight women to every man, a gringo with a little hard currency goes a long way. The handful of men, all over fifty, were wearing Hawaiian shirts, shorts and flip-flops. Lounging back on cane chairs, they sipped beer from chilled glasses as doting young ladies fondled them. It was gringo heaven.

A giant Scandinavian called Lars tried to befriend me.

'Going to Jivaro country?' he asked, pushing a girl off his lap.

I nodded, impressed that even he, a complete stranger, knew my travel plans.

'Hope you're taking gifts,' he said.

'We've got all sorts of things – food, clothes and lots of Fanta bottles.'

Lars flinched.

'What about Vicks Vapour Rub?'

'What about it?'

'You'd better stock up with it.'

'Why?'

Gulping a mug of Cristal lager, Lars looked over earnestly.

'The Jivaro warriors rub it into their genitals,' he said. 'They think it gives them more stamina with women.'

*

A fleet of *motocarros* were needed to ferry the nineteen sacks from Punchana down to the docks. César and his three young brothers met me at the quay. The rusting hulk of a ship was being mobbed by a throng of people. It was a scene of utter desperation. Hundreds of passengers were fighting to get up a narrow gangplank. They were carrying everything they owned like refugees – wicker chairs and chests of tools, wheelbarrows, stepladders, pots and pans and, of course blenders.

César's brothers pushed their way onto the boat, and formed a relay to get the loot aboard. César and I followed. Greasing an official's palm with a few extra *soles* secured us two cabins. They were located beside the main lavatories, but were still a far better option than sleeping out on the decks, like everyone else. I stowed my bags under the bed, chaining them to its frame. Then I barged into César's cabin.

One of the boys was lying on the bed, naked. César was standing over him with his trousers down. I looked at them. They looked at me. Time seemed to stop. I opened my mouth, but no words came out. Somehow I managed to get out of the cabin, and shut the door behind me.

17

Saigon of South America

I leant on the river ferry's railing, looking out at the pandemonium on the quay. Even more passengers than before were fighting to get aboard. As I stood there, staring, still in shock, I considered what seemed like an unreal situation. How could I set off in search of a wild tribe with a paedophile as a guide? Worse still, this was a paedophile molesting his own brother. The decision was an easy one. I returned to César's cabin. Although almost unable to look such a degenerate in the eye, I said that we would not be going into the jungle together.

To my surprise, he didn't seem at all perturbed. He told me to take the supplies, and that he would return the money I had paid. He'd be glad to pass up such a dangerous journey, he said.

Feeling as if a prize-fighter had punched me in the face, I rattled back to Hotel Selva with a convoy of *motocarros*. The receptionist supervised, as the sacks were taken to my old room.

Words cannot express my sense of defeat.

I told the receptionist what had happened, what I had seen on the ferry.

'*Bueno sí*, oh yes,' she said freely, 'everyone knows that Señor Vargas likes his little boys.'

'*Do they?*'

'Of course they do,' she replied, 'there are no secrets in Iquitos.'

'But they're *sus hermanos*, his brothers!'

'Is that what he told you?'

I admitted it was.

'That's a lie. They aren't his brothers, but *sus novios*, his boy-friends.'

Over at Ari's Burger, I was in no mood for Florita's pouting. She must have sensed this, because she brought over a banana milk-shake and hurried away. I sat in a corner facing the wall, unable to speak.

The old American chain-smoker came over.

'Heard you just found out about César,' he said.

'Why didn't anyone tell me César was a paedophile?'

He thought for a moment.

'You were so happy with him,' he said, 'no one wanted to spoil your trip.'

The fact that César liked children was bad, but it was just the tip of the iceberg. He was the most wanted man in town. He had been convicted dozens of times for ripping-off tourists and acting as a pimp, for theft, drug dealing and a range of sex offences.

'César Vargas,' he said, snorting, 'he's the Dennis the Menace of the Amazon.'

In the afternoon I sat on a bench in Plaza de Armas with my head in my hands. The usual scrum of boot boys and chewing-gum dealers hung well back. Word had spread of my misfortune. Whatever the circumstances, I couldn't allow myself to do business with a known paedophile.

The first drops of rain splashed onto the tiled surface of the square. In the Amazon, where it pours almost every day, the rain can drench you in under three seconds. But it isn't seen as the scourge of nature it is in the West. Rain is the lifeblood of the jungle.

I left the bench and sought refuge in the Gringo Bar.

A smattering of young women were carousing with older foreign men, to the sound of the Bee Gees. As I entered the bar, there was silence. Everyone turned to look at me. The girls stopped fondling, the glasses ceased clinking. Even the Bee Gees fell silent.

The barman, an old American with a bald head and a Hawaiian shirt, slapped a tumbler of *guaje* juice down in front of me.

'It's on the house,' he said.

I thanked him and sat down in the corner. A middle-aged man asked if he could join me. He had grey hair, fleshy white legs and a sunburned nose. He was an American called Max. Everyone would tell you behind his back that he was CIA, an 'active cell'. He said he had retired from the Agency, and that he bred snakes. Like most of his fellow countrymen lying low in Iquitos, I suspected he had been lured by the cheap beer and the inexhaustible supply of available jungle women.

As far as Max was concerned, I was now one of the boys. I'd been bitten by the jungle, as he put it. I'd been initiated.

'But even if I can get some more money sent,' I said, 'I haven't got a guide. I need someone who knows the jungle, someone who has no fear of the Shuar.'

Max called out for another drink.

'You need a man who can trek through the rain-forest in the dead of night,' he said. 'A man who can kill an anaconda with his bare hands; who can live on a diet of tree grubs washed down with his own urine; a man who's taken *ayahuasca* a hundred times, who'll protect you if it means sacrificing his own life ...' Max paused, 'a man who has no fear.'

'Does such a man exist?'

Wiping the froth from his mouth, Max glanced at the wall clock.

'He should be here in five minutes,' he said.

The Texan I'd met at Ari's swept in out of the rain and slapped a soggy dossier on the table.

'The police have been after César Vargas for a long time,' he said. 'He's at the top of their list, he's a prime target. We're going to clean up this town. This place is the best kept secret on Earth, and we ain't gonna have it tainted with paedophile scum.'

'He's dealing in insects, too,' I said limply.

The Texan screwed up his face.

'Low life scum!' he barked.

At that moment, the door of the Gringo Bar swung back with such force that it almost broke free from its hinges. Standing in the frame was a ferocious-looking foreigner. A shade over six feet, he was as lean as a race horse, with a back so straight as to be unnatural. He was drenched with rain and dressed from top to toe in camouflage. His boots, his khaki fatigues, and torn *ninja* singlet were caked in fresh mud. A bandanna had been tied tightly over his head. His unshaven face was daubed red in warpaint, its long chin etched with a diagonal scar. Around his neck were military dog tags.

His searing malachite-green eyes scanned the bar with robotic precision. Then he made for our table.

'Here's your man,' said Max under his breath, 'Richard Fowler: Vietnam vet', jungle expert, and occasional guide.'

The soldier pressed his callused hand into mine. My first handshake since Huancayo. His palm felt like coarse grade sandpaper.

He sat down and drank a mug of Pilsen in a single draught. I asked him what had brought him to Iquitos.

'Been living in the woods for a long time,' he said, in a voice moulded by Marlboros. 'Signed up for 'Nam back in '68. I was with 101st US Airborne Division Jungle Operations – long range reconnaissance. Tet Offensive, Battle of Hue, Hamburger Hill, all that shit.'

Richard lit a cigarette, sucked hard, and expelled a jet of smoke through his nose.

'The jungle's my turf,' he said. 'I tried livin' back in the US, but it doesn't love me, and I sure as Hell don't love it.'

'Do you know anything about *ayahuasca*?' I asked.

Richard cackled menacingly.

'*Ayahuasca, sanango, chacruna, datura*, I've done 'em all.'

'What are *sanango* and *chacruna*?'

The Vietnam vet gulped down a second beer in one.

'They're nerve agents.'

'What about the Shuar, the Jivaro?'

'Jivaro?' he echoed, lighting another Marlboro. 'They make the Vietcong look like pussy cats.'

'Would you take me to them . . . to the Pastaza?'

'Can I bring Francisco?'

'Who's he?'

'My shaman.'

'You can bring anyone you like, as long as there's no paedophilia or insect dealing.'

Richard looked deep into my eyes, his pupils dilating in a sea of green. It was not a conventional Iquitos stare.

'I promise you one thing,' he said.

'What?'

'I promise that if you hire me, I will keep you alive.'

The Vietnam vet' loosened his laces and leant back on his chair.

'The Amazon isn't a kid's playground, you know,' he said. 'If you come with me you live the jungle, you breathe it . . . you eat it.'

'*Eat* it?'

He sucked at a dried callus on his hand.

'If you don't eat it,' he said ominously, 'it'll eat you.'

'But I've got lots of canned food.'

'Screw the canned food,' said Fowler, 'I'm talking about fresh chow ... peccaries, caimans, larvae, anacondas. You can leave your supplies behind. They're dead weight. In the jungle you only need one thing.'

'What's that?'

'A sharp knife,' he said, tugging a collapsible Ka-bar blade from its sheath on his belt.

I boasted about the size of my nickel-coated Alaskan moose knife. The Vietnam vet scoffed.

'Leave that behind, too,' he said.

Fowler needed two days to put the jungle expedition together. He suggested we hire our own boat and take it right up to the Pastaza. That way we wouldn't have to rely on the river ferries. But before he could do anything, he'd need to catch up with his belle, Señorita Jane. Like the other foreigners in Iquitos, he had succumbed to the unrealistic gender ratio. Jane would be due out of high school in a few minutes.

'How old is she?'

'Sixteen,' he sniffed, 'but she looks old for her age.'

'Isn't that rather young?'

The Vietnam veteran slipped his knife away.

'Are you crazy?' he drawled. 'Sixteen's a damn fine age.'

*

At eight the next morning I found myself sitting at my usual table at Ari's. With my back facing the wall, I had a clear sweep of all the staring faces. The first die-hard patrons were already sipping Nescafé, black as crude oil. Florita's colleague was mopping the floor. Noticing me, she mopped her way over to my table. She said that Florita was sick. It wasn't an illness caused by disease, but one derived from true love. Florita was getting weaker all the time. A trip to Gringolandia was the only antidote. When she was strong enough, *if* she survived, she'd travel with me to Europe.

'Her bag is packed already,' said Florita's friend. 'You must buy her a ticket. Then you can be married.'

'But I'm already married!'

'So?' she said, 'you can have two wives.'

The waitress slunk back across the room, probing the mop between the legs of the chrome chairs. A salesman slipped his way over. He was offering a new range of tarantulas in frames. They came in sets of three – small, medium and large, and were designed to be hung together on a wall in order of their size. I asked him about *Titanus giganticus*. He looked nervous.

'*Expensive*,' he mouthed.

'How much?'

'Seven hundred dollars each, maybe more.'

'Why so expensive?'

'Hard to get,' he replied. 'There's only one man in Iquitos who can get them.'

'Who's that?'

'A man called César Vargas,' he said.

The salesman broke off, grabbed his tarantulas, and scurried out of Ari's. I looked round to see what had scared him away. César was coming towards me.

He sat down and began to berate me.

'Why did you say you were going to have my legs broken?'

'I never said such a thing!'

'Well, everyone in town's saying it.'

'César, I don't want to harm you.'

'God will judge you,' he said, 'He knows how bad you are and how good I am.'

César had stopped eating. It was his own form of hunger strike. He wouldn't swallow another mouthful of food until his name had been cleared. Meanwhile, he'd turned to God for guidance. His conversation was heavy with religious remarks. César had been born again.

'Meet me tonight at the bandstand in Belen,' he said, 'and I will give you the money I owe you.'

*

Since hiring Richard, my confidence had been bolstered. He looked like the sort of man one could do with having along on a dangerous mission. I admired his devotion to the jungle, and was secretly jealous of him. Even with the most rigorous military training, I would never be as hardy. He was from different stock – tough as nails, with honed muscles, a foul mouth and an iron gut. He was the kind of man who could live on mealworms and termites, with no fear of insects with more than six legs. I was thankful Richard had turned up, and that César had been exposed in the nick of time.

At nine o'clock sharp I felt a muscular hand on the base of my neck. The Vietnam vet' had crept up, and was looming over me. He was chewing on the end of a cigar.

'You love this town, don't you?' he said.

'It's all right,' I replied. 'It grows on you.'

'*All right*? It's more than *all right*,' said Fowler, slapping his hands together. 'It's the Saigon of South America!'

Three men were standing to attention beside him, waiting to be introduced.

'Meet my buddies,' Richard said.

I shook their hands.

'This is Cockroach.'

He motioned to a teenager with an innocent face. 'He'll be the cook. And this here is Walter, he's your *motorista*, he owns the boat.'

'Who's the third man?'

Richard moved the cigar to the left corner of his mouth.

'That's Guido.'

'And what does Guido do?'

'He's an odd job man.'

We left Ari's and went down to the floating market at Belen. A battered speedboat was waiting to take us down river, where the *Pradera* was waiting to be inspected.

'She's as sturdy as any craft on the Amazon,' Richard bragged as we bounced our way downstream. 'She's got a big engine and the space we'll need for a long river trip.'

'She's very strong,' said Walter, the boat's owner. 'She's only six months old. You will not regret hiring the *Pradera*.'

Two hours later, with the afternoon rain lashing down, the speedboat swerved off the Amazon and down a tributary. The current was much slower, the river-banks abundant with wildlife and breadfruit trees. We veered into a backwater off the river. The craft's aluminium hull sliced through fields of water lilies. Then, taking a right hand bend widely, the pilot brought the speedboat to a sharp halt. Bobbing in the wake was a rotting monstrosity of a riverboat. It reminded me of the *African Queen* shortly before she was destroyed.

Forty feet long, it was clinker-built, with open sides and a flat roof. The lime green paint was chipped, and the woodwork was in a pitiful state. An unskilled hand had daubed in red paint at the bow the name, *Pradera*.

I climbed up and had a look at what would be our home for weeks, possibly months. From the moment the soles of my shoes touched the floorboards, I knew this boat was trouble. The beams were covered in cobwebs; like all the other timber, they were rotten to the core. The problems were not only structural – the battery was dead, the steering mechanism was held together with fragments of string, and the engine wouldn't start up. Rats could be heard dashing about in the cavity between the boards and the hull.

At the stern there was a medicine cabinet. I opened it optimistically. It was filled with giant red beetles, and had no medical supplies. Beside it was a Johnson 65-horsepower engine with a damaged propeller and, beyond that, was a makeshift toilet . . . a hole in the floor.

Richard sucked on the end of a cheap cigar.

'Great, isn't it?' he said whimsically.

'What do you mean? Could it get us to the Pastaza?'

''Course it could.'

'There's no way this boat's six months old,' I said. 'It's falling to bits. The wood's all rotten, it's leaking like a sieve, the battery's flat, its engine doesn't even work . . . and it's infested with rats.'

The Vietnam vet' struck the *motorista* on the shoulder-blade with his fist.

'It's a fine boat,' he said. 'We'll take it!'

*

Richard dropped by my room at Hotel Selva later that day. The *Pradera*'s owner would bring it to Iquitos at night, he said, ready to set off at dawn. The rotting vessel was going to cost $25 a day, plus petrol. I regarded it as highway robbery.

Once he had picked his way through the nineteen sacks of loot, Richard swore violently.

'César said we'd need all that stuff,' I said. 'I admit the Fanta bottles were my idea. They're an invaluable tool.'

Fowler froze me with his green eyes.

'You gotta understand something,' he said, 'people in the jungle don't want pretty little combs and mascara, they don't care a toss about mirrors, beads or fuckin' Fanta bottles. They only want one thing . . .'

'What's that?'

'Sixteen gauge shotgun shells,' he said, 'that's what they want.'

Lugging some of the gifts and tins away to swap them for ammunition, Richard said that he'd catch us *fresh* meat during the trip. Canned food, he said, was for wimps.

A little later, when the evening air was ringing with the buzz of miniature wings, I made my way to Eiffel's bandstand at Belen, to wait for César. Squatting nearby was Rosa, the woman whose face had been dunked in acid. She smiled shyly when she saw me, covering her cheek with her hand. I bought a peeled *guaje* from her and sunk my teeth into its yellow flesh.

Why wasn't she at home with her husband?

'*Esposo*, husband?' she replied, 'what man would marry someone as ugly as me?'

'I'm sure many men would,' I said.

Rosa offered me another *guaje*.

'*Cógelo*, take it, I have so many and no one wants to buy them.'

I asked about the *maestro*, the one who'd had the premonition.

'He was not a good man,' she said tenderly. 'He seduced young women. He often made them pregnant and said the Devil was the father. He would try to get me to sleep with him. He was disgusting. So I scorned him. But my parents believed in his magic.'

'The *maestro*'s dream?'

'*Sí* ... my mother threw acid on my face when I was sleeping. He told her to do it.'

César arrived at the bandstand an hour after Rosa had gone. He said he couldn't stay long. The police were after him.

'They're saying I'm a criminal,' he said weakly. 'They want to throw me into jail and beat me up, and rape me. They want to break my legs.'

'Why did you tell me the boys were your brothers?'

'They're *like* brothers,' said César. 'Our friendship isn't a crime.'

'Please give me the money back and I'll leave you alone.'

César sat on the edge of the bandstand. He was very frail, no doubt a result of his hunger strike. He was holding a pair of Tupperware boxes. They were white and familiar.

'Is the money inside them?'

César ducked his head subserviently, and blinked.

'Not money,' he sighed. 'I'm still waiting to be paid, and all the money you gave me was spent. Debts, so many debts.'

'So what's in the boxes?'

César held them out towards me.

'Have a look,' he said.

Somehow, I knew what the Tupperware boxes contained even before I prised off their lids. In each one, paralysed with fear, was an enormous black beetle. They were over five inches wide.

'*Titanus giganticus*,' said César proudly. 'They're little more than babies. I'm giving you them in place of the money,' he said. 'They're worth $800 each.'

18

Green Hell

I do not know why, but the *Pradera* was supposed to meet us alongside the dance-floor of an Iquitos disco. The nightspot stood precariously at the Amazon's edge, beside a quay. In the middle of the night Richard, Cockroach, Guido and I ferried our sacks through the disco to the water. A wild Brazilian salsa band was in full swing. We weaved in single file amid the throng of sweaty dancers. Richard had bought 300 gallons of pure drinking water, 100 gallons of petrol, and almost 1,000 shotgun shells. They had to be shuffled through the disco along with the rest of the supplies. The *motorista*, Walter, had promised to be there dead on 5.30 a.m.

I had tried to find someone to look after the giant beetles in my absence. Max, the CIA snake man, said he didn't look after anything with legs; Florita said it was against her religion to babysit beetles, and the receptionist at Hotel Selva said her husband would feed them to the chickens. So, with great reluctance, I took the two Tupperware boxes down to the quay, along with all the rest of the goods. The pair of baby *Titanus giganticus* would just have to come along with us to meet the Birdmen.

By about 9 a.m. the band had packed up their instruments and sauntered off home. A handful of people stayed to dance even though there was no music. They were salsa fanatics.

Quite suddenly Richard picked a fight with Guido, the odd-job man. He accused him of lying, stealing and general dishonesty. Guido ran away with his knapsack. When I asked Richard why he'd disgraced the man so publicly, he replied: 'It's a warning to the others. If I don't make my mark right at the start, they'll take us for all we've got.'

Richard treated Cockroach to a few drinks. I was touched by his generosity. He said it was also important to keep the men watered. Well-watered men had high morale. And without it the journey would end in disaster.

At three o'clock that afternoon we were still waiting for the *Pradera*. I sensed myself losing control of the trip again. I was about to march back to Hotel Selva with the beetles, when I spotted a dark green hulk fifty feet out. It was heading towards the quay, low in the water, moving in slow motion. It could only be the *Pradera*.

Once she had docked, I moored the guy-line to the disco's bar, and supervised the loading. We struggled to haul the sacks, the water, and the barrels of petrol on board. Only then did I throw my own bags up, before climbing aboard, with the beetles' boxes tucked under my arm.

The departure from the disco quay at Iquitos lacked pomp and circumstance. But then, some of the greatest expeditions in human history, I mused, must have had no send-offs at all. As we ventured out, into the beds of water hyacinths, I made a solemn oath. I would not return to Iquitos until I had spent time with the Shuar, with the Birdmen of Peru.

I gave Cockroach the Tupperware boxes and explained what was inside. The valuable jungle commodity was being entrusted to him, and him alone. He would have to establish what *Titanus giganticus* liked to eat. Under no circumstances was anyone else to be permitted access to the precious insects. Cockroach nodded his head repetitively, indicating that he had understood the instructions. He cleared the common red beetles from the medicine cabinet, and stowed the plastic cartons inside.

The *Pradera* bobbed along up the right bank of the Amazon, heading upstream towards the great river's source. The size and current of the river were truly daunting. Even in the Upper Amazon, it's at least a mile wide. Richard said that, at any one time, a fifth of the Earth's fresh water is flowing through the waterway.

Gradually the log dugouts, the shanties, and the fishermen's canoes fell away. The grumble of the outboard motor broke the silence. I sat on the roof, filled with elation. The journey had at last begun.

Richard smoked three Marlboros, and drank four cups of cold Nescafé. I sensed that his body needed fuelling up with toxins before it was ready to take command.

'We'll go up to the village of Tamshiyacu,' he said, 'that's where we'll pick up Francisco, my shaman.'

Cockroach dragged the cooking gear and some of the food to the front of the boat, next to the driver's seat. He and the others were busy staking out their space. I wondered where to sling my top-of-the-range, British-made, jungle hammock. I didn't want to be too close to the engine, the toilet, or the cooking area. Eventually, I found the perfect spot, put it up and climbed in. A second later there was a distressing ripping sound, and I flipped onto the floor. Richard led the others in a bawdy round of laughter.

'That's English tourist shit,' he said. 'I told you to leave that crap behind.'

Cockroach probed about in one of the sacks. He pulled out three tins randomly. They contained tuna fish, butter, and condensed milk. I watched from a distance as he opened them with a steak knife, tipped the contents into a saucepan, and cooked for twenty minutes. Then he filled the pan to the top with water, cracked in five eggs, stirred, and announced that the *soup* was ready.

As it was dished out, I asked Richard if Cockroach had cooked before.

'He's used to fresh food, not this tinned shit,' he said.

*

Just before dusk, the *Pradera* moored at the jetty of Tamshiyacu. A man was standing there ready to catch the rope. He was about five feet four with a mop of tangled hair, spindly legs and an over-sized mouth. It was filled with the kind of joke teeth you get in a Christmas cracker. He looked like a child, but must have been in his forties, and was naked except for a pair of Y-fronts and a buttonless shirt. Piled up next to him was an assortment of pots, cloth bags, and a metal-framed rocking-chair. He tossed up his belongings, the chair, and came aboard.

When he had greeted the American, he lit a home-made cigarette. It was as thick as a cucumber. The lower deck was engulfed in smoke.

'Meet Francisco,' said Richard.

'How did he know to rendezvous at the quay?'

Richard took a puff of the giant cigarette.

'He saw us coming in a dream,' he said.

I was about to make some condescending remark, when the shaman handed me a package. It was wrapped in newspaper. I opened it up. Inside was a hammock. Francisco whispered something to the Vietnam vet' and pulled up his underpants. Their elastic had gone.

'What did he say?'

'He saw your crap limey hammock in his dream too,' said Richard, 'so he brought you a new one.'

Having seen many awe-inspiring feats of illusion performed by Indian godmen, I am suspicious when it comes to suggestions of mind-reading or one-in-a-million coincidence. But, grateful for the hammock, I told Cockroach to unload some canned food and supplies for the shaman's family.

'Does he want to wear some of the clothes we've brought as gifts?'

'Francisco doesn't need clothes,' said Richard, coldly. 'They cramp his style.'

I told the Shaman of our planned route up to the Pastaza region, in search of the Shuar. He obviously hadn't seen our journey in his dream. I know this because he grasped his unshaved cheeks, and emitted a high-pitched shriek.

'¡*Muy peligroso*! So dangerous!' he yelled.

'That's why we've brought them gifts ... we've got lots of shotgun shells,' I said.

'The Shuar don't use guns,' riposted Francisco. 'They use poisoned darts and black magic. Everyone knows they eat the brains of babies and shit on the bodies of their victims. They'll murder us and shrink our heads!'

Making excuses, the shaman hurried from the boat. As he scrambled to the jetty his Y-fronts fell down. Richard watched, disappointed at the sight of a grown man fighting with his underwear.

'If he's so frightened, let's leave him behind,' I said.

'We're not going another inch without Francisco,' Richard replied. 'The Shuar have no respect for anyone who travels without a shaman. And besides, he can cook up some nerve agents along the way.'

The veteran disappeared into the darkness of Tamshiyacu, returning an hour later with Francisco. I was unsure how he'd tempted the shaman to join the expedition. It may have had something to do with the food.

Cockroach squatted over my titanium Primus stove, cooking meals back to back. As soon as the pot of buttery tuna soup had been gobbled down, he set to work on another creation. Like an artist experimenting with colour, he dolloped equal amounts of corned beef, porridge oats and strawberry 'Fanny-brand' jam into the pot. Then, gritting his teeth, he stirred the concoction over a moderate heat until it bubbled.

Before serving, he threw in a handful of uncooked rice.

As we choked down the dish, the *Pradera* moved away from the jetty, heading upstream once again. It was now pitch dark. High above us, the stars glinted like light shining through the holes of a sieve. I lay on my back on the boat's roof and gazed upwards. The Southern Cross heralded the way into uncertain waters. I cannot remember ever feeling so overcome with expectation. And I was filled with fear. The realm of giant insects, venomous reptiles and die-hard tribes, the jungle and its kin prey on the ignorant. I was dreading the journey ahead, but the trail of feathers had brought me here. And, besides, Richard Fowler – who seemed to roar with laughter in the face of danger – had promised to keep me alive.

At least, I pondered, we were now steering a clear and definite course. I had come far on my haphazard route since the auction of shrunken heads: across the mountains, the desert, and into the jungle. I cautioned myself to have courage, and to take the jungle in my teeth. Soon, I hoped, we would meet the Shuar, and fly with them ... and reach conclusions.

Francisco and Richard climbed up onto the *Pradera*'s roof and smoked another giant cigarette. The shaman thanked me for the food which, he said, was the best meal he had ever eaten.

'This is for you,' he said, taking a string of beads from his neck. I held them in the candlelight. They were curious, odd-shaped beans, flame-red on one side and black on the other. Richard explained that the beads were from the bean-pod of a jungle tree, and that shamans prize the spot where they fall to earth. There is no place, they say, more sacred to take *ayahuasca*.

'They're *wayuro* seeds,' said Francisco. 'You must wear them until you reach your home. They'll protect you. Do not take them off.'

'Why not?'

Francisco spat into the water.

'Take them off and you will meet death,' he said.

*

My first night on the Amazon was among the most uncomfortable I can remember. Part of the problem was getting used to the hammock. But far worse was the jungle night-life. The boat was tethered to a low-hanging tree in the early hours. I shone my torch into the water and made out the eerie orange reflection of alligator eyes. But the caimans were not an immediate danger, unlike the nest of furious hornets hanging above the boat. As they struck, we desperately untied the boat and sought a safer spot upstream.

Slouched in my hammock, I tossed from side to side, thinking about the entire food chain's eagerness to consume me. As I tossed, the *wayuro* seed necklace choked me. I would not have taken the shaman's threat seriously, but I'm a sucker for superstition.

Pulling my sleeping bag over my head, I prayed for daylight. But Cockroach's *plat du jour* was surging through my intestines at an alarming pace. My bowels were warning of impending catastrophe. I had to relieve them without delay. In one distraught movement I unfurled myself from the sleeping-bag, put on my shoes, and shuffled down the boat.

Getting from my hammock to the loo involved a complex obstacle course. First, there were the hammocks, which criss-crossed the body of the boat like nets on a tennis court. After the hammocks lay the oil drums and water barrels, which had to be scaled. Beyond them was the Johnson 65, which was passed by walking a narrow plank of wood running beside it.

After the plank, you found yourself in a snug, faeces-caked corner alive with cockroaches. This assault course was made even more difficult by the lack of light, and the uncertainty of a rogue bowel. Once squatting in that vile privy, you had to avoid falling down through the hole into the water. Flick on the torch and you'd be dive-bombed by insects.

On that first night I made the sombre pilgrimage to the end of the boat five times.

Long before dawn, Cockroach began preparing breakfast. He switched on my yellow camping lantern and banged about with the pots. I think he wanted to show his enthusiasm for the job. Richard got everyone else up before 6 a.m. The Vietnam training must have had something to do with his insomnia. He disliked it when people slept too much. He'd sit on the roof all night, rocking back and forth in a chair, smoking Marlboros.

I unzipped my sleeping bag, and checked the air for insects. All was clear on the bug front, so I dangled my legs over the hammock's edge and fumbled for my shoes. Rats had feasted on the left one in the night. I told Cockroach to get rid of the rats at all costs.

Up on the roof, Francisco was gulping down his second helping of tuna and jam casserole. He said he'd had good dreams. The river mermaids would leave us alone.

'*Mermaids*?'

'*Sí, las sirenas*, the mermaids,' he said, licking the bowl with his tongue. 'They are evil. But I will keep them away.'

'What are they like, these mermaids?'

Francisco lit his pipe and looked over at me in surprise. I must have been the only person on the Amazon who didn't know about the mermaids.

'They have blonde hair and teeth made of gold,' he said. 'If they fall in love with you, they lure you to their kingdom under the water. You can never escape. There are so many fishermen who live down there.'

I asked Walter if he'd heard of the mermaids.

'*Por supuesto*, of course, Señor,' he said, 'everyone knows of them. One of the fishermen who worked on this very boat fell in love with *la reina de la sirenas*, the queen of the mermaids. She sent hundreds of fish for him to sell, then she took him.'

'Where is he now?'

Walter pointed over the edge.

'*Ahí abajo*, down there,' he said.

Every so often we passed a cluster of thatched houses set back from the water's edge. Children skipped through the grass, their mothers ground clothes against the rocks; their fathers checked the fishing nets. They used green nets at night and white ones during the day, as the latter reflected the moonlight, making them visible to fish.

The main body of the Amazon carried an endless stream of flotsam. Entire tree trunks and branches frequently careered towards us. I had been keen to travel by day and by night, but the risk of running into a submerged tree trunk made night travel very hazardous indeed.

Walter said we had already got through ninety gallons of petrol, and that we'd have to load up with more at Nauta. It was impossible for so much fuel to have been used in less than a day of travel, but I couldn't prove any wrongdoing. When we reached the small village of Nauta in the early afternoon, I said I would spend my remaining money on petrol. After that it was Walter's job to get us to the Pastaza and back. I passed around my empty wallet. If we ran out of fuel up river we would all suffer.

Richard told me that pilfering supplies on a jungle expedition was considered as a perk. César, he said, had bought nineteen sacks of merchandise for a reason.

'You'd find a few cans of tuna missing here, a sack of salt or a load of soap there,' he said, 'and before you know it you'd have nothing left. César would have had it all skimmed off and sold en route.'

The theft of supplies has been the bane of expeditions for centuries. When Stanley, the 19th century explorer, set off on his great African voyages, he'd take enough food and supplies to sink a ship. He knew very well that within months, even days, eighty per cent of the stocks would have disappeared. Only a regime of total ruthlessness, he said, could prevent failure. Any man found stealing was slapped in chains and fed on gruel. Taking Stanley's example, I proclaimed that anyone found stealing would be left on the river-bank.

While waiting for fuel at Nauta, I sent Cockroach to spend my last ten *soles* on a high quality mosquito net. The one I'd brought from London was no good for the Amazon, where anopheles mosquitoes are unusually small.

When we had loaded aboard 430 gallons of fuel, Walter climbed into the pilot's seat and started the engine. A crowd came to the quay to see us off. It was made up of Nauta's football team, dressed in their blue and green strip, five or six prostitutes from the local bar, and a class of schoolchildren. One of the kids ran down to the boat and handed me a chicken as a gift.

I stayed on the roof for most of the morning. The Amazon had become the Marañon. Near Nauta the Ucayali River merges with the Marañon to form the Amazon proper. It has 2,300 miles to run before reaching the Atlantic. The water had already travelled so far from the snow-capped Andes that its reserves of oxygen were depleted. As a result, some species of fish had adapted. We saw them jumping out from the river to breathe the air. One large fish even jumped onto the deck. I said we should throw it back. But Walter took it down below where Cockroach was cooking a great pot of bony stew. The fish was cleaned and tossed in. I couldn't understand how the crew could so enjoy such disgusting smelling fare.

'This is much better than that tuna fish,' said Francisco. 'It's fresh food. We like *fresh* food.'

When I asked Cockroach what he'd cooked up, he pointed at my feet.

'Las ratas que se comieron sus zapatos. The rats which ate your shoes,' he said.

*

From the roof of the *Pradera* there was a fine view of the jungle. The trees were laden with creepers, their overhanging branches shrouded in moss and lichens. God knows how far back the undergrowth extended. It was as alien to me as it must have been to the Spanish Conquistadors when they first sailed up the Amazon, four and a half centuries before.

The plants, the animals, and the people they found, defied all that the Spanish understood. They had come in search of El Dorado, a fictitious metropolis, rumoured to be made from gold.

They had heard the legend of a great monarch, called El Dorado, whose kingdom lay in the Andean Cordillera, in what's now Bolivia. At festivals, he would adorn his naked body with gold dust, before washing it off in Lake Guatavita. As he bathed, his adoring subjects would scatter jewels and sacrificial offerings into the water. From 1538, the Spanish combed the area, but found no trace of El Dorado. For some insane reason they moved the search to the New World's most inaccessible region, the Amazon jungle.

At the same time as the frenzied search for the golden city was taking place, the Conquistadors came upon another legend. Francisco de Orellana was travelling down the Amazon River in 1542 when his party was attacked, he said, by an army of wild women, wearing grassy Hawaiian-type skirts. The Greek poet Homer had been the first to record the myth of a ferocious tribe of female warriors, known as Amazons. They were thought to reside in the Caucasus. But over the centuries the myth moved westward. Some said the Amazons lived in Scythia and Cappadocia, then Africa and, after that, the Americas. Of course we now know that Orellana wasn't attacked by warrior women at all, but men in grass skirts.

When Orellana reported to Phillip II of Spain, the King assumed he'd been attacked by the Amazons he had read about in Herodotus's narrative. Accordingly, he named the waterway after them, and not Orellana.

With their armour, horses and heavy weaponry, the Spanish must have been a hopeless sight in the jungle, a place they knew as *El Infiero Verde*, The Green Hell. Hundreds were struck down by terrible diseases and were left where they collapsed. Around them the jungle seethed with life, waiting to devour those who survived. The imaginations of tortured European minds ran wild. Few expected to escape with their lives. Cannibals and poison arrows were just two of many fears. No one had ever seen people as savage.

Sir Walter Raleigh's work *The Discoverie of the large, rich and bewtiful Empyre of Guiana* contains a startling woodcut illustration of two headless figures, with faces on their chests. Raleigh said they were 'Ewaipanoma' people, whose 'eyes were in their shoulders and their mouths in the middle of their breasts.'

Such legends persist. In her book *Witch-Doctor's Apprentice*, Nicole Maxwell wrote of a common belief – that the USA was conspiring to take Indians from the jungle. Their bodies were melted down, and their fat, which was skimmed off, was taken away as a key ingredient in making atomic weapons. The practice, she said, was known in Peru as *Pishtao*. Maxwell's book was first published in 1961, about the time when nuclear weapons were on everyone's minds.

But she links the story to a much earlier legend. In the 16th century, lard was used to polish the Spanish armour, to ensure that rust didn't set in, especially important for soldiers in a tropical climate. One tale, passed from generation to generation, told how the Conquistadors were unable to find any pigs to make lard. Instead, they captured some Indians, killed them, and melted down their corpses to obtain fat. I was impressed that the legend could have continued for more than four hundred years, transmuting over time.

When Cockroach had finished washing out his cooking pot, I asked him if he'd ever heard tales of Indians being boiled up for fat.

'Yes, it is true,' he remarked earnestly, 'my mother told me when I was a child not to go in the jungle after dark. She said the *Sendero Luminoso*, the Shining Path, took children and boiled them up. They dipped their bullets in the fat.'

19

Two Wishes

Two days further up the River Amazon we reached New York.

Despite the ambitious name, it was little more than a collection of thatched long-houses, with a tin-roofed church. The hamlet was a short distance north-west of the Marañon, up the River Tigre. We got down onto the muddy river-bank and greeted the chief. He was a fragile looking man with rounded shoulders and a pronounced limp. I told him we were going to the Pastaza, in search of the Birdmen.

'A Shuar man used to live near here,' he said, 'in a *maloca* in the jungle. But he disappeared, about three months ago.'

New York was arranged around a square of grass, at one end of which stood a home-made goal post. Most villages we visited were laid out in a similar way, with a football pitch in the middle. All Amazonian men were football mad. On the Tigre, Sunday-best no longer consisted of feathered capes and grassy skirts, but of a Manchester United football strip. No one asked why I, who had so much, didn't wear football gear all the time. But I knew that in their heart of hearts they were desperate to know.

The chief said he would take us to the Shuar's *maloca*, but first he directed us to his own home. It had a raised bamboo floor, open sides, and a densely thatched roof. His hunting dogs sounded the alarm as we approached, but with a whistle he called them to heel. Three or four stools were borrowed from neighbours' houses. Thanking the chief, Richard, Francisco and I sat down. Cockroach and Walter had instructions not to leave the *Pradera* under any circumstances.

A meal of roasted meat and *yuka*, manioc, was set before us. The chief shouted at his wife to bring more food. She was a lazy woman, he said, and had been nothing but a burden since the day of their marriage. In time he hoped she would drop dead. Then he would find another wife, a woman with big breasts. The chief picked out a hoof. He passed it to me. I gnawed at it spiritedly. Had he been married long?

The chief thought for a moment or two.

'*Demasiados años*, so many years,' he said. 'I cannot remember how many. But our wedding was before we built New York.'

'You built the village?'

'Yes, with the missionaries' help. They have given money for so many villages along the Tigre – Brussels, Egypt, Los Angeles, Great Britain and others, too.'

Glance at any detailed map of the region and many familiar names jump out at you.

Richard chewed a chunk of the roasted meat. He asked our host what he knew of the Shuar tribe. The chief spat through a hole in the floor.

'Shuar will cut off your heads,' he said. 'They'll eat you, just like you're eating that meat.'

'Are they cannibals?' I asked.

'*Caníbales*, cannibals? They're much worse than cannibals. The Shuar are Devil Worshippers.'

'Even the Shuar man who lived here,' he said, 'he pretended to be a good man, but we all knew the truth.'

Richard, Francisco and I waited to hear that truth. The village chief called his wife to bring more meat. He cursed her for being so slow, for having small breasts, and for bearing him no sons.

'Señor Rogerio was seen talking to the Devil,' he said with wide eyes. 'He would walk in the jungle at night. He had no fear because Satan was protecting him. It's fortunate that he disappeared.'

'Where did he go?'

'He vanished one night,' said the chief subversively. 'I think the Devil took him to Hell.'

After the meal our host swore at his wife again. She was ugly and no better than a thief, he said. Were he not a Christian, he would have slit her throat years ago. Lucky for her, the missionaries had converted them. He put on his Wellington boots and led us across the football pitch, with its lop-sided goal post, and into the jungle.

Wellingtons have a special place in an Amazonian man's wardrobe. Although far below a Man United football strip, they are regarded highly. No one could understand why I chose to wear handmade leather hiking boots when I could obviously afford Wellingtons.

The curtain of green descended with tantalising effect. Twenty feet beyond the football field we were lost in another world. A realm of fallen tree trunks and shadows, bottle-green moss, lichens and leaves the size of louvre doors, spanned out before us. High above the canopy shielded out the rain, pierced by only the harshest streams of light.

Francisco and the chief tracked expeditiously through the undergrowth. Richard, too, moved swiftly. Clearly an expert in jungle matters, his confidence mirrored my unease. He was a walking pharmacopoeia as well. There wasn't a single plant or creature he couldn't identify by both Linnaean and dialect name. At first I'd mistaken his camouflage dress and military background for signs that he enjoyed the ways of war. But, although he had been trained as an élite soldier, I soon realised that he was a naturalist at heart. He would only ever kill an animal for food, and he delighted in the preservation of life. Above all, he basked in the mysterious ways of nature.

'It's stuff you just can't make up,' he often exclaimed.

'What is?'

'Nature!'

He pointed to a tarantula cowering on a branch.

'It looks like just another tarantula, doesn't it?' he said, 'but it's in a coma, paralysed by the venom of a tarantula wasp. The wasp lands on the top of the spider and bores a hole into it, in which it lays its eggs. When the eggs hatch they'll feed on the live tarantula.'

I had to agree that even my over-vivid imagination was stumped by such nature.

Taking my place again behind Richard, I struggled forward, tripping clumsily like a convict bound in chains.

After five minutes of stumbling I had lost my bearings altogether, and was gripped by a great thirst. Sweat drenched me. Richard called back, telling me to lift up my feet, and to not fight the forest, but to become part of it. Every twig, every branch, vine, and pool of stagnant water, every ant, spider, and rotting trunk of wood, he said, were part of the system. Each element was linked to and dependent on the next.

How could I ever become part of such a thing? A European is an intruder in the jungle. He can't help it. He's ignorant of the sounds,

the smells, the sense of unity – just as the precise detail of a modern
city would be lost on a tribesman from the forest.

As we tramped through the undergrowth, Francisco gathered leaves,
flowers and sections of vine for his potions. He squirrelled them away
in a cotton bag, tugging up his Y-fronts as he walked. I asked why he
was only taking a few leaves from each plant.

'Lore of the jungle,' said Richard, 'take only what you need. Anyway,
that shit's so strong it'll blow your mind.'

'What is it?'

'Hallucinogens,' he said dreamily, 'lots of hallucinogens.'

Eventually we reached the hut where Rogerio had lived. It was set
in a narrow clearing, edged with banana trees. The roof was tattered
and had let in the rain, causing the floor to rot and grow moss. An
enormous termite mound had developed nearby. The chief said that
it was a sign.

'A sign of what?'

'That *el Diablo*, the Devil, has been here.'

In all his years in the jungle, Richard hadn't heard of the superstition. To him termites were an invaluable commodity. He strode
over to the mound, kicked off its top with his boot, and grabbed a
fistful of the insects.

'Rub 'em on your skin,' he said, 'and you've got yourself a natural
insect repellent. They live on tree resin which keeps the bugs off.'

He ground a handful of termites onto my bare arm. Their mashed
wings and bodies soon rubbed away, leaving my skin smelling of the
sticky resin.

Richard led me to the house. We climbed up onto the raised stage.
A few of Rogerio's belongings were still in the house. His machete,
a blue and red checked shirt, a box containing ammunition, and
a pair of Chinese-made Wellington boots. His gun appeared to be
missing.

'Those are good boots,' said the chief.

'Why don't you take them, or any of the other stuff?'

He laughed.

'We do not need the possessions of Satan,' he said.

'Are you certain he was a Devil Worshipper?'

'Of course,' said the chief of New York, 'that's why he disappeared.'

'Maybe he died while out hunting, after all his shotgun isn't here.'

The chief jumped down from the house.

'His gun might be missing,' he said, 'but no man would go hunting without his rubber boots.'

*

Back on the *Pradera*, Cockroach reported that the *Titanus giganticus* beetles had been fed. He had put them on a diet of rotten wood, scraped from the underside of the boat's floorboards. The chicken had been tied to the ledge, with her bottom pointing over the edge. She was being fattened up to eat. I named her Rosario. She was, after all, now a member of the crew.

We gave the chief of New York some old clothes, some rice, soap and sugar and a couple of tins of tuna fish. He and the other villagers came to see us off. A last request was that we drop one of the young men off at the next village, so that he could play football there. He climbed onto the boat, dressed in a luminescent green and yellow outfit. He was barefoot and carried a wicker basket. In it were his precious football boots.

From New York, we had decided to continue on the River Tigre, before journeying west up the Corrientes River to the Pastaza. This route would act as a shortcut, taking us deep into the backwaters of the region. The Amazon's tributaries had much more wildlife than the main river. But my route planning came out of worry over the fuel situation. As ever, we were getting through far more petrol than expected.

I spent the afternoon sharpening my Alaskan moose knife. One never knew when it might be needed. Richard swore loudly when he saw the nickel-coated blade.

'It was very expensive,' I said. 'It's sharp enough to skin llamas.'

He swayed back and forth on his chair.

'Seen any llamas around here?'

I changed the subject.

'What about Vietnam?' I asked.

To anyone else it might have been a strange question. But to a man who'd lived through the Tet Offensive and the Battle of Hue, it was a subject of endless possibility. Richard never volunteered his tales of battle but, if asked, he would talk.

'I volunteered for 'Nam,' he said, 'cos I wanted to be in the deep jungle. As far as I was concerned it was an all expenses paid, two year snake hunt, with unusual and additional hazards thrown in.'

'Weren't you frightened?'

'You bet your ass,' he said. 'I was shit-scared. On the first day I was dropped into a combat situation. It was early '68, just before Tet. I knew the only way I was going out of there was in a body-bag. The first two weeks on the ground were the worst of my life.'

Richard paused to light a Marlboro.

'Then I came to a realisation,' he said. 'As I was gonna die I'd better make the most of the time I had left. You bet I was sorry when buddies were killed but, hey, all I can say is that I'm glad they took the bullet rather than me. We all went to 'Nam with the same fuckin' odds of survival. Sure I was brainwashed,' he said. 'Too much John Wayne shit.'

Our conversation was interrupted by Cockroach, who said dinner was ready. He had cooked a pot of spaghetti. Like virtually everything else prepared in his kitchen, it was boiled in oil. He served my helping in my lightweight aluminium mess tin. I'd spent hours teaching him to disinfect the tin and my green metal cup with rubbing alcohol. Richard had shown me the merits of 70 per cent clinical alcohol. He washed his hands and toothbrush in the liquid all the time. It protected him, he said, from common jungle diseases, as well as from chiggers.

The six-legged chigger fly was a constant threat. It burrows under the skin of an unsuspecting victim where it reproduces. The larvae hatch under the skin, causing excruciating pain. Dousing the body in alcohol prevents visits from the chigger fly. Nicole Maxwell had her own special way of keeping the pest at bay. She would dab bright red nail varnish on her skin, to prevent the larvae from hatching out. God knows what she was doing taking nail polish into the Amazon.

*

For a squeamish landlubber like me, life aboard the boat was one of hardship. But before I knew it an entire week had gone by. I had no idea how much further we had to proceed. Nor did anyone else. As the days passed, life on the *Pradera* entered a well-structured routine. Richard would sit up on the roof, rocking back and forth, smoking. When his supply of Marlboros ran out, he turned to Francisco's stock of *mapacho*. Most nights the shaman and he would smoke themselves senseless. Then Francisco would lead him on a spiritual journey, with the aid of some jungle decoction. They hardly ever slept. Before dawn,

Richard would be up, prancing back and forth on the roof, practising *ryuku kempo*, an Okinawan martial art based on pressure points. He rarely came down into the body of the boat. He liked to watch the jungle, which he called 'the biggest widescreen TV in the world'.

Walter was usually at the wheel, although everyone took turns from time to time. Throughout the day and late into the night, Cockroach spent his time cooking. The others regarded his cuisine as nothing short of Amazonian Cordon Bleu. They mistook quantity for quality. I was constantly worried that the supplies would run out. Some of the meals used more than twenty cans. Richard was keen to give the crew fresh food. He didn't want them becoming even bigger wimps than they already were. The thought of fresh food, which meant roasted jungle rodents, made my stomach turn. It was my greatest worry of all.

One day mingled into the next, each one a cycle of rain, heat, and darkness, filled with animated insect wings. The boat became infested with cockroaches. The cook said it was my fault, as the rats had always eaten the roaches. When the rats were turned into stew, the boat's fragile food chain had been broken.

Safe in the medicine cabinet, the precious *Titanus giganticus* beetles were growing even bigger, weaned on their diet of rotting floorboard. Rosario the chicken was getting plumper as well, a fact frequently drawn to my attention by the crew. I refused to let them kill her.

Hour after hour I lay on my hammock, staring zombie-like at the rot above my head. I'd never come across such decay. But the floorboards were not the only thing to be rotting. The nightly storms had drenched us, and the boat's limited size meant that airing out belongings was near-impossible. Fungus and mildew now covered everything. All my stuff was decomposing – my clothes and sleeping-bag, my self-inflating mattress, hammock, and the Force Ten high altitude tent, were all scarred with mould.

When I was not watching the rot, I was sprinkling my feet with powder. Most of the jungle expeditions I'd read about had failed as a result of trench foot. Another concern was genital infestations. The best explorers have been stopped dead in their tracks by genital lice. So I doused the area frequently in 70 per cent medical alcohol, and hoped for the best. With time, I got used to the burning sensation.

Each night I would cocoon myself in the mosquito net, and dream of a fast food restaurant far away from the Amazon. I'd almost given up ever coming to a firm conclusion about primitive flight. Such thoughts were the preserve of a well-fed person wearing clean clothes.

Now we were on the Rio Tigre, there was a wider variety of fauna to be seen. The jungle was flooded – higher than at any time in living memory. Hundreds of trees on the river-bank had fallen, the soil softened by the high water. Many of the mammals had moved inland to higher ground. But in the trees howler monkeys, three-toed sloths and brightly coloured birds were abundant.

Cumulus clouds hung above the jungle, growing darker until they could hold not another drop. When they ripped open, they drowned us in rain. As afternoon became dusk, the coral-red sky was reflected in the water, heralding nightfall. Before the last rays of sunlight had dissipated, Venus became visible. Although so far away, she was a companion, a point of familiarity.

Like those who lived on the river's silent banks, I started to go to bed at dusk, waking at dawn. The idea of staying up past 7 p.m. seemed insane. Only a madman would have wanted to expose himself to the night's onslaught of bugs.

One evening, as he steered a course along the right bank of the Tigre, Walter told me about a wish that had come true.

'Nine years ago,' he recounted in his brusque voice, '*Yo era muy desgraciado*, I was a very unhappy man. I had no work. My family were almost starving. Then my wife left me, taking our sons. She'd found out that I was going to prostitutes, and wanted a divorce. I didn't know what to do.'

Walter steered the boat to the opposite bank.

'I had even thought of killing myself, or running off to Lima. But a friend suggested I visit a shaman who was known to him. He lived in the floating village at Belen. As he owed my friend a favour, he said he'd give me a consultation for free. So, one night I went to see him. I explained my problems: that I had no work and a wife who was angry. The *maestro* told me to take two beans and bury them in the dirt under the floor of our house. I was to water them every morning with lemon juice. When a month was over, he told me to dig up the beans and eat them one at a time. But, before doing so, I was to make two wishes.

'Although it sounded mad, I did as the shaman had told me. I had no other choice. A week went by. Then another. I was just going to curse the *maestro*'s name, when a remarkable thing happened.

'My wife came back home with our three sons. She said an angel had come to her in a dream and told her that I was a good man. The angel said she should give me another chance,' continued the *motorista*. 'But the next week,' he said, 'an even more incredible thing happened.'

He stopped mid-story to steer the boat across the river.

'*What?* What happened?'

'Well, I used to go to the market and sell bracelets made of beads and that sort of thing,' he said. 'It made me almost no money, but kept me occupied. One day, an American woman from Tennessee asked me for directions. We started talking and she bought all my necklaces. She was very friendly. Before she went back home, I gave her my address. The next month she wrote me a letter. She said she wanted to help me. She asked that I write to her once a week, and in return she promised to send me a cheque every month. That's how it's been for nine years,' said Walter. 'Her cheques come as regularly as clockwork. It's meant I've been able to send my boys to school instead of having them work with me. But best of all,' he said, 'it meant I could buy the *Pradera*.'

'I thought you said this boat was only six months old!'

Walter swept back his hair with his hand.

'She's six months and a few years,' he said.

*

Since the first night, when I had experienced the trauma of the *Pradera*'s loo, my digestive tract had seized up. We had now been on the boat for nine days, and my colon was plugged with an assortment of wretched meals. My medical kit – supplied by London's Hospital of Tropical Medicine – didn't contain anything to relieve constipation, only diarrhoea. At first I kept the problem to myself. After all, it's a private matter. But Richard and the others were fascinated by my lack of bowel movements. On a close-knit river expedition, one man's bowels are another man's business.

Cockroach brewed me a cup of coffee, made with seventeen table-spoons of Nescafé. I slugged it back in a single gulp. The crew clustered around me. The only reaction to the coffee was a surge of adrenaline. Walter suggested I drink a litre of vegetable oil. Holding my nose, I did so. Still no result. Francisco said I was a fool for resorting to caffeine and oil as laxatives. He could, he said boastfully, cure my dysfunction with a simple two-part treatment.

First I was to drink a strong tea made from the bark of a tree. He called it *mololo*. Only later was I able to have the bark identified. Known in the West as 'Cramp Bark', it's been used medicinally for centuries in North America. Tribes like the Meskwaki and the Penobscot once prescribed it to cure chronic constipation. It's curious that Francisco used a North American plant.

The *mololo* tea, which was quite pleasant, warmed me to the shaman's expertise. I was rather looking forward to the second half of the remedy. He said it would take time to prepare, but should be ready some time that afternoon. I went to my hammock to stare up at the rot.

In the early evening the shaman came down from the roof. He was holding my green mess mug. It was full to the brim with a hot liquid. Francisco said he'd just finished making the medicine and I was to drink it at once. Following his instructions, I took a deep draught of the liquid. It was very salty and had undertones of tobacco.

'*¡Bébetelo!* Drink it up!' said Francisco impatiently. 'If it gets cold it will not work.'

I asked him what the beverage was made from.

He didn't reply.

'Quickly, finish it,' he barked.

'Tell me what's in it?'

Still the shaman refused to answer.

'If I tell you what it is, you won't drink it!'

Cockroach looked up from a pot of boiling oil.

'*Es sus meaos.* It's his urine,' he said blankly, 'you're drinking Francisco's urine.'

20

River of Lies

After the coffee, the oil, the *mololo* tea, and half a cup of the shaman's urine, I spent most of the night huddled over the *Pradera*'s putrid hole. It was unpleasant, but I was very pleased that the state of constipation had been reversed. Richard was on the roof lying out under the stars. He had taken an extra-strong dose of *sanango*, his favourite nerve-agent.

'You oughta try it,' he said cheerfully, next morning. 'I'll get Francisco to make you up a batch. It clears your head like nothing else.'

'I've had enough of Francisco's medicine,' I replied, 'and, after all, I'm saving myself for *ayahuasca* with the Birdmen.'

Richard wasn't listening. Sliding his knife from its sheath, he poked at something in the rot above my hammock.

'That's all we need!' he exclaimed.

'Horrendous damp rot,' I said. 'Never seen anything like it.'

'Not the rot ... the nest.'

'*Nest*?'

'Arachnid. Looks like it's just hatched. In a day or two this boat'll be running with wolf spiders. It wouldn't be a problem if we had some fuckin' rats on board!'

Some say that these hairy brown spiders get their name from their wolf-like technique of chasing and hunting their prey. Few others of the species can match their extraordinary speed. Richard showed me how to identify them by their unique arrangement of eyes. He was an arachnophile of the first degree. Wolf spiders have three rows: the lowest has four small eyes, the middle has two much larger, and the upper row has a pair of medium-sized ones.

The plague of spiders was bad news, but was just one of many problems. Our stores of food were going down fast, largely because the crew were eating five cooked meals a day. A valuable sack of flour had mysteriously fallen overboard in the night. And a bottle of bleach had ruptured, ruining most of the sugar. Meanwhile, Walter was complaining that the Johnson needed a new propeller. Without one, he said, we'd be scuppered upstream.

In the cooking area, Cockroach brought another problem to my attention. The boat was sinking. A two-foot crack had developed in the starboard side. I suspected endemic wet rot had something to do with it. I ordered the crew to take it in turns to bail water. They'd have to bail day and night. Fortunately, Richard had a roll of industrial tarred tape in his pack. He said it was 'core' equipment. The bailing and the tarred tape kept us afloat. But they were a short-term solution.

Vietnam training had taught Richard the importance of core equipment. His few possessions were super-durable military issue. Army stuff was cheap and tough. He scorned anything made in the private sector, calling it 'civilian shit'. All my luggage fell into that category. In his book, civilian shit was for wimps, like canned food. Everything he owned from his watch-strap to his underpants was army issue, and came in camouflage green. Camo' mimicked nature, he said, and nature was all that mattered.

When he was digging out the tape, Richard emptied the contents of his canvas pack onto the boat's roof. I was struck by the cleanliness and good condition of his gear. He had a US army flashlight with a Morse code button, a fork which doubled as a knife and can-opener, a US army water bottle filter system with drinking straw attached, and a litre of medical alcohol. There was a chipped tin cup as well, and an 18-inch carbon steel machete, a coil of nylon rope, a condom, and two fishing hooks.

'The condom's for carrying water,' said Richard sternly. 'That is, unless I meet a cute señorita in the jungle.'

I asked about his boots. He rarely took them off.

'They're standard US army Altama jungle boots,' he said. 'They've got a valve which pushes out the water when you walk. They're the only boots worth having out here.'

'Is US army gear the best?'

'Some of it,' he said, 'but the French make the best clothing. Look at these trousers I'm wearing, they're herringbone, with reinforced knees and double-lined pockets. They're fuckin' handmade!'

Richard had found a last packet of cigarettes at the bottom of his pack. He tore off the cellophane wrapper and was soon inhaling the air of Marlboro country. The shaman was squatting nearby. He had been working on another batch of *sanango*, but now he was going through his own bag of loot.

Francisco was the *Pradera*'s magpie. He'd scoop up any unwanted junk he could find, and tuck it into his voluminous duffel bag. Amongst other things, he was collecting empty tin cans, dead batteries and strands of my used dental floss. When I asked why he needed such things, Walter murmured *'Para la magia'*, for magic. Francisco's unconventional dress sense and his strange behaviour had made a great impression on Walter and the cook. They were terrified of him.

The Vietnam vet' had great respect for Francisco, but he didn't fear him like the others did. They were an odd couple. The shaman would sit at Richard's feet in his droopy Y-fronts, talking about the shamanic world. He would scowl when Richard lit up a Marlboro. To Francisco, tobacco was a sacred product. He was disgusted that such a hallowed plant could have become an icon of addiction and branding. Francisco despised Marlboros and everything they stood for. But he viewed me with even greater contempt. As far as he was concerned, a man who didn't smoke at all had no soul.

*

On the thirteenth day, with the boat going slower and slower against the current, the crew begged Richard for some fresh food. They were, they said, sick of eating canned gruel and spaghetti boiled in oil. They hated each meal more than the last, they claimed, and were only choking them down to please me. This failed to explain why they were eating so much. Richard told Cockroach to fetch an empty sack. He then instructed Walter to tether the boat on the river-bank. Taking his machete, the sack, and a bottle of drinking water, he set off into the jungle.

Cockroach abandoned bailing duty and slunk down the boat to slaughter Rosario. I managed to wrestle him to the ground just before he snapped her neck. She would remain alive as long as I was there to protect her. Francisco was sprawled out at the back of the boat on the drums of petrol. He lit his pipe and was soon lying in a fug of smoke. I kept to the other end of the *Pradera*, hunting for wolf spiders, which were now crawling everywhere.

Three hours after setting off, Richard marched back out from the jungle, the white nylon sack strung over his shoulder. Thanking him, the cook dragged it below. I sat on my hammock and watched as the contents were pulled out one at a time. First came a black-feathered bird. I wasn't sure what it was. Then, a *paca*, a giant nocturnal rodent, with bucked front teeth and clay-coloured hair. It had been gutted with Richard's knife. Swishing away the flies, Cockroach delved again into the sack. He pulled out a pig-like peccary, then a *mahasse*, a rodent whose meat is a delicacy in the Upper Amazon.

That night Cockroach cooked up a rich stew made from fresh meat. Walter had six helpings of it, and Francisco ate so much that he had to throw up over the side. I'd been concerned that the meat would go to waste, but it was soon finished. Cocooned in layers of mosquito netting I resisted the stew. Instead, I boiled a pan of water and cooked up a sachet of Lancashire Hot Pot.

Walter went on and on about the propeller and the crack in the boat's side. But I ignored him. There was nothing I could do except to commandeer Francisco's cauldron for bailing. The shaman asserted that the pot was a magical tool. If it were used for bailing we would, he said, end up at the bottom of the river. As it was we were heading that way, so I told him to leave me alone. The village of Grande Bretagña, Great Britain, was marked on the map. With a name like that, I hoped it might have a resident mechanic. I buried my head in Flornoy's book *Jivaro: Among the Head-shrinkers of the Amazon*, printed in 1953, and tried to forget about my troubles.

Before the Spanish arrived in the Americas, I learned, the Incan Empire bordered the Shuar land on its west. Just before the Conquistadors arrived, the Inca, Huayna Capac, led his armies against the Shuar. The year was 1527. The Incas were routed so fiercely that they were forced to flee back to the Andean highlands. As a way of saving face, the Inca declared the Shuar unworthy of being his subjects.

A few years later, in 1549, the Spanish commander Fernando de Benavente made the first European incursion into the Shuar territories. He had heard of the jungle's abundance of gold, and was still eager to find El Dorado. His party is thought to have followed the Rio

Upano, south from its Andean headwaters, down to the junction of the Rio Paute.

Benavente had planned to establish a town in the region, but fled when he realised that the locals were about to butcher him. However, another Spanish expedition did found two settlements nearby, in about 1552. Crazed with gold fever, they came across some gold deposits. Soon they had built mines, enslaving local tribesmen to work them.

The Spanish forced the Shuar labourers to pay a tax in gold dust which, supposedly, was to be sent as a gift for King Phillip III's coronation. The levy grew greater and greater. Finally the Shuar could stand no more.

One night, in 1599, a group of them slunk into the Governor's house and pulled him half-naked, from his bed. They dragged him by his hair into the courtyard, and said it was time for them to pay their taxes, as they had been told to do. Emptying the Spanish gold reserves, the Shuar leader, Chief Quirruba, ordered his warriors to melt down the gold in small crucibles.

Meanwhile the Governor was stripped naked and tied hand and foot. Once the gold was liquefied, his mouth was prised open with a bone and, one at a time, the crucibles of molten ore was poured down his throat. At first the Governor screamed, but his tongue was soon burnt away. The liquid gold passed through his body and out via his bowels, killing him in agony.

All around, the Shuar went wild with delight. They slaughtered most of the Spanish contingent and danced until dawn.

From then until the 1850s almost no white man dared to enter the Shuar lands. In 1767 a group of Spanish missionaries strayed into the region. They were presented with the skulls of their Catholic brethren, slain in a previous attack.

Francisco's shouts drew my attention away from the book.

'Grande Bretagña!' he called. 'We have arrived at Great Britain!'

I popped my head over the edge of the hammock. A boy was running along the river-bank. All he was wearing was a tattered tee-shirt decorated with the triumphant face of Mohammed Ali. But I could see no sign of Great Britain. The shaman pointed to three dilapidated shacks, one of which was missing its roof.

'That's Grande Bretagña,' he said.

'But it doesn't even have a football pitch.'

Ten minutes after mooring at Great Britain, we had established that no mechanic lived there. In fact, it was home to only two families, each with six sons. They had no work, they said.

'If only the oil mining company would come here,' said one youth, 'like it has come to Trompeteros.'

'Where's that?'

'*Arriba*, up river.'

'How far?'

The young man snatched at a fly.

'A day or two from here,' he said. 'In Trompeteros everyone's rich. The oil company gives them money, and the women are very sexy. They wear pink lipstick. And ...' he continued, making sure his parents were out of ear's reach, '... at Trompeteros they have a disco.'

As I thanked the young man for his information, his father came over. The man was in his forties. He had a wispy moustache, bucked teeth and an unusually flat nose.

'Life here in Grande Bretagña is very difficult,' he said softly. 'We are poor people. There's no school and no doctor. And the neighbouring villages laugh at us, because we don't have a football field.'

I sympathised with the man.

'We do not need help,' he said proudly, 'but there is one problem which needs attention. We were expecting the missionaries to come, but they have forgotten us.'

I braced myself to be asked for money.

'My youngest son has a lump on his head,' said the man. 'It has been growing very big, and we don't know what to do.'

'If you would cut it off,' said his wife, 'we would pay you what we can.'

We asked for the boy to be brought. Shyly, he came out of the house and into the sunshine. His name was Juan, and he was about six. Although shy, he was smiling. That is, until he saw our expressions. Nothing could hide our shock at seeing such a tremendous tumour. The skin around the growth had been shaved. Juan started crying when he saw how worried we looked. I told his father that it wasn't anything too serious.

'Then will you cut it off?' asked the mother. 'You must have a sharp knife on your boat.'

I suggested that we take Juan and her up-river, to Trompeteros, where the oil company would surely help. The boy's mother was hesitant. She pushed her husband forward. He would come with us, she said.

Father and son stepped aboard the *Pradera* and we set off up the River Tigre once again.

*

The blurb on the back of my map said it was the *crème de la crème* of Amazonian maps. Richard and the others made great fun of it. They didn't trust maps. As the days passed, I began to understand why. The few places which were plotted, were way off the mark. Most villages weren't featured at all. I insisted that we stop regularly and get the locals to sketch us maps from their own knowledge. Once I got back to Europe, I'd mail their drawings to the map company. The crew thought it was a crazy idea. They knew something I did not. In the Amazon no one has a clue what lies more than five miles in any given direction. More importantly, no one cares. The idea of mapping out an entire region or, for that matter a country, is an example of the Western mind working on overdrive.

The lack of accurate maps did not, however, prevent the art of speculation. Ask someone in the remotest village where Lima is, and they'll give you an answer without flinching. 'It's two hours that way,' said one man motioning up stream. 'Three days after Nauta,' said another, pointing the opposite way. No one would ever admit they hadn't got the faintest idea. As in India or Central Asia, an Eastern form of hospitality was at work. To admit ignorance was considered impolite.

The end result was that this made navigation and budgeting for fuel virtually impossible. Worse still was the elasticity of truth. The goalposts never stopped moving. One minute Walter would boast he had plenty of fuel to get us back to Iquitos, and the next he'd say that we were down to the last drum. Cockroach claimed his grandmother was a Shuar chief's daughter, then a few days later he was bragging she came from Guatemala. And Francisco was no better. At first he said he had four children, but then changed it to six.

Walter spoke for the others: '*Mucho naka-naka,* so many lies,' he said, running the wheel through his hands. 'In Peru lying is a national hobby, it's something to be enjoyed. Peruvian women like a man who can tell a big solid lie.'

'Why?'

Walter put his hand on his chin.

'They think it's sexy,' he said.

Juan's father said the lies were bringing disaster to the jungle.

'People have learned from the politicians,' he said. 'They've learned that lies protect them ... that the truth is a dangerous thing.'

I was touched by the man's perception. He hugged an arm around his son's shoulder, coaxing him to be brave.

'The missionaries taught us to believe in God,' he said. 'They told us God will cure all our problems. Well, look at Juan, look at his head. Bibles and hymns haven't helped him.'

Again, I tried to reassure him that the oil company would take care of little Juan. They would have a doctor who could treat his tumour.

Richard jumped down from the roof. He cast a disapproving eye over Cockroach and Francisco who had deserted their bailing stations and were playing cards. The shaman was taking alternate drags from a pipe and a *mapacho* cigarette. He cheated mercilessly and everyone knew it. But fear of his magical powers kept the cook from protesting.

While Juan and his father enjoyed a bowl of stew, made from the rank-smelling legs of a jungle pig, I sat on the roof with Richard. We watched the sun set. And, as we did so, Walter guided the *Pradera* west from the Tigre, down a narrower waterway, the Rio Corrientes. Its name meant 'current', although the river's surface was as smooth as glass. Twisting and turning like a snake on its back, its banks were veiled in the thickest jungle we had yet seen.

'It'll be a miracle if this is the right fuckin' river,' said Richard. 'Walter's never been this far away from Iquitos before.'

'The boat's leak has got worse,' I said. 'If we don't get to Trompeteros soon we'll be in trouble.'

The Vietnam vet' put his hands to his mouth and made the solemn call of the squirrel cuckoo.

'*Aukcoo! Aukcoo!*'

As he rocked back and forth, the faint sound of a female echoed through the twilight.

'She's in love,' said Richard. 'You can always tell when a female's in love. But they're foxy little suckers – they like to keep you guessing. Just like women. You think you understand them and they go and do something stupid.'

Long before meeting Señorita Jane in Iquitos, Richard had been married. In the short time he'd lived in the United States since

Vietnam, he had been married twice. His second wife, twenty years younger than he, was a former stage magician's assistant.

'She did all that stupid shit with the doves and the juggling balls,' he said. 'She had the tight skirts and the blinding smile. We've got the cutest little girl. We named her Harmony. That's what our marriage was, Harmony. I delivered her. She popped out like a little paratrooper.'

Richard called out to the squirrel cuckoo again.

'Harmony's all that matters,' he said under his breath.

Juan's father asked which engine was powering the boat.

'It's a Johnson 65.'

'A *Johnson*,' he said quietly, 'a Johnson could get you to the end of the world.'

'We're going to the Pastaza, to meet the Shuar,' I said.

The man replied without turning his head: 'They're dangerous people.'

'That's what I've heard.'

'They're the Antichrist,' he said curtly. 'When they kill a man they drink his blood, and eat his kidneys. It's human kidneys they like most. If the kidneys taste bad, they carve out the eyes and eat them.'

'Have you met any Shuar?' I asked.

The man didn't reply. He hadn't finished his rundown of Shuar cuisine.

'They like to eat caimans' gall bladders, and dogs' tongues boiled in urine,' he said with revulsion. 'If you don't eat the food they give you, they'll poison you with *ampihuasca*.'

He asked why I was so interested in the Shuar.

'They fly,' I said. 'They are Birdmen.'

Juan's father swatted a baby wolf spider on his cheek.

'*Ayahuasca* ... you are speaking of *ayahuasca*?'

I nodded.

'*Es una medicina muy potente*, it's very powerful medicine,' he said. 'Take it and you'll fly like a great white *jabiru* stork. Your wings will take you to the other world. You'll see wonderful visions. But *ayahuasca* can be dangerous,' he mused, 'be careful, you must be careful!'

'Of what?'

'*Cuidado con el aterrizaje*, be careful how you land,' he said.

21

Gold Teeth

Trompeteros is a small town in the Upper Amazon whose reputation beats all the rest. Nestled on the north bank of the Corrientes River, the community surpasses even Iquitos when it comes to vice and depravity. Ask at the remotest jungle village and they're sure to have heard the legends. They will tell you of the underdressed women, the *chuchuhuasi* liquor, and the discotheque.

For three days Walter, Francisco and Cockroach spoke of nothing but Trompeteros. They harped on and on about the taste of its gut-rot brews, the *mapacho*, and the supply of seductive under-age women. There was no question that their speculation couldn't answer. Remarkable, I thought, considering none of them had ever been near Trompeteros before. I wasn't interested in the vices available, but I'd heard that the town had one of the finest hotels in the Amazon.

As the *Pradera* navigated the remaining few miles up river, Francisco imparted a last piece of valuable lore. Go for the girls with gold teeth, he said. The more gold they have in their smile, the better they can satisfy a man in *certain* carnal ways. White teeth were a sign of frigidity. Walter agreed – sexual acumen and teeth went hand in hand. His wife, he boasted, had no white teeth at all.

We had been on *Pradera* for too long; shore leave was well-deserved. With the crew running wild after the gold-toothed women, I was uneasy that the boat might be robbed. Although much of the food had been ruined or already consumed, there was still valuable fuel and equipment, not to mention the Johnson 65. As well as guarding the *Pradera*, someone would have to look after the *Titanus giganticus* beetles, and Rosario, who needed regular feeding. Until the repairs were done, bailing also had to be done constantly.

The crew would take it in turns to stay on the boat. I drew up a roster and pinned it to the medicine cabinet. Anyone found abandoning bailing duty would go without food for two days. Richard and I were exempted. He wanted to go walkabout in the jungle, and I planned to spend my time ashore, ordering room service and taking hot baths. But before getting too comfortable at the hotel, I promised to take Juan to the oil company for treatment. I gave him a cherry-flavoured lollipop with bubble gum inside.

*

Cockroach took the first shift to bail and keep watch. I'd cautioned him to protect the giant beetles beyond all else. Nothing was so important as their survival. If there were any problems, he was to defend himself with my moose knife. Walter went to look for a man to repair the hole in the boat's side. He was desperate to get the repairs done quickly, so that he could hunt for gold-toothed women. Tying a bandanna over his head, Richard set off into the undergrowth. I asked when he would be back.

'When I'm ready,' he replied.

After making enquiries, I learned that Plus Petrol, the oil company, had its offices on the southern bank of the river. I took Juan and his father across in a dugout. We were received at a steel-framed jetty, and escorted into the plant. All Plus Petrol employees had identical yellow construction helmets and American-made Wellington boots. Everything they wore, or held, carried the gleaming Plus Petrol logo. They looked as if they'd stepped out of a TV commercial for their firm.

The oil plant was bordered on three sides by the jungle, and on the fourth by the Rio Corrientes. Three giant satellite dishes were clustered at one end of the area, beside the low tin-roofed residential quarters. Opposite stood offices, and beyond them an industrial complex. The man with a yellow helmet and rubber boots wrote our names on a clipboard. When he saw Juan's tumour, he called his superior.

Two minutes later we were sitting in the reception area. A single door divided the two worlds. Outside lay the jungle: suffocating, damp, seething with life. Inside there was central air-conditioning, thick pile carpets and neon lighting. An American water cooler stood in one corner of the room, beside a potted jungle plant. On the coffee table were crisp copies of the *New York Times*, and *Newsweek*. In the background I recognised the hum of a photocopier.

Juan and his father were as threatened as I was comforted by the surroundings. They stood to attention when the bearded plant manager greeted us. He said that their doctor would take a look at the boy. A biopsy of the tumour would be rushed to Lima. When I thanked him, he pressed his hand into mine.

'Thank God you didn't go to a doctor in Trompeteros,' he said.

'I didn't expect there to be one.'

'Everyone in town is suffering from the same thing,' he said, 'the quack rubs toothpaste on the infected parts.'

He roved a hand through his beard, muttering: 'I doubt he's ever treated a patient's head.'

*

A concrete path formed the main street of Trompeteros. It being in the middle of the jungle, there were no cars. The path ran the length of the town, a total of about four hundred feet. Either extremity ended in foliage. At the path's westernmost edge stood *Hostal de Milagros*, Hotel of Miracles. A man with leathery cheeks and swollen eyes stumbled from the entrance and down the steps. He was doing up his flies. On his face was a broad grin and, on his arm, a young woman. Her hair was pushed up in a bouffant style, her heels were high. All her front teeth were gold.

The hotel's reception was decorated with a number of moth-ravaged leopard, panther and snake skins. A display cabinet above the counter was stocked with dark bottles of beer. I told the man in charge that I needed the best room in the house.

'*¿Dónde está su mujer*? Where's your woman?' he snarled suspiciously. 'Do you need one?'

He clicked his fingers and, before I could blink, three scantily-clad girls with gold teeth were standing in the doorway.

'You don't understand,' I said, 'I just want to sleep.'

The local beauties protested for a moment or two, before slinking away.

Room number three was basic, but a welcome change from a hammock infested with wolf spiders. The stench from the blocked lavatory, the lack of sheets, and the pool of dried blood in the far corner, were hardly worthy of mention. I sat on the bed, flicking the light switch on and off. Electricity was a great novelty.

In the stifling heat of the early afternoon, I found Walter and Francisco spending their savings at Trompeteros's small emporium. It was packed from floor to ceiling with shiny merchandise. Everything was wrapped in crumpled cellophane. The usual supplies of Nivea cream and oxblood-coloured boot polish were complemented by an array of more enticing products – imitation Barbie dolls, pink plastic hair clips, ping-pong balls and tubes of superglue. But the boat's crew weren't interested in cheap trinkets. They'd come for ingredients.

When I asked them what they were making, they looked at each other and cackled subversively. Walter said a man was mending the boat's leak, but the work would take three days. This gave them some time. He turned to the shaman. They pooled their money to buy half a dozen bottles of Chinese 'Shanghai brand' body lotion, and a tin of Colman's English mustard powder. Then they hurried away into the shadows behind the shop.

At the centre of the concrete path, past the boss-eyed barber's stall and a makeshift bar, lay Trompeteros's most celebrated feature – the disco. Widely acclaimed as the sleaziest establishment in the Upper Amazon, its bamboo swing doors were never closed to business. The single ultraviolet light never wavered, and the distorted music never waned. In the moist atmosphere a horde of lascivious gold-toothed women hunted for custom.

Outside the nightspot a boy of about five was sucking on a syringe. He said the doctor had given it to him. When his mother exited the surgery, opposite the disco, she cursed the physician. She said the medicated white cream he prescribed to all his patients didn't do any good at all.

Further down the concrete path I came across a man touting giant Amazonian snails. He was cutting them up live to make *ceviche*. Beside him, another man was trying to sell some daffodil-yellow lingerie. He said it was imported specially from Paraguay.

I was admiring the size of the snails when a well-dressed man strode up to the salesmen, and handed them each a dozen red sachets. All over town the tomato-coloured packets were being passed around. You could have as many as you wanted for free. Indeed, the more you were seen to take, the more praise you attracted. The sachets contained condoms.

The people of Trompeteros were a wily lot. Privately they frowned on using the prophylactics, but this didn't stop them grabbing as many of them as they could. Men, women and children alike had found that a condom had a thousand uses. Food could be stored in them, and liquids carried; they made fine markers for fishing nets when filled with air, and they could be burned to keep insects away, or roped together to form a lightweight clothes-line. Some women used them to tie back their hair. And no child was without a home-made condom whistle.

The electricity, the running water, the condoms and the disco of Trompeteros were all made possible by the oil company. Without the multinational, the town would have shrunk back to being another insignificant village on the Rio Corrientes. And yet, everyone in Trompeteros despised the oil workers and their production plant. One man told me that they were low life workers from Argentina; another that they were polluting the river and killing the fish. A third, a haggard man resting on the steps of my hotel, revealed another reason to hate the oilmen. They were so snobbish, he said, that they wouldn't sleep with the local women.

Back at the Hotel of Miracles, a line of beauties were waiting in the corridor outside my room. There must have been about thirty of them. All had mouths chequered by gold teeth. I feared that news of a foreigner had tempted the most infected of Trompeteros's femmes fatales from the humid confines of the disco. But, as I edged down the hallway, none of them even looked at me.

They had been lured by room number four. Thinking no more of it I went into my room, flicked on the light, and got ready to go to bed. I tried to hang my shirt on a hook mounted high on the wall. But, to my surprise, the hook snapped off and fell onto the cement floor. It was then I realised that it wasn't a hook at all, but the chrysalis of a giant moth.

I lay on the mattress coaxing my back to embrace the flat surface. Occasional sounds disturbed me from next door. I could have sworn I heard Francisco's raspy voice through the wall. The thought of the chrysalis twitching with larvae disturbed me, too. But before I knew it, I was asleep.

By the time the sun had risen above Trompeteros's pair of street lamps, a stage had been constructed at the centre of town. The boards of the podium were made from yellow mahogany, its backdrop was a screen of woven banana leaves. Once the stage was prepared, it was decorated with inflated condoms. Nearby, another team were rigging up speakers, and scrappy red bunting, strung together with yet more prophylactics.

I asked the barber what was going on. He looked at his watch.

'It must be carnival,' he replied, vaguely. 'In Trompeteros it's always carnival. Prepare yourself ... the *fiesta* is very wild.'

An hour later, a horde of people was massing at the far end of Trompeteros, dressed in a multiplicity of costumes. Mothers and wives were prodding the menfolk into line, as the last stragglers arrived. Peruvians like nothing more than to put on a fabulous parade, which they can do at the drop of a hat. It's a way of showing off their finest clothes, and is a great booster of morale.

A band shuffled forward, their home-made uniforms tattered by years of wear, the dents in their instruments reflecting the light. As they assembled, silence prevailed.

Then, with the clash of cymbals, the jamboree began.

The theme was the jungle. Many had dressed as tribal warriors. The painted faces, feather crowns and blowpipes suggested that it wasn't fancy dress at all. There were animals, too. One man had dressed as a toucan, another was wearing a panther skin, and a skinny woman was wrapped in a cape made from sloth skins. Behind her was a sinister young man. He was dressed as a giant rodent.

After the rodent came a clutch of gold-toothed girls in seductive clothes. They had come as themselves, day and night dancers from the disco. And, after them, followed a wave of men and young boys dressed like Rambo. They wore the ripped black clothing of guerrilla fighters, and carried home-made guns. Their faces were blacked with charcoal, and they had bandannas tied around their heads. They had come as members of the *Sendero Luminoso*.

At the front of the crude parade, was a little girl of about nine. She was set apart from all the others, for she'd spurned the pageant's theme. I recognised her as the type of little girl that every normal child loathes. Her hair, adorned with pearls, was neatly tucked behind a silver comb, and her prim little ballet shoes were free from dirt. She wore a velvety alabaster tutu, lace gloves, spotless white stockings and bright red lipstick. As she marched, her miniature hands juggled a silver baton faultlessly. I prayed that the giant rodent would nudge her into the mud.

When the parade ended, the tribal men paced off into the jungle to go hunting; the loose women slunk back into the disco; and the giant rodent meandered away home. The little prima donna pulled the lace gloves tighter up her wrists. Then she barked a string of orders to her brow-beaten father. I wondered what her future might be in Trompeteros.

I took a stroll down to the *Pradera*, where a robust carpenter was at work fixing a brace into position over the crack. Cockroach still hadn't been relieved by Walter or Francisco. He said they were up to no good. Even before stepping off the boat, they had been hatching a plan to woo the sleaziest women in town.

'No sensible girl would be interested in them,' I said, 'They're both uglier than Quasimodo.'

'This isn't like other countries,' said Cockroach, apologetically. 'Here in Peru, the ugliest men get all the most beautiful women. It's a fact.'

This may have explained why I had attracted advances from so many Peruvian women. As I pondered the thought, Cockroach suggested we let the beetles out of their boxes for a few minutes, to stretch their legs. I commended him on the idea, after all they had been locked away inside the medicine cabinet for days. I stood well back as he tapped out the huge specimens into a shallow cardboard box. Although still juveniles, their size was truly astonishing.

When I got back to the hotel, the queue of women waiting outside room four had grown. It now snaked round the corner, up the stairs and through the reception. I asked the manager what was going on. He put a hand on his groin and murmured '¡Milagros! Miracles!'

Having been unable to find Walter or Francisco, I slumped on my bed. That night a jungle beauty pageant was going to be held, I'd been told, in the centre of Trompeteros. I knew that the event would be sapping to the senses.

As my cheek pressed deep into the stocking-stuffed pillow, I heard noises radiating from room four. Sounds of arousal were mixed with instructions from a rasping, familiar voice. It sounded like Walter.

But, as I reasoned it, no self-respecting woman would have given him the time of day. Then Cockroach's words came to mind. I stepped out into the corridor and called Walter's name. The sea of gold-toothed girls parted as the room's door opened no more than a crack. A frenzied eye jerked about, straining to focus. It was Walter's eye. Before I could ask how he was attracting such large numbers of local women, he volunteered his ruse.

'*Una cura*, a cure . . .' he whimpered, 'we are curing the women.'

'*We?*'

'Francisco and me.'

'He made a medicine, a cream . . . and I'm giving it to the women.'

I asked if, by any chance, it contained 'Shanghai-brand' body lotion, and Colman's English mustard.

Consulting with his accomplice, Walter said that those were just two of the many ingredients. Francisco's head poked up.

'We're curing the disease,' he said, proudly. 'These women all have a disease.'

'And what good is Chinese body lotion and mustard powder at curing their afflictions?'

The shaman slapped his hands together and spat.

'*Una cura milagrosa y gratis*, it's a free miracle cure,' he said, beaming, 'after all, this is the Hotel of Miracles.'

I might have dismissed Francisco's potion as a sham, but the last free miracle medicine I had come across had miraculously cured me of asthma. It was being dispensed in the old city of Hyderabad, India. On the first day of the Monsoon each year, the Gowd family, who live there, hand out a remedy to anyone suffering from chest infections. Having developed asthma myself, I took advantage of the physic, along with more than half a million others, from all over India.

Everyone who turns up for the miracle cure makes their way to the Gowds' two-storey whitewashed house. They each bring with them a live *murrel* fish. After days of queuing, they hand the fish to one of the Gowd brothers, who fills the creature's mouth with a glob of foul-smelling yellow paste. The afflicted person opens their own mouth very wide and, before he knows it, the amateur physician has stuffed the live fish down his throat. Words cannot adequately describe the hateful nature of the experience.

Despite the lack of medical evidence and basic hygiene, I have not suffered from asthma since gulping down that innocent fish. Perhaps,

I thought to myself as I left the hotel, there might be something in Francisco's miracle cure as well!

*

An old woman moved between the rows of chairs, wiping each one with a rag. Her hands were trembling, her brow beaded with sweat. Nearby, her granddaughter was skipping with a home-made condom rope. Last minute preparations for the beauty pageant were underway. A great banner was suspended over the stage, coloured lights and a crude sound system had been rigged up. A thousand condoms were strung in clusters, as balloons, adorning the stage. And, now that the audience's chairs were clean, the woman hurried home to change into her best clothes.

A hard-boiled egg seller could hardly contain his eagerness.

'The women of Trompeteros are the most beautiful in Peru,' he imparted with a toothless smirk. 'But beware! You may go mad when you see their soft skin, or when they seduce you with their eyes.'

My informer displayed his eggs in a wicker basket, putting the freshest ones at the bottom. Licking his broad tongue over his palm, he mimicked the local beauties' seductive skill.

'After tonight you'll forget your wife and your country,' he disclosed, 'you'll want to live here forever. That's *el embrujo*, the spell ... the spell of Trompeteros.'

As the blood-red riot of dusk defused over the Rio Corrientes, the audience slipped from the shadows and took their seats. So familiar were they with the ritual, I suspected beauty shows to be a common feature of Trompeteros life. Gone were the wild costumes of the parade, replaced by respectable clothing and wetted-down hair. In my grubby, half-rotting shirt I felt distinctly under-dressed.

The hard-boiled egg man edged up and handed me a free egg. He asked me to advertise its good taste loudly. If a foreigner was seen enjoying his wares, he said under his breath, everyone would want one. I sunk my front teeth into the egg and groaned with pleasure. Then the show began.

An officious man swept up onto the stage and grabbed the microphone. He went through an elaborate routine of testing the acoustics. This involved pressing his lips to the microphone and making bird calls. When the technical tests were at an end, the official announced the evening's programme. The most beautiful women from the state of Loreto had been gathered, he said, and were waiting on the other side of the banana leaf screen. They would show off two costumes – formal wear and natural. But first, as a warm-up, members of the audience were invited to take part in an amateur talent show.

Thirty gold-toothed women pushed their offspring up towards the podium. Even in the jungle the glare of the limelight is strong. The compère selected a dozen children at random and lined them up. Before they demonstrated their talents, he introduced the pageant's sponsors. A luscious woman in a scarlet sequinned top swaggered onto the stage. She held up a tomato-coloured sachet, and announced the benefits of Inca-brand condoms. When it came to protection, she said, Inca-brand was the only name to remember. Tossing a handful of the sachets to the crowd, she made way for the young actors.

Were they not starved of even amateur entertainment, the audience might have protested at the performances which followed. There were a series of gawky song and dance routines, three mimes, two Michael Jackson impersonators, and a boy of about six attempting to walk on his hands. Instead of hissing the performers from the stage, the spectators applauded with great verve. They voted the Michael Jacksons as the winners.

After another word from the sponsors, the insect-loaded light-bulbs were dimmed. A backing track of savage, techno' music echoed around us, as the first of the beauty queens stepped from behind the screen. In Trompeteros formal wear meant swimsuits. The first belle was wearing a striped gold bikini, her slender legs ending in a pair of white stilettos. Across her chest was a sash bearing the name of her village, *Cuchara*, which means 'spoon' and from her wrist dangled tag number one. As soon as they saw her, the audience went wild. The men whistled, and the women whooped.

The second girl prowled like a panther onto the stage, blowing kisses to her admiring fans. Her leopard-skin print swimsuit was complemented by a cowry shell necklace, and a pair of dangerously high-heeled white shoes. Behind her, contestant number three emerged. Unlike the others, she was thick-built and bulky, with a tremendous neck, and hands the size of pudding bowls. The hard-boiled egg man tapped me on the knee and pointed. She was one of his best customers, he said. The audience appreciated the display of obesity. They applauded furiously.

The contestants kept coming, ever more seductive in their swim-suits and white high-heels. When all nine beauties were on the stage, they marched in a circle pouting, and blowing kisses to the swooning men below. Every few minutes, the compère would lower the music and proclaim the high quality of Inca-brand condoms. The beauties on the stage, he declared, were examples of clean-living girls who always used an Inca condom.

After the formal wear, the girls slipped away to change into some-thing a little more casual. Contestant number one reappeared a moment later dressed in a real leopard skin, with red face paint and a spear. Gone were the white high-heels, replaced by bare feet. The next contestant modelled a fibre skirt, her hair embellished with a simple feather crown. As they paraded round the stage, each one would mime out a jungle scene – gathering water, carrying bananas on her head, or hauling in a fishing net. The formal costumes had been a big hit, but nothing like the natural wear.

To the audience, every girl was a sensation. But the routine of contestant number six mesmerised them beyond words. First, she danced across the stage, wriggling her hips and stroking her thighs. Then, dropping to her knees, while still dancing, she pulled a leaf pouch from her back and emptied its contents – a smattering of white specks – onto the stage. I craned my neck to catch sight of what was going on. The others knew the routine. It was their favourite. Clasping her arms behind her back, the girl writhed forward like a limbo dancer, lowering her face until her lips touched the boards. As I watched entranced, she sucked up the white specks and swallowed them. The spectators were ecstatic. Unsure of what she was eating, I asked the man sitting beside me.

'¡Gusanos vivos!' he exclaimed. 'She's eating gusanos.'

I made him explain what a gusano was exactly.

He scrunched up his face, disturbed at my lack of basic Spanish.

'Gusanos vivos,' he repeated, 'live tree grubs.'

22

Wawek

Seven days after disappearing into the undergrowth, Richard arrived back at the *Pradera*. His fatigues were caked in mud, as when I had first met him. On his walk in the woods he had, he said, tasted the scent of nature on his lips. He had drunk water from the *cipó d'água* vine, had eaten fresh brazil nuts, and had spotted a young ocelot prowling through the trees.

'A man who has trod softly on the jungle floor,' he said with uncharacteristic poetry, 'has the blinkers pulled from his eyes. His lungs breathe purity, and his mind is honed to right and wrong.'

So surprised was I that Richard had uttered such a sentence, that I jotted it down. As I scribbled in my notebook, Cockroach handed the veteran a boiled *mahasse's* leg. The dish was one of Richard's favourites. He clambered back into position in the rocking chair, and chewed at the wild pig's hoof.

The week-long sojourn at Trompeteros had given me time to dry my clothes and regroup. I was ready for another bout of tortuous river travel. With the beetles stowed in the medicine chest, Richard on the roof, and Cockroach frying *tsampunta*, grasshoppers, in a pan of oil, things were getting back to normal. Only Walter and the shaman were missing, unable no doubt, to prise themselves away from the Hotel of Miracles. I sent Cockroach to hunt down his shipmates.

When Walter finally slunk back onto the *Pradera*, he was boasting of his philanthropic work to rid Trompeteros of venereal disease. I dreaded to ask how many women he had ravaged in the process. The oil workers' liaisons with the gold-toothed girls were, he said, responsible for the spread of great disease. Similar claims had been made against the rubber barons and their labourers, a century ago.

But thoughts of the girls were now far from Walter's mind. He was more interested in getting me to foot the repairman's exorbitant bill. I let him inspect my empty wallet. In the Amazon, a journey's financier is responsible for covering every cost.

'No one keeps money in their wallet,' Walter said knowingly. 'In Peru everyone puts their cash in their shoes.'

I tugged off my rat-gnawed shoes. He and the others poked about under the insoles. Nothing. They searched the bottom of my sleeping bag. All they found was mildewed underwear.

Reluctantly, Walter called for Francisco to fire up the engine. On the tenth jerk of the starting-cord, the Johnson 65 lurched into life. The river-bank was soon masked in dense, oily blue smoke. As it dispersed, I made out three figures standing at the water's edge. They were each holding laundry bags. All three were young women. The youngest one, who couldn't have been older than fifteen, was asking for Walter.

She and the others begged the *motorista* to take them on the journey. They would work aboard the boat, they said, and would tolerate any discomfort as long as they could be with him, the man they loved. I wondered if I was hearing right. Walter was hardly a fine example of manhood. Cockroach nudged me in the ribs.

'See what I was telling you,' he said, 'the most ugly men in Peru get all the women.'

Walter told the girls that he would return. He didn't know when, or how, but he would come back to Trompeteros. Nothing would stand between them. It was a poignant moment. I was almost touched by Walter's promises. I asked Cockroach to give the girls a couple of *mahasse* legs each. It was one way of disposing of the vile-smelling meat.

Without pausing any further for pleasantries, Walter pulled back the throttle and steered the *Pradera* towards the left bank of the river. Three black vultures circled above us, a grim omen of things to come. Cockroach and the others had no interest in such signs. They waved back to the gold-toothed girls, and wished them luck. I sensed that the disco's depraved atmosphere would soon erase their memories of Walter.

*

The boat was now so infested with wolf spiders that you had to

14. Vietnam veteran, naturalist and jungle expert Richard Fowler, who promised to keep me alive.

15. Richard drinking *masato*, fermented manioc liquor, in the Upper Amazon.

16. The author wearing a shamanic costume.

17. The *Pradera*: despite being infested with rats and wolf spiders, it was an ever-faithful craft.

18. A *paca*, a large jungle rodent, brought aboard the *Pradera* and dished up as stew.

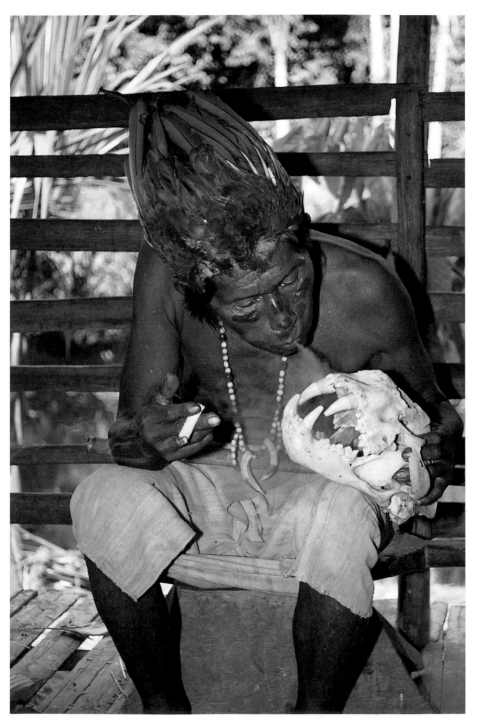

19. The master shaman and *ayahuasquero* Ramón, performing a purifying ceremony – which involves blowing smoke into a jaguar's skull.

20. Ramón's wife preparing a pot of *masato*. She takes handfuls of the cooked manioc from the cauldron, chews them and spits them back. The enzymes in her saliva cause the beverage to ferment.

21. The raw ingredients of *ayahuasca* mixed with river water, ready to be cooked.

22. The mixture is brewed for several hours.

23. After filtering out the leaves and bark you are left with the dark tea-like drink hallucinogenic, *ayahuasca*.

check every spoonful of food before putting it in your mouth. The cockroaches tended to keep back, but the wolf spiders – *wolfies* as we called them – would jump suicidally onto your spoon when it was raised to the lips. The rafters were swarming with them. There were so many that the shaman suggested reintroducing rats back onto the boat to curb their numbers.

Two days after pushing off from Trompeteros, Francisco jumped from his string hammock and ran up and down the roof, squealing. I supposed he was just having a bad reaction to the food. But Richard recognised the outburst.

'He's seen something,' said the vet'. 'He's had a premonition.'

'About what?'

The shaman froze and plunged his fingers into the front of his underpants. 'The Shuars,' he said. 'We are near them. There's danger The Shuar have sent a dart to harm us.'

I would have ignored the warning, that is if I hadn't already read about the Shuar's bewitching techniques. In their society, bewitching shamans are called *wawek*. The reference books said they were usually the richest people in the village, as everyone gave them gifts. You can't do too much to stay on the good side of a *wawek*. Usually, a Shuar shaman could swallow a little tobacco water, then regurgitate a *tsentsak*, a magical dart. Part live and part dead, such darts are the most feared of all shamanic tools. If hurled at someone, they can pass right through his body. Oblivious that he's been bewitched, the victim drops dead soon afterwards.

When a shaman wants to bewitch someone from a distance, he can use the help of the *wakani* bird. Acting as a spirit-helper, it will carry the dart and toss it at the victim on the shaman's behalf.

Most shamans in the Upper Amazon conserve one aspect of their power as a thick white phlegm. Kept in the upper part of their stomachs, the phlegm is said to contain magic darts and spirit-helpers, used in curing or bewitching. It can be regurgitated at will, and can even be drunk by a shaman's pupil, when a master wants to transfer power to the apprentice. Francisco boasted that his phlegm was more powerful than any other; he could create limitless supplies of it. Given the amount he smoked, this seemed hardly surprising.

He said that he'd seen the Shuar's darts pierce our bodies. To us they were invisible, but he – with his special shamanic perception – could see them lodged in our chests. The darts were in all of us. When

I asked him what he could do, he stuffed a pipe with *mapacho* and filled his lungs with its sable-coloured smoke.

'He'll smoke the darts out of us,' said Richard. 'And later, when the boat is lost in the darkness, we'll take *sanango*.'

The thought that we were at last entering the country of the Shuar, boosted my own morale. I kept thinking back to Dr Cabieses' office, with its fine shrunken head, and the talk of allegorical flight. Had the doctor not coaxed me to continue, to seek out the Birdmen, I would not have been sailing up the Corrientes in a rotting, spider-infested boat. Nor would I have been duped by César, or have crossed paths with a Vietnam vet.

I lay out on the roof. On a long journey, I mused, the line between resounding success and unimagined failure is no broader than a hair's breadth. I prayed that the Shuar, my beloved Birdmen, would welcome us, and initiate me with a flight on *ayahuasca*. I prayed, too, that the crew would stick by me. Their loyalty was always in question. But my greatest fear was of offending the proud warrior tribe. For this reason, I read and re-read the two books about the Shuar, and memorised as many points of etiquette as I could. The list of don'ts was long: don't mix with the Shuar if you are sick; don't refuse to eat their food, however grotesque; don't ask too many questions, touch a child's head, discuss the river, or show the soles of your feet.

Between the 1930s and '50s, a wide variety of books and publications were written about the Shuar. Most dwelt sensationally on the tribe's achievement in shrinking heads. Some masqueraded as works of anthropology, but even they contained pictures of their tall, white authors posing with a *tsantsa*.

For thirty years, any amateur explorer worth his salt hurried down to Shuar country, to pass around Lucky Strikes and get his hands on the shrunken heads. Such men came from all kinds of backgrounds. Some were socialites or treasure hunters, others former insurance salesmen or bankers' clerks. I had long since resigned myself to the fact that, as a collector without a collection, I wouldn't come across any *tsantsas* in the jungle. There were none left.

Despite the collective obsession for head-shrinking, very few explorers – amateur or professional – bothered to understand Shuar society. It wasn't until decades later that anthropologists grasped why heads were shrunk at all. The trailblazers had come for a freak show – a true life *Ripley's Believe It or Not*: shrunken heads for the sake of shrunken heads. They claimed to have found rare examples, too, including Caucasian, Negroid, and Chinese *tsantsas*, and even entire shrunken bodies. While the world yearned for newer and stranger shrunken exhibits, taxidermists' workshops worked overtime.

Thousands of fake *tsantsas* clutter the shrunken head market, today. Take a look at one of the internet auctions and you find them. Most are crudely made from goat or monkey skin. Study the real thing carefully and you soon notice the tell-tale signs of a fake. Most have skin which is too leathery and hairy to be human; their noses lack nasal hair, and their ears are poorly sculpted. But at the turn of the last century a few taxidermists across the Americas were making superior fakes.

Procuring heads from morgues in the poor parts of town, they shrunk them expertly. This probably explains why there are so many fake Negroid *tsantsas*. Later they invented a provenance and sold them as rare artefacts to leading museums and private collectors. Genuine *tsantsas* always have the lips sealed with thorns or by pins, made from the chonta palm. Those which have been honoured at *tsantsa* feasts, and are fully complete, have long cotton strands hanging down from the mouth (different from the scrawny strands of twine on fakes). Most also have a hole at the apex of the head, for a cord. Genuine examples tend to have oily complexions, and are lacking facial hair. This gets singed off during the shrinking process.

Up De Graff, in his book *Head Hunters of the Amazon*, talks of an expert taxidermist in Panama who had shrunken human heads, and even entire bodies. One of them, he said, measured no more than twelve inches in length. Flornoy also mentions a shrunken body, that of a Jesuit monk. The story goes that the friar upstaged a Shuar shaman by healing patients whom he had been unable to cure. In a 'sacred frenzy, drunk with *natema*', the Shuar denounced the Christian, murdered him with 'savage passion', before shrinking the man's entire body.

As far as the Shuar are concerned, it would be sheer folly to shrink the head of a foreigner. There would never be occasion to do so. The reason is the soul. The head of a victim is shrunk so that the man who cut it off isn't followed by the victim's *musiak*, his 'avenging soul'. The *tsantsa* itself isn't regarded with much reverence for it is a means to an end. The Shuar traditionally believed that only they and neighbouring tribes had souls. Foreigners were soul-less and so, as far as the Shuar were concerned, you didn't have to protect against an avenging spirit if you killed one. The idea of a genuine white man's *tsantsa*, is therefore unlikely in the extreme.

*

As we progressed at walking pace north-west up the Corrientes, the river became increasingly narrow, twisting more with every mile. The banks were abundant with flora. Giant *punga*, kapok trees, clung to the water's edge, their branches spread-eagled over the river, their red pods ripe and ready to fall. Some still had their magnificent ivory flowers, which Richard told me were pollinated by a species of fruit bat.

The sunshine of mid-afternoon was so bright that I was unable to sit on the roof. I lay in my fetid hammock, trying to ignore the wolfies, which scurried across my chest like rats running from a cage. At my feet, Cockroach was boiling up a toucan he'd traded with someone. Although uncertain why, I was surprised to see that the bird's meat was blue.

Richard wasn't discouraged by the bright light. From his vantage point on the roof he broke the silence, calling Walter to bring the *Pradera* to an immediate halt. At first I thought he'd spotted a sand-bank, although this was unlikely as the river was so high. I shouted up to him.

'Dolphins,' he called back. 'Dolphins at three o'clock.'

I climbed up onto the roof, screwed up my eyes and peered off the starboard side. Through a break in the kapok trees, Richard had glimpsed a lagoon. In it he'd seen the ridge of a dolphin's back.

There was only one thing the crew feared more than mermaids – dolphins. As soon as they heard the word *delfín*, they started pleading. Cockroach protested we'd all die if the creatures saw us; and Walter cried out that his brother-in-law had been taken by dolphins on the Rio Nanay, while trying to kill one. Many fishermen wear love charms, he said, made from the dried genitals of a female dolphin. If the fisherman touches a woman while wearing it hidden under his shirt, she'll fall in love with him. His brother-in-law had been taken by the dolphin princess before he could kill her and make a pendant from her genitalia. Now he lived under the waves, a prisoner in the dolphin realm.

After Walter's outburst, Francisco piped up, urging us return to Iquitos.

'The Shuar have sent dolphins to kill us,' he blurted, 'they're a sign, *un mal augurio*, an ill-omen.'

'Nonsense!' I barked. 'I'm sure you'll learn to like them.'

The shaman froze me with a deranged stare.

'They're *demonios*, demons,' he said. 'They will kill us.'

Richard delved into his camouflage bag.

With the crew still protesting, he told Walter to take off his precious Wellington boots, and steer the *Pradera* through the waterway into the lagoon. With great reluctance the *motorista* complied.

From his camouflage bag, Richard had taken out a large black Walkman with a built-in speaker. He seemed abashed at owning such a thing. I had never seen him using it.

'What do dolphins love most?' he asked me.

'Fish.'

'Well, other than fish?'

I shrugged.

'They love ZZ Top,' he said.

Once the boat's engine had been cut, and the frenzy of ripples had calmed, Richard clicked on a ZZ Top cassette, set the Walkman at full volume, and dropped it into one of Walter's Wellington boots. Leaning over the edge of the boat, he held the boot's foot under the surface of the water.

'Waitin' for the Bus', a hit ZZ song, vibrated out through the water. By the third track, Cockroach was frantic. He had taken the miniature silver crucifix from around his neck, and held it to his lips. Francisco was crouched over the titanium Primus stove, setting fire to toucan feathers. Dolphins abhor the smell, he confided.

But the burning feathers did little to keep the animals away. By the fifth track, the slender dorsal fin of a grey Amazonian dolphin was cutting through the water towards us. A moment later, Richard noticed another swivelling about on the port side.

Had I not witnessed it myself, I would not have believed the extent of the crew's terror. Walter poured a cup of petrol over his head. He suggested I do the same. Dolphins, he claimed, hate petrol even more than burning toucan feathers. But I didn't want to escape from them.

Richard and I eased ourselves into the cool water. Despite my fear of piranhas, I swam towards the middle of the lagoon. The smaller of the pair circled me, diving below the surface time and again. It swooped through the water like a swallow darting through the late summer air. Again and again it passed us, racing at full speed with the other, before peeling away and doubling back. The force of its sweep, and the vacuum which followed it, sucked me down below the surface. As it brushed me I felt its sleek rubbery skin on my hand, and saw the rows of scars which covered its back. Like scratches from a set of long fingernails, the scars marked the dolphin's place in the group's hierarchy. I was struck that anyone could equate such a peerless creature with evil, or would want to cut out its genitalia and wear it as a pendant.

We had left the Walkman aboard the *Pradera*. Even though the music had stopped, the dolphins continued to play. The smaller one charged me repeatedly, careering to a stop inches from my face, cackling through its blow-hole. A third one appeared. It was not like the first two – it wasn't grey, but pink.

Much larger than the grey dolphins, it didn't have a dorsal fin, only a low ridge along its arched back. River dolphins once thrived in many of the world's great rivers – including the Mississippi, the Ganges and the Nile. But the pink variety of the Amazon, known to fishermen as *boutu*, are regarded as the most ancient species of river dolphin. Their colour, still a mystery, may be derived from their diet, like that of the flamingo, which turns pink through eating shellfish.

Richard and I swam across the lagoon, the dolphins lunging through the water either side of us. Their movements, precision, and urge to communicate, were captivating. With the sun so brilliant above us, shining on the lagoon's mirror-like surface, I could have swum there all afternoon. The veteran eventually called me back to the boat. It would be dangerous, he said, to stay in the water too long.

'Piranhas?'

'No,' he riposted, 'not piranhas, they'll only come if they sense blood.'

'Then what's the danger?'

'The *camero* fish. It's very inquisitive ... it swims up the body's orifices and *that* attracts piranhas.'

Once back at the boat's side, I tried to pull myself up onto the deck, but was too weak to do so. There was only one solution. I had to dive down and swim up the lavatory hole, which was lower, but slippery with excretion.

The moon was full that night. It hung above the jungle like a tre-

mendous ring of gypsum. By its ivory light we navigated a passage up
the right side of the river. Walter was fearful that the Shuar might
attack. After all, we were now firmly in their territory. Rather than
pull in and spend the night nestled up to the trees, I insisted we
continue to the next village.

Shortly after nine p.m., Cockroach spotted a row of shacks in the
distance, set high above an embankment. I gave the order for the gifts
to be made ready. I took warning from Fitzcarraldo's example: when
dealing with the Shuar, be prepared. Cockroach trawled through the
bags. He took out a selection of clothing, odds and ends of food,
shotgun shells, Fanta bottles, and the Vicks Vapour Rub. He made up
three or four individual gift bags.

Once we were in line with the village, Walter killed the engine and
drew the boat up to the bank. Unease gagged us all. We had heard so
many stories of the Shuar and most ended with the visitors getting
their throats slit. Now we had arrived at our first Shuar village. I
wondered how we ought to progress. Richard said the best course of
action would be to lie low during the night.

I climbed onto the roof. My Maglite was at the ready, but I dared
not use it. As I scanned the shacks, the dark roofs absorbing the
moonlight, I heard something. It was singing, shrill and harmonious.
I motioned to Richard.

'The ancient Shuar songs,' I croaked. 'I've read about them! They sing
of the heads they've taken and the glorious battles they've fought.'

The Vietnam vet' rubbed a hand across his face. Even he appeared
to be moved by the songs. He was just about to say something,
when I noticed the slender form of a man running down the steep
embankment towards us. I strained to see him clearly. He was carrying something. I asked Richard to get his revolver ready; he retorted
that threatening behaviour would be suicide.

'Let's wait and see what happens,' he said.

The man called out to us well before he reached the boat.

'What's he saying?'

Richard didn't reply to me, but called out to the man in Spanish,
inviting him to come aboard. Cockroach put the boarding plank
down. Stooping his head in respect, the young warrior welcomed us
to the village, which was called San Jose. He had brought us a gift, he
said in broken Spanish. The villagers would be honoured if we
accepted it.

The warrior passed something to Richard. It was about the size of a small dog and was covered in scorched fur.

'What is it?'

Praising the man's hospitality, Richard ripped off an arm and handed it to me. It ended in a miniature hand, with fingers that were scrunched up into a fist.

'Get your teeth into that,' he said, 'and make it sound like you're enjoying it.'

'What is it, though?'

'Roasted monkey.'

23

Ancient Ballads

During the night I had a dream. Actually, it was more of a nightmare. I dreamt that the chief of the Shuar village was displeased with our gifts. Canned food, Vicks Vapour Rub and Fanta bottles were, he said, useless products from a world preoccupied with comfort. He craved a commodity far rarer than the ones in our nylon sacks: he was longing for a set of American dentures. The chief had seen a poster for *Gone with the Wind* and wanted Clark Gable's smile. American was best, he said. So angry was he that we'd not brought dentures, that Richard, Cockroach, and I were tied up with *ayahuasca* vines. Then our heads were chopped off with a flint-edged axe. Francisco and Walter only managed to escape the brutal treatment by promising to treat the village's venereal disease.

I woke from the fantasy as water gushed through the rotting roof onto my hammock. Torrential rain was cascading down, flooding the decks. Cockroach was doing his best to lower the blue plastic sheets which acted as primitive blinds.

Three hours later, with the rain still lashing down, I woke again. This time Francisco was bending over me. He was spitting saliva onto my face. Before I could tell him to back off, he spoke.

'You will need my protection,' he said. 'The tribe have been singing all night. I have heard them.'

'The ancient Shuar ballads,' I replied, stirring from my hammock.

'No,' said the shaman. 'Not ballads, but war songs. They're going to kill us, with stone axes. I have seen it in a dream.'

I knew that mention of my own nightmare would have led to mutiny. One word and the crew would swing the boat round and head for Iquitos at full speed. So I bit my lip and asked what was for breakfast.

Cockroach served me a chunk of toucan on a bed of sticky rice. The rubbery blue meat had no taste at all. I had learnt to overcome the dullness of his cooking by sprinkling Pepé's *Ajinomoto* powder liberally over the food.

When I had swallowed as much of the toucan as was physically possible, I crawled up onto the roof to discuss the plan with Richard.

I asked if he'd had nightmares.

'Slept like a fuckin' baby,' he said, rocking back and forth.

'Aren't you worried that we might have our heads chopped off? After all, everyone's warned us of the Shuar.'

The Vietnam vet' leant over and tapped me on the knee.

'No one messes with Richard Fowler,' he said.

I looked at him in silence. He was stripped to the chest, his dog tags reflecting the morning light. His torso was lean, rippled with muscle and pocked with scars.

'Did I ever tell you 'bout the bear at the zoo?'

'Don't think so.'

'I was wavin' my ice-cream through the bars,' he said, 'taunting this great fat grisly. He came over, lurching at the ice-cream. He wanted that sucker bad.'

'Did he get it?'

'He would've done, if...'

'*If* what?'

'If I hadn't grabbed his fuckin' tongue in my fist. I pulled that sucker till his face was pressed up against the bars.'

I tried to draw morals from the story, but Richard had more to impart: 'The monkey last night was a sign,' he said.

He slung one of the gift bags over his shoulder and jumped ashore. I followed in his footsteps. The crew made excuses why they couldn't accompany us. There were suddenly pots and pans to be scrubbed, floorboards to be repaired and spells to be cast.

'They're a bunch of fuckin' girls!' Richard shouted as we headed up the steep embankment. 'Rule number one of war,' he cautioned, 'keep the floozies behind the front line.'

I had donned my best mouldy clothes, powdered my feet and doused myself liberally with *Eau Sauvage*. But even that couldn't mask the scent of rot. As we walked up through the tiger grass, Richard reminded me not to rush the tribe.

'Don't mention *ayahuasca* or shrunken heads until they've accepted us,' he said. 'And make sure you eat whatever they serve.'

A few minutes later we had conquered the bank, and gained our first glimpse of the village. Rectangular in shape, the four sides were edged with *malocas*, traditional houses, about fifteen in total. A communal field stood at the centre of the village. The dwellings were raised on stilts, their *irapai* thatch roofs supported by central posts. Typically, all four sides were open, allowing the air to move freely, and neighbours a view into each others' lives. A morass of mud lay around every *maloca*. Chickens and ducks rooted about in the slime, scratching for whatever they could find.

The village seemed abandoned. Smoke was spiralling from fires in one or two huts, but there were no other signs of life. I feared that the villagers had hidden and were waiting to mount a surprise attack. A pair of hunting dogs were tethered at the far end of the quadrangle. They sounded the alarm, but no one came.

'We'll go to the chief's house and wait for him,' said Richard.

He led me through the grass square and up to what he supposed was the leader's dwelling. He explained later that the floor of the house was higher than the others, indicating elevated status. We stood outside the house and waited.

After almost an hour, the villagers appeared from a large building on the edge of the jungle. Its walls were made from banana leaves and bamboo, and its floor was at ground level.

Like the other people, the Shuar chief was wearing simple Western clothes. An old man, his complexion was amber-brown; his eyes almond shaped, their whites flecked with blood. Flame-red lines ran across the lower part of his cheeks, like a cat's whiskers. The oily paint derived from the *achiote* seed, which is said to protect the wearer from demons. On his head, he wore a crown, made from the breast feathers of a scarlet macaw.

With warm greetings, he welcomed us to his *maloca*. We ascended the plank ladder and sat cross-legged upon the bamboo floor. I cast an eye around the room. It was about thirty feet long and half as wide; its rafters were masked in cobwebs. At the far end of the room, a fire was burning on a flat stone. Three equal lengths of wood met on the stone in a triangle. The floor was clear, except for a few wooden bowls and a blackened cauldron. All other possessions were stowed in the rafters.

We sat in silence for ten minutes or so. Only when his wife had filled the two largest wooden bowls with a white beverage, and stirred them with her hand, did the chief begin to speak.

'You must be thirsty,' he said in rudimentary Spanish, '*beba*, drink!'

Richard took the bowl in his hands and pressed its rim to his lips. It had been a long time, he said smiling, since he had been honoured with *masato*. He took a deep draught of the milky liquid, draining the bowl. I assumed the drink was milk, although we had seen no cows in the area.

The chief's wife took the empty bowl and filled it, and stirred the mixture again with her fingers.

'Drink up,' said Richard sternly. 'Every drop.'

I put the rim to my mouth and took a sip. The moment it touched my tongue, I realised it was not milk. I couldn't make out the exact taste, except to say it contained a trace of alcohol. Richard and the chief watched as I gulped down the bowl's contents. When I had finished, I licked my lips.

Richard smiled at the chief, and thanked him for the refreshing beverage.

Soon after our arrival in San Jose, I discovered the cryptic process by which *masato* is made. The women peel and wash a number of *yuka*, manioc, at the river-bank. They then grate the roots and wash water through the coarse mixture, sieving it thoroughly. This removes a poison, a form of hydrocyanic acid, which occurs naturally in the tuber. After grating, it is cooked and crushed with a wooden spoon. Two or three women often sit around the pot, mashing while they chat. As they mash, they pull out handfuls, chew, and spit them back into the pot. The enzymes and bacteria in their saliva cause the *yuka* to ferment. After four days the paste has fermented. It's mixed with water, then served. The drink, a weak alcohol, is traditionally consumed in enormous quantities. In Shuar society, *masato* is presented to guests before any conversation takes place. To refuse it would be an unthinkable insult.

Once Richard and I had each downed a second bowl of *masato*, the chief introduced himself. He said his name was Enrique. It struck me as an odd name for the leader of a proud, head-shrinking tribe. He welcomed us formally to San Jose, and said he hoped we would stay in the village for many months. I pointed to the white nylon sack.

'We have brought you a few things,' I said. 'They are tokens of our gratitude.'

My basic Spanish, and Enrique's own unfamiliarity with the language hindered our conversation. But he smiled, bowed his head, and opened the bag.

He pulled out the box of shotgun cartridges first, and held the box up to his nose.

'Good,' he said, 'they are dry ones, very good.'

'They're 16 gauge,' I replied, but Enrique was too busy looking through the sack.

He pulled out the assorted packets of salt, rice, flour, tea, the cans of tuna fish and butter, the soap, loo paper, and fishing hooks. He praised each item for a moment, thanked us, and called for his wife to bring more *masato*.

Then the Shuar chief thrust his right hand back into the sack. He fished out a small tub made of blue glass.

'Vicks Vapour Rub,' I said. 'I've heard you all like it.'

Enrique narrowed his eyes, prised off the lid, and sniffed the oily cream. He asked what it was used for.

'For coughs,' I said. 'But I've heard you have another use for it.'

I chuckled. Richard chuckled. But Enrique didn't understand. I wondered whether the Scandinavian in Iquitos might have been having me on. I hoped not, as I'd spent a small fortune on thirty tubs of the mentholated cream. Enrique looked over at me quizzically, then sniffed the ointment a second time.

'*You know*,' I said casually, pointing to my lap, 'it's for rubbing down there. It'll make you strong.'

To put an end to the awkwardness, I fumbled in the bottom of the sack, and pulled out one of the Fanta bottles.

'This is a very special object,' I said, 'with so many uses. It's a rolling-pin, a pestle for crushing bananas, a musical instrument, and even a weapon.'

The Shuar chief straightened his macaw-feather *corona*, and licked his thin tongue across his lips.

'*¿Pero de qué habla*? What are you talking about?' he said. 'That's a Fanta bottle.'

'You've seen one before?'

'*Por supuesto*, of course,' Enrique replied. 'The missionaries bring us Fanta whenever they come here.'

Richard and I exchanged troubled glances.

'*Missionaries*?'

'They're our friends,' said the leader. 'They taught us about God.'

'You're Christians?'

'*Evangelists*,' he corrected.

'What about the ancient beliefs of the Shuar?'

'The traditions were important in my childhood,' said Enrique, 'but with time they disappeared.'

He passed Richard more *masato*.

'We used always to be at war with other tribes,' he said. 'A Shuar would never sleep without his knife, or walk in the jungle without watching for attackers. Life was very dangerous. But then the missionaries came.'

Enrique paused to take a draught of the white, creamy liquid.

'They told us that killing was wrong,' he said. 'God doesn't want us to kill. He wants us to pray, to pray for Jesus.'

When all the *masato* was over, a roasted *paca* was brought out. The creature, which had obviously been shot, was peppered with lead pellets. The Shuar don't serve food until the *masato* has been finished.

Enrique took us on a tour of the village. He showed us the water tank which the missionaries had built, and the rustic church at the end of the village. When we arrived, the villagers had been praying there, as they did every Sunday morning.

Every villager received us with hospitality and more *masato*. As we drank it, they welcomed us with the same line: 'We thank Jesus for sending you'. There was no mention of killing, feuds, war, or of shrunken heads. I wondered if these people really were the Shuar. Were they my fearless Birdmen?

Unable to stand the suspense, I asked the chief about *ayahuasca*. Now they were evangelists, had they any use for it?

'*Natema*,' he said, through his clenched teeth. '*Es muy importante.* That is very important. Of course we use it. How do you think we get into the *other* world?'

'The world of the spirits?' I asked.

'No', said Enrique softly, 'the world of Jesus.'

Remarkably, the missionaries hadn't outlawed *ayahuasca*. They must have known that its prohibition would have led to revolt. But the more I saw of their evangelistic faith, the more disturbed I became. In little over a generation the core elements of Shuar society had been stripped away. Virtually everyone I met in the region had a Spanish Christian name, although their spoken Spanish was frequently limited. From the loss of Shuar names to the knowledge of medicinal plants, ancient ways were disappearing fast. Perhaps it was right that the culture of taking and shrinking heads had gone. But to replace elaborate rituals with evangelism, or any alien religion, seemed insane. By making subtle changes, the old ways collapse, like a house of cards.

With shotguns, there was no longer a need for fibrous shields, once carried by every warrior to protect against axe attacks; or *manguaré*, log drums, as a shotgun blast carries further over the jungle. Without *tsantsa* raids, there was no need for lookout towers either. Traditionally built on the roofs of houses, they doubled as missile posts when the village was under attack. And, with the cessation of *tsantsa* raids, there wasn't a need for *tsantsa* feasts, which were crucial in transferring folklore and songs from one generation to the next. With the introduction of Western clothing, ancient methods of weaving died out. I asked if traditional textiles had ever been embroidered with designs of men with wings and trophy heads, but gained no definite answer. Even if there had once been burial chambers with textiles, there was little hope of finding them intact. Unlike the ultra-dry sands of the Atacama desert, anything buried in the Amazon jungle is devoured by its acidic soil.

Enrique introduced us to his daughter and son-in-law, who lived nearby in a *maloca* overlooking the river. I recognised their son as the man who had brought down the monkey the night before. I thanked him.

'Please stay with us,' said the man, whose name was Ignacio. 'Your boat must be very damp.'

Richard and I accepted the hospitality. Ignacio's own son, José-Dias, took a message down to the boat for me. It asked Cockroach to send up a gift bag and a few of my things.

Ignacio's wife put her newborn baby into the hammock, suspended across the room. Like many of the other Shuar women, she wore a faded red skirt, and a tee-shirt. She welcomed us, saying they were honoured to give strangers shelter in their Christian home. The Bible, she said, tells us to care for visitors as if they are your own kin. She hurried off to fetch a bowl of *masato* and some meat.

Fifteen minutes later she returned with a gourd of the beverage and a shallow wooden tray, which held a large quantity of rodent meat. As before, the *masato* was drunk first. Then the meat was passed to me. Ignacio's wife had a flare for cookery. She had decorated the rim of the dish with the rodent's tail and feet. I wondered whether I was supposed to eat them. Perhaps, I suggested to myself, they had another purpose. We have all heard of how the Bedouin of Arabia serve camel and sheep eyeballs to important guests. The tradition of eating the eyes came about as a result of a misunderstanding. They were not a delicacy to be eaten at all, rather the eyes were an indication of the freshness of the meat. In a desert climate animal flesh goes bad quickly. A bright eye is a sign that the meat is fresh. British dignitaries visiting Bedouin encampments mistook the eyes for choice morsels, and gulped them down.

Thankfully, everyone steered clear of the rodent's feet.

'Tonight we have a special prayer meeting in Church,' said Ignacio, once we had eaten, 'we hope that you will join us.'

At San Jose, the busy cycle of village life came to a halt on Saturday night, and didn't start again until Monday morning. Sunday was for prayer, and prayer alone. Christian evangelism might have come to the land of the Shuar, but some things hadn't changed. The young men would still creep from the village long before the sun had brought the dawn. With their weapons at the ready, and a little *masato* paste packed in a leaf, they'd go hunting, dogs at their heels.

Although shotguns were the most sought after product from the outside world, they were expensive. And shot had severe disadvantages. It ripped the prey's flesh to pieces, peppering it with lead. Worse still was the sound. One blast from a gun and all the surrounding wildlife was frightened away.

Ignacio reached up into the rafters and took down his preferred weapon. It was a blowpipe, about ten feet long.

'I use this to hunt monkey,' he said, holding it to his lips. 'I tip the darts with *curare*, and make a notch just before the end. When the monkey tries to pull out the dart, it breaks there, leaving the poisoned end in the animal.'

A quiver of darts could be made in a few minutes, tipped with *curare* and with a band of kapok as a flight. The high quality of the weapon was matched by the warrior's accuracy. The Shuar are regarded as great masters in making and using blowpipes. Most can hit a bird or mammal at a distance of up to a hundred feet.

One story tells of a prominent American ornithologist who was collecting jungle birds in the 1960s, for a museum in the United States. The local people were keen to help him catch specimens, which would later be stuffed. One morning they brought him a selection of dead birds. He refused them politely, explaining that he required specimens without dart holes. Next day the hunters returned with more examples. There were no marks on them at all. The warriors had shot the darts through the birds' eyes.

At dusk we escorted Ignacio and his wife to the church. My aversion to missionary practice led to a sense of unease. As far as I was concerned, an alien faith was eroding the traditions which had enabled the Shuar to survive for millennia. As we strolled down to the tin-roofed house of worship, Ignacio agreed that there was more illness now, than before.

'In the old days,' he said, 'with feuding between one tribe and another, only the strongest people survived. The *cuandero* could save some people with powerful jungle plants, but anyone with a very bad wound, died. The missionaries told us not to use plants, but to take the pills which they bring. Now people are forgetting which plants cure which illness. And,' Ignacio continued despondently, 'there's so much illness.'

I asked what kind of afflictions.

'Last year tuberculosis came to the village, and then whooping cough,' he said. 'More than ten children died. Soon after that, three more died from malaria.'

Ignacio's wife looked at the ground, and wiped her fingers over her eyes.

'Our eldest son died two years ago,' she said. 'He was so weak that nothing could save him.'

We entered the church. A number of uneven benches were laid out in rows on the mud floor, facing the front of the room. Although there was no electricity in the village, an expensive-looking hurricane lamp was hanging from the central beam; a gift from the missionaries. As no one else had yet arrived, Ignacio took the lamp down and lit it. Outside, dusk was turning to darkness, and the jungle's nocturnal creatures were readying themselves to feast.

Gradually, as darkness cloaked the village, the congregation gathered at the church. The benches were soon crammed with honest faces. I could almost hear the missionaries bragging. They'd civilised a tribe of head shrinkers, and made God-fearing evangelists out of them.

Dressed in their best clothes, some in Wellington boots, the congregation of San Jose began their evening service with a prayer. They asked that the Devil keep away from their community. Then they thanked God for sending Richard and me to them. That night, as every night, they praised the Lord, fluttering their hands in the air, crying, 'Hallelujah! Hallelujah!'.

With the hurricane lamp roaring in the rafters they ran about, jerking their arms hysterically, just as the missionaries had taught them to do. Only then, as a tambourine marked out a hypnotic rhythm, did they begin to sing.

They pounded out one hymn after the next, some in their Shuar language, *Achuar*, others in Spanish. The parts I could understand, spoke of truth, justice, temptation and of Jesus. Pausing between hymns, they shrieked in unison, over and over: 'Hallelujah! Hallelujah!'

The tambourine stirred back into action. The church was soon resounding to a Shuar translation of *When the Saints Come Marching Home*.

Sitting beside me, Richard rolled his eyes.

'The ancient Shuar ballads,' he whispered...

24

Trumpets of the Devil

After late morning prayers Enrique took us to meet the village shaman. He lived away from the other houses, in a clearing on the edge of the jungle. It surprised me that such enthusiastic evangelists would still find a role for the *maestro*. Perhaps, I reflected, he was needed for his knowledge of *ayahuasca*. The missionaries had replaced natural remedies with little white pills, but had turned a blind eye to the Vine of the Dead. Mixing mind-altering flora with religion is nothing new. Many faiths throughout history have incorporated hallucinogens into their creed. Among them, the Zoroastrians of Persia, who once used the mysterious plant-based hallucinogen *haoma* in their rituals.

Christianity has accepted hallucinogens, too. I'd heard of the Native American Church, which was founded on the ritualistic use of the peyote cactus. It has more followers today than at any time in its history. The Church's practitioners believe that the cactus enables them to cure sickness and to speak to Jesus.

Richard told me of a Christian *ayahuasca*-using sect, called Santo Daime.

'It was started in the 1920s,' he said, 'when a rubber-tapper called Raimundo Irineu Serra was invited to take *ayahuasca* by Indians in the Brazilian Amazon. In a vision he saw a beautiful woman. Supposedly she was the Virgin Mary. Irineu called her "Queen of the Forest".

'Through visions she taught him hymns,' he went on. 'She told him to base a religion on her songs – which became his church's doctrine. And she ordered him to spread her message to others. Santo

Daime is enormously powerful over the border in Brazil,' said Richard. 'It's swept across the US and Europe, too.'

'But the Shuar's faith is different,' I said. 'Evangelism and *ayahuasca* don't mix, but coexist.'

The Vietnam vet' swiped a furry caterpillar from his leg.

'Those missionaries are clever as shit,' he said. '*Ayahuasca*'s been around a lot longer than they have. Screw with it and they'll be kicked all the way back to Tallahassee. They know that.'

Richard's emerald eyes shone with anger.

'When they messed with the Shuar,' he said, 'the Spanish and the Incas had their butts kicked. But the evangelists have won the battle, and without a single death. They didn't need weapons. Theirs was a different kind of war,' he said, tapping a finger to his brow. 'They fucked with their minds.'

*

Bolts of sunlight ripped through the surrounding canopy, blinding me as I walked. A few feet into the undergrowth and I was gripped by the jungle thirst again. I put it down to dehydration brought on by the overpowering humidity. As I stared up at the light, I glimpsed a mossy branch of a *carapanuaba* tree. On it were growing a dozen orchids with rich yellow petals. Richard identified the alluring flowers as *Mormodes rolfeanum*. He said that each one represented a bird in flight. High above them, a nest of spider monkeys were calling. I wondered if it was their relative whose arm I had eaten two nights before.

Enrique pointed to a long-house in the distance.

'That's where Alberto, the shaman . . .'

Before he could complete his sentence, a slender man slipped from behind a *cecropia* tree. He was holding a sloth by the armpits. At first I didn't look at the man, the shaman, as I was so captivated by the sloth. It moved in slow motion, wielding its wiry, hair-covered arms through the air like sickles reaping wheat. Its expression was haunting, wide-eyed with dimpled cheeks. Never had I come across an animal with a face so trusting, in circumstances so uncertain.

As we tramped down the path towards Alberto's *maloca*, I took my eyes off the sloth, and looked at the shaman. Like the other Shuar, his features were delicate and exact. Had I met Alberto, or any of the other villagers, on the Mongolian Steppes I wouldn't have looked twice. The only difference was the ring of macaw feathers which crowned him. His face was typically East Asian, testimony to his ancient ancestors' march across the frozen Bering Straits ten millennia ago. His hands were curiously scarred, their skin chequered with uneven lines.

When Enrique introduced us, I asked what would become of the sloth.

'I am taking him to Ramón,' said the shaman, 'my teacher. He lives two days up the river.'

'What will *he* do with it?'

'Ramón needs its head,' said Alberto.

Richard silenced me before I could protest.

'Is your teacher an *ayahuasquero*?' he asked.

Alberto snapped a cecropia twig as he walked, stowing it under his arm.

'Of course Ramón's an *ayahuasquero*,' he replied. 'He's known throughout Loreto. He's old, with many children, but his visions are strong. When he takes *ayahuasca*, his spirit flies across the jungle.'

'He flies?'

'Yes,' said Alberto, 'he flies ... over the trees, across the water, like a bird, to the other world. To the real world. There is no greater *ayahuasquero* alive. Some people say that at night he flies ...'

'In his mind?'

'Not only in his mind,' said Alberto. '*Por el aire*, through the air.'

A rush of blood warmed my back. Although I disliked the idea of taking the sloth's head, the thought of the great *ayahuasquero* was uplifting.

The shaman welcomed us to his house. He led the way up the ladder onto the bamboo floor. I climbed up behind him, followed by Enrique and Richard. The sloth was deposited in one corner with the *cecropia* branch. He curled an arm around the leaves, drowsily hooking them up to his mouth.

No *masato* was served at the shaman's *maloca*. He was not married and so had no one to prepare it. I thanked God for his bachelorhood. A pot had been left in the middle of the room. Inside it were a dozen or so long flowers, yellowy-orange in colour. I recognised them as *datura*, the plant of which Cabieses had forewarned me. He had called *datura*'s tubular flower 'The Trumpet of the Devil'. I learned later that, in Europe, they are sometimes known as 'Angels' Trumpets'.

Alberto noticed my interest in the flowers.

'The missionaries bring bottles of syrup and pink and white pills,' he said, 'but they have nothing as powerful as *toé, datura*. Their medicine is like a child before it has learned to walk. It has hope, but is so young and frail.'

I made note of Alberto's remarks. But it wasn't until I read a book by Mark Plotkin weeks later, that I realised how right he was. Plotkin (in *Tales of a Shaman's Apprentice*) says that of the world's 250,000 or so plant species, only about 5000 have been screened in the laboratory to determine their therapeutic potential. There are, he says, 120 plant-based prescription drugs currently on the market. They are derived from only 95 species.

The shaman picked one of the *datura* flowers from the pan and held it in his fingers.

'*Toé*,' he said, 'it can give life or take life. Like *ayahuasca*, we trust it and have learned from it. And we have used it to travel, to fly . . .'

'To fly to Jesus,' said Enrique.

Alberto regarded the chief with a poisoned stare. I sensed his hatred of the missionaries, and all they had brought. He invited me to take *datura* with him; he was about to prepare some. Richard, a die-hard test pilot when it came to hallucinogens, backed away. He added to Cabieses' warning.

'Half a cup of the stuff and you'll be dicing with the fuckin' Devil,' he said. 'It'll send you flying up through the trees, over the clouds, to Lalaland.'

Sitting there in the shaman's *maloca*, looking at the *datura* flowers, I was naïve about the plant's effects. Only with further research, did I find an astonishing connection, linking *datura* with Europe's medieval tradition of flight.

The Shuar took *datura* very seriously. Everyone was aware of its ability to kill or its tendency to drive sane men mad. Despite its extraordinary potency, the Shuar have always had a place for this hallucinogen. At one time, a child who didn't behave might first be spanked with a nettle. If he continued to be disrespectful to his father, the parent would prepare a weak solution of *datura*, called *maké*, and feed it to him. Falling into a trance, the child would hang between life and death. Supposedly transported to the nether world, he'd learn that he was wrong, and his father was right. There are reports, too, that hunting dogs would be fed *datura* to imbue them with supernatural powers.

Datura is a member of *Solanaceae*, the potato family. Occurring in both the Americas and Asia, it contains the powerful alkaloid *atropine*. The compound is credited with a sensation of flight, similar to the one provided by *ayahuasca*. So powerful is the atropine, it can be absorbed through the skin. This explains why preparations made from it are frequently taken by rubbing an ointment onto the skin.

The Algonquin once made a beverage with it, called, *wyoccan*, which they gave to those entering puberty rites. The Zuni Indians of New Mexico applied the ground-up roots of *datura* to their eyes. They said that it allowed them to see at night, and to commune with spirits and birds. Like civilisations before and since, the Incas used *datura* to fly.

The plant's natural history is linked firmly with the Americas. But its initial arrival in Europe is both curious and intriguing. On their triumphant return to Madrid, after a long voyage of exploration, the Conquistadors brought with them all kinds of exotic species. Potatoes, tomatoes, tobacco, and other *Solanaceae* were presented to the king. Among them was *datura*.

One can only imagine how the alluring trumpet flowers were received. Flirting as they do with the ignorant observer, it wasn't long before society found a use for the flowers.

Witchcraft and magical flight have always gone together. While the tower-jumpers and the likes of Roger Bacon, and others, were trying to fly by understanding physics, European witches were resorting to magic. The battery of New World flora fuelled what was undoubtedly the most active period of witchcraft in Europe's history.

These days, witches appear quite unaware of how their ancestors used psychotropic plants. Covens across Europe and North America still cling to the ritual and ceremony, but have lost their knowledge of hallucinogens. The besom, a twig broom, commonly ridden by witches, is today nothing more than a symbol.

Many medieval flying ointments contained *Brugmansia arborea*, a tree-like *datura* species brought from Peru. A variety of herbs and solanaceous compounds would be mixed together and rubbed on an area of the body where the skin was soft. Sometimes the salve was rubbed under the arms, on the face, or on the inner thighs. One theory is that a witch would apply the ointment liberally over her inner thighs and genital area, before climbing onto the besom. The action of riding the broom rubbed the cream into the skin.

After a few minutes, the *datura*'s potency would take effect. The witch would usually pass out. When she came to, she would assume that she had flown. Some writers in the 16th century realised that magical flight was all in the mind. A colleague of Galileo, Giovanni Porta, wrote a detailed account of a witch rubbing flying ointment on herself. She soon collapsed. When she was revived, the woman insisted that she'd actually been on a magical flight. Medieval witches habitually claimed to have transformed into a bird, such as a goose or an owl. Similarly, when the Shuar take *datura*, and even when drinking *ayahuasca*, they profess that animal transformation has occurred.

A number of recipes for medieval flying ointments survive. Some include human and animal extracts, and ingredients like, 'the fat from a baby freshly dug from its grave'. In the early 1960s, the German anthropologist Dr Will-Erich Peuckert prepared a flying ointment from a 17th-century witch's formula. As a folklorist, he was interested in social use of *datura*, and its role in the illusion of flight. The recipe he used contained deadly nightshade, henbane (both members of the potato family) and *datura*. Peuckert rubbed the salve on his forehead and armpits. Very soon he was experiencing a sense of flight, interspersed with falling sensations. Then he fell asleep for twenty-four hours.

*

Two days after climbing the embankment up to the village, I went down to check on the boat. Ignacio's wife had been trying to drag me to a special prayer reading in church. Visiting the *Pradera* was an easy excuse. Ignacio's family, Enrique, and the other villagers were eager to pray for their shaman's soul. They appreciated the *ayahuasca* he made, as it took them to Jesus. But they strongly disapproved of his hostility towards the missionaries.

On board ship, Walter, Cockroach and Francisco were on the lower deck playing cards. They were surprised I was still alive. I told them that I'd prayed for their souls, for better food on board, and for an end to my constipation. My soul had been saved by the Shuars, I said, but Richard hadn't been so lucky. His head had been chopped off by a crazed Shuar warrior. Walter cackled demonically.

'That means I can have his Walkman,' he said.

No words of comfort could get the crew to leave the boat. They refused even to jump down onto the river-bank, let alone come to the village. The Shuar, they said, would cut out our tongues and eat them with salt. Francisco was in charge of spreading the lies. He'd had another dream. A panther had emerged from a violet mist. Right away he'd grasped it was no ordinary cat.

'It was *wawek*,' said Francisco, 'the bewitching shaman. He'd come to kill us with *anamuk*, the bewitching dart.'

'Who did he kill first?'

Francisco tossed four aces onto the table.

'We all died together,' he said. 'The *wawek* threw the special dart into the river, as we were going down stream. The dart was made from armadillo bone. As it touched the water, it turned into a giant boa constrictor, which flipped *Pradera* upside down.'

'*Nos ahogamos todos*, we all drowned,' said Walter, coldly, peering up from his cards.

I am not sure what Richard said to Alberto to gain his trust. I had expected the shaman to be mistrustful of white men, especially after the destructive visitations from foreign missionaries. But Alberto agreed willingly to introduce me to his teacher, the *ayahuasquero*, who lived two days up the Corrientes. His willingness may have stemmed from the fact he would receive a free trip up river. As usual, I couldn't establish if – by *two* days – he meant two days by dugout, or by a boat powered with a Johnson 65. In the Upper Amazon, any suggestion of time is nominal. Alberto cautioned me not to mention missionaries if we met his teacher, Ramón. The great shaman despised evangelism, a fact that endeared him to me even before we had met.

Clearing a space on the bench for Alberto, I made an announcement to the crew. We would leave at once, I said. They applauded. Walter dealt another hand of cards in celebration. Then I told them that Alberto, the Shuar shaman, would be joining us along with his sloth. Anyone who didn't approve would be left on the river-bank.

Back in the village, Ignacio wanted to show me something. As his wife prepared a fresh batch of *masato*, he pulled a manila envelope from the eaves of the house. Inside were three colour photographs. Damp had stuck them together and, as a result, their emulsion was rubbing off. The last picture was so badly damaged I could hardly make out the central figure, a child.

'It was my son,' said Ignacio, 'the one who died from malaria. This is the only picture we have of him. The missionaries took it with their camera.'

When a bowl of *masato* had been passed around, Ignacio suggested we say a prayer. He, his wife, Richard and I stood in a circle holding hands. Ignacio led the invocation. He prayed for the souls of the ones we love. Then he prayed for Jesus to lead us through times of uncertainty.

'*Ojo con Ramón*, beware of Ramón,' Ignacio said after the prayers. 'He is not an evangelist like us. He's *wawek*, a bewitching shaman. Some people say he is *Iguachi*, the Devil.'

*

Alberto came aboard the *Pradera* with the three-toed sloth and a basket brimming with *cecropia* leaves. Zombified as before, the sloth didn't appear disheartened at the prospect of coming along. At the end of the boat, nestled up against the fuel tanks, the crew were playing cards and sharing a pipe of *mapacho*. They pretended that the bewitching shaman's presence didn't bother them. Francisco had encouraged the others into a frenzy of hostility. Walter said he couldn't be responsible for any Shuars who joined us. Cockroach was equally unfriendly. He said he would feed everyone and everything aboard, including the *Titanus giganticuses* and the chicken. But not a morsel from his pot would be served to the *wawek* or his sloth.

Just before we pushed off from San Jose, Enrique hastened down the embankment. A pair of hunting dogs were tearing alongside. His prized blowpipe was at hand, held like a javelin above his head. He asked if he could join us, as the hunting was better further upstream.

Enrique and the dogs scrambled aboard. A few seconds later the engine was fired up, and we pushed off into the dazzling waters of the Corrientes. Behind us, the village rang out with another evangelist ballad. The God-fearing community had met in church to pray for our journey.

Leaning into his rocking-chair, Richard inhaled on a fat *mapacho* cigar, back in position on the roof. Down below, the deck had become Noah's Ark. The beetles, Rosario the chicken, the three-toed sloth, and the ferocious hunting dogs, all had their assigned places. There were three rats, too, which I had reintroduced from the village. They set to work hunting the wolf spiders. The only problem now was that Enrique's dogs tore about in a whirlwind of teeth and claws, trying to kill the rats.

Francisco curled up in his hammock, muttering under his breath. He loathed having competition, especially from a Shuar. As Cockroach had refused to cook for the guests, I ripped open a few packets of Lancashire Hot Pot and served them up. The chief bowed his head to say grace before starting. He and Alberto liked the food so much they requested seconds. After the meal, Enrique took one of the empty packets. He said he'd tell the missionaries to bring lots of Lancashire Hot Pot, when they next visited San Jose.

I asked Richard what we could do to break the ice between the two shamans.

'Teamwork!' he yelled, 'get them on some exercises together. In 'Nam,' he said, 'you learned to look after the next guy's butt. It was as simple as that. You watch his butt and he'll watch yours. I learned that on Hamburger Hill.'

'Was it anything like the movie?'

Richard cupped his head in a camouflage bandanna.

'Fuckin' movie,' he said. 'They made it seem as though the Vietcong really wanted the hill. The fact was they were trapped up there like rats. They had no place to fuckin' go.'

'What about the battle?'

'It took thirteen days,' he said. 'There was rain, logistical problems, casualties, all that shit. But we kicked ass. You never saw a bunch of Americans lying around dead like in the movie. It didn't happen like that. We hammered their asses.

'Hamburger Hill was a mountain which straddled the line between Laos and Vietnam,' he continued. 'I was in the 1st Brigade LRRPS – Long Range Reconnaissance, 101st Airborne Division. Before the actual battle, we got intelligence that the place was crawling with Commies. Six guys from our team were put on the hill. Picture it. They can't move. There's trails with Gooks all around them, like they fuckin' own the place. When our team radios in, they're told to hold still.

'During the night there's a severe fuckin' storm. On an operation like that you sit back to back, put up trip wires and Claymore mines. So in the night, lightning hits the fuckin' radio. Blows the fuckin' thing up, igniting the grenades on some of the guys' belts. Kills three of them right off. The other three are deaf, they've got broken bones, these guys are fucked up.'

'Did they die?'

'No, no, no,' said Richard sharply. 'We sent in another LRRP unit and got their asses out of there.'

He inhaled on the crude cigar, staring out across the jungle.

'That, my friend, was teamwork.'

25

Love the Jungle

Morale on the *Pradera* had never been high, but when the Shuar came aboard, it plummeted. There was hostility in the air. The crew had become so embittered that they shunned me as well as our guests. Sensing mutiny to be a real possibility, I dug out my Alaskan moose knife and strapped it to my thigh. For the first time, the crew had started complaining about the boat's miserable living conditions. I was just as uncomfortable as everyone else. The *Pradera* stank of human, dog, chicken, sloth and now rat excrement.

Enrique's incessant praying was getting on everyone's nerves. When he wasn't thanking Jesus for saving our souls, he was spitting over the edge. His dogs went for the heels of anyone trying to cross the middle area of the deck. It had become their territory. Getting to the loo in the night was now far too dangerous to attempt.

From time to time the craft came under fire from a barrage of pebbles, thrown no doubt by wicked boys. Enrique shouted out at the invisible attackers. He blamed their parents for not instilling in them Christian morals. If they were his children, he said, he'd feed them *datura*.

Two days after pushing off from San Jose, Cockroach said we needed fresh meat. Enrique volunteered to hunt a monkey or two, but the others didn't want anything caught by a Shuar's hand. In the early evening, as the cacophony of bird cries rang out over the canopy, Cockroach and Francisco jumped down and scurried off in search of meat.

Richard and I had no faith in their ability to hunt. So the surprise was all the greater when they returned with the body of a young *capybara*. The creature, which had short brown hair and a blunt-ended snout, must have weighed more than fifty lbs. It's said to be the biggest rodent in existence, thriving near the water on aquatic vegetation. Cockroach hacked up the animal and washed its meat in the river. He said that he'd speared the creature, having spotted it hiding at the base of a tree. I found this strange, particularly as he hadn't had a spear with him. It was far more likely that Cockroach had discovered the creature already dead – jungle road kill. Francisco, too, had found something in the jungle. It was a dark resin, scraped from a tree. He said it was *curare*.

He assumed I didn't know what the substance was. But my enthusiasm for detective thrillers had introduced me to *curare* long before. One of the tranquillisers most favoured by Amazonian tribes, Indians have smeared it over the tips of their arrows and blow-darts for millennia. By interfering with electrical impulses, it stops the muscles from working, causing the diaphragm to relax. Coma through suffocation follows. Hunters prize the resin for hunting monkeys. Hit one with a *curare* dart, its grip loosens, and it falls from the tree. The animal, which is only tranquillised with a speck of *curare*, is quite fit to be eaten.

Francisco wrapped the resin in a damp cloth, and hid it under the floorboards. When I asked him whom he was going to tranquillise, he squirmed, stuck his hands down the front of his underpants, and giggled nervously. I cautioned him. If the Shuars or their animals were found in a comatose state, I said, he'd be the first suspect.

The morning after he had cooked up the *capybara*, Cockroach climbed up onto the roof. His expression was taut, his eyes swollen with worry. One of the beetles had stopped eating flakes of rotten wood, he said. He feared for its life. A moment later, Alberto said we'd arrived at Ramón's.

The famous *ayahuasquero* lived nearby on another river. I wasn't going to take any chances with the *Titanus giganticuses*, so I packed them in my rucksack, along with key equipment. The crew had no intention of venturing through the jungle to Ramón's village. They volunteered to guard the boat and its remaining supplies.

Richard bundled up a sack of assorted merchandise and threw it onto the river's bank. The dogs, the sloth, Enrique and Alberto followed. We bid farewell to the others, and pushed into the undergrowth. I had no idea how long we would be gone.

Alberto had advertised the journey through the forest as a 'short walk'. He said that we would follow a path to the village, one which he knew well. The route was severely overgrown, forcing us to hack a way through with our knives. I suggested to Richard that no one could have visited Ramón for a very long time. He replied that in the jungle plants grow fast. Someone could well have hacked the route a week before, and we would never have known it.

After five hours trekking beneath triple canopy, I was wondering how much further there was to go. Although by far the youngest in years, I handicapped the rest. My jungle technique was non-existent. Alberto led the way with the sloth in one hand and his machete in the other. He cleared a slim path. Behind him was Enrique. So skilled was he at moving through the undergrowth that he had little need for a machete. I'd unsheathed my Alaskan moose knife, proud at last to have a chance to use it. But its extraordinary weight made it a very clumsy tool.

Richard had cut an awkward figure on the paved streets of Iquitos. Even on the boat he was restless. But as soon as his US army boots stepped into the fierce undergrowth, he was at ease. No moment went by without him pointing out the detail, the kind which was not naturally revealed to my anxious, amateur vision. He pointed to the smooth lichen-free trunk of the *capiruna*, explaining that the tree had evolved to shed its bark to keep parasites and lichens away. He showed me how to make a poultice for cuts with the leaves of tropical mistletoe, which we often saw high in the trees. Then he taught me how to tell termite and ant nests apart; and said that leaf-cutter ants, which follow a chemical trail, are blind.

Most tourists who venture to the Peruvian Amazon love the idea of the jungle. They want it just like they saw it on TV – a place which can be muted or switched off by a remote control. Some expect nothing less than air-conditioning, a mini-bar, laundry service, and satellite television. Fortunately for them, there are a variety of 'jungle' lodges with such amenities a stone's throw from Iquitos. Few foreigners are willing to endure the kind of exacting expedition which Richard Fowler leads. The rough reality of his journeys wards away most civilians. He said that the US military sometimes ask him to train élite SEAL units in jungle survival. Infrequent adverts placed in *Soldier of Fortune* bring him a few more battle-hardened adventurers, tough enough to withstand what he calls the *real* jungle.

The difference between Richard and the others, and me, was that they understood the rain-forest. They loved it. They were a part of it. As far as I was concerned that abyss of green was something to fear; something to despise. From the moment I took my first jungle steps, it sensed an intruder had violated its boundary. I was soon drenched with sweat, my mouth cold and rasping, parched beyond words. I followed in Richard's size 11 footprints, focusing on them and nothing else.

Let your eyes strain too closely at a branch or twig, and you start seeing the hideous detail. With fear, the jungle closes in, the insects get bigger, magnified by the mind. How could Richard have prowled through the forests of Vietnam, hunting and being hunted at the same time?

When I asked him, he told me to concentrate on the five rules of jungle travel. One: chop stems downward and as low to the ground as possible; then they'll fall away from the path. Two: go slow, as speed only snags you on fish-hook thorns. Three: rest frequently and drink liquid. Four: love the jungle, don't hate it. Five: check your groin for parasites twice an hour.

Our Shuar companions must have thought I was mad. Whenever we stopped, I'd pull down my trousers and forage about in my boxer shorts. The area was inflamed by chafing and sweat. But there were no bugs. To tell the truth, I didn't really know what parasites to expect. I'd seen some cocoons which Richard had eaten, and plenty of 'roaches and wolfies, but surely they were too big to nestle comfortably in my crotch. Richard said any self-respecting grub would want to burrow into my private parts – it's what they are programmed to do. I told him of the inflammation and the chafing.

'The rawer and bloodier it is down there,' he said, 'the snugger the larvae will be.'

We marched on, but the chafing only got worse. I tried lubricating the area with Vaseline. Then I sprinkled it with mentholated foot powder. But a dark purple rash developed. Alberto asked to see the inflammation. While Enrique held the sloth, the shaman scraped a fingernail over the rash. He made a clicking sound, tramped off into the jungle, and returned with a mass of foliage. Then he rubbed the thin milky sap from the leaves onto the inflammation. The itching was soothed immediately. A couple of hours later, the rash was gone.

'*Huayra caspi*,' said Richard. 'It's a tree with red bark; the milk eases irritations. It's especially good for venereal disease.'

We moved forward for another hour or so, until about four o'clock. Then Alberto said we should camp for the first night.

'*First* night? How far is Ramón's village?'

The shaman fed the sloth a clump of *cecropia* leaves.

'Two or three nights more,' he said.

I sat on a sheet of plastic while Richard built a basic shelter from branches of yarena palm. I dared not move. The Shuars had never been to a city, but they knew I was a city type. My hands weren't scarred like theirs, and I jumped at any sound. They enjoyed my reaction to giant spiders most. I whimpered when I saw them. All around in the darkness spiders' eyes reflected my torchlight, thousands of them, glinting like pearls. Pink-toed tarantulas were everywhere. They were out hunting. Richard caught one and tried to make me watch as it scurried over his face and his back. He drew my reluctant attention to the tips of their legs, which looked as though they had been coated neatly with pretty pink nail varnish.

I wondered how I would go on. Nature had become my tormentor. I had begun to regard it with absolute loathing. But then I spotted something wonderful squatting on a low branch. It was a frog, like none I'd seen before. Its skin, which glistened as if coated with lacquer, was indigo-blue, marbled with splotches of black. Most of the other animals I had come across were timid, expecting imminent death. The indigo frog was far more self-assured. He sat on his branch, looking out at the green world.

So impressed was I with the little creature's confidence, I told Richard to come and have a look. He wiped his machete on his fatigues and peered down at the frog.

'*Dendrobates azureus*,' he mumbled, 'they're fuckin' wild suckers.'

'What's wild about 'em?'

'Poison arrow frogs,' he said. 'When they get stressed they secrete nerve toxins onto their skin. Any predator not warded off by the bright colours gets floored.'

As far as Richard was concerned, the indigo frog was dangerous but not unfriendly. The reptile's yellow cousin, living over in the jungles of Surinam, was another story altogether.

'They call it *Phyllobates terriblis*,' he mumbled, 'the *terrible* one.'

'*Terrible?*'

'They've got enough toxins to kill 20,000 mice. They look like glazed lemons. They're kings of the jungle.'

While we were admiring the indigo frog, Enrique strode over. Before I could stop him, he jabbed a sliver of sharpened stick through the reptile's neck, until it came out its back. The creature didn't die, but exuded a thick foam onto its back. Mindful not to touch the frog, the Shuar chief dipped three or four darts into the foam. Then he headed away into the jungle with the dogs.

By the time the shelter was completed, it was getting dark. The fluorescent green of glow-worms glimmered in the undergrowth, hinting at secret life. Alberto helped me find some rotting wood to feed the beetles. The smaller one looked very forlorn. Its powerful mandibles uninterested in crushing any food. I considered tossing the *Titanus giganticuses* back into the jungle then and there. But, unfortunately for them, they'd become pawns in a despicable human game. Too much money was at stake, and I still hoped to recoup my funds. I whispered to them that in Tokyo or in New York a big bug lover was waiting to pamper them.

Alberto told me to skewer the beetles on a spike and roast them. He said they tasted nutty, like Brazil nuts. At that moment Enrique stepped from the undergrowth, his blowpipe in one hand, a young *paca* in the other.

We lit a fire and roasted the *paca* on a spit. The flames lit up the night, shooting sparks into the trees. The smoke, and the smell of charred meat, kept the insects away. I was in no mood for another rodent meal, so I sprinkled a few grains of *Ajinomoto* powder onto my tongue and thought of roast beef. As I had expected Ramón to live close to the river, I hadn't brought much equipment. With no insect repellent or sleeping-bag, and little drinking water, I prepared myself for a tortuous night.

I hunkered down beneath the shelter, praying for the giant insects, the snakes and the poison-arrow frogs to keep away. Richard slept soundly, snoring beside me. Alberto and Enrique bedded down on a natural platform in a *lapuna* tree, making mattresses of its dark green foliage. As I tried to sleep, I cautioned myself never to return to the jungle. This, the real experience, was the preserve of the professionals. People like me should stay at home and watch it on TV.

The morning was slow in coming. Only when the last shadows had been wrung from the night did the first stream of sunlight break through the canopy. I started the day by checking for genital intruders. The tips of my fingers had mastered the art of probing for maggots and chrysalids. I poked about, still half-asleep. Something was lodged there. As I tried to extract it, it turned into mush.

'Hope it wasn't burrowing,' said Richard. 'If there's still some in there, you're up shit creek.'

Reluctantly, I allowed the Vietnam vet' to inspect the area. The last thing I wanted was a grubby GI rooting about in my boxer shorts.

Richard identified the problem. He said something had indeed been burrowing into my upper thigh. He suspected it was the larva of a chigger mite (the organism that Nicole Maxwell had dabbed with scarlet nail varnish to destroy). Alas, we had no nail varnish. I asked Richard for more information.

He gave me an uneasy glance and looked away.

'Of course, there's always the possibility,' he said delicately, 'that it's not going in, but coming out.'

I grimaced.

'It might be a guinea worm boring to the surface,' he said. 'But let's hope it's not that.'

'Why? What's wrong with guinea worms?'

'By the time they're boring to the surface,' said Richard, 'they've reproduced, filling you with millions of larvae.'

We dabbed the area with clinical alcohol and foot powder, and hoped for the best. Then it was time to move on.

*

For two more days we hacked our way through the jungle. Our odd procession made slow progress. My moose knife was blunt, but I wasn't much of a trailblazer anyway. I swung the great blade from left to right in an arc, pretending to cut. The sloth was kept satiated with a ready supply of kapok leaves. Fortunately, no more of the hole-boring parasite reared out from my thigh. My worries returned to the smaller of the beetles which was tucked away in my pack. It was still refusing food, making me fear for its life.

In the jungle, life was cheap. Our own world hides from death, and considers it as an unnatural condition. In the Upper Amazon nothing could be more natural. On the third night, as we gnawed at the bones of another oversized rodent, Enrique told of life fifty years before, in his youth.

'There was much killing,' he said, his cinnamon eyes reflecting the firelight, 'my father was a great *kakaram*, a warrior. He had taken so many heads. I remember when they came back to the village with the heads. They held them high, and would sing. Then we would have the *tsantsa* feasts.'

'Did the villagers make the heads into *tsantsas*?'

'The warriors started making them on the way back through the jungle,' Enrique said. 'The skin was peeled from the skulls and boiled in water. Then it was filled with hot pebbles, and after that with sand. But there was danger...'

'What danger?'

Enrique threw the rodent's leg bone to one of the dogs.

'Warriors from the village which had been attacked,' he said, 'would be chasing my father and the others through the jungle. The *tsantsas* had to be started. They couldn't wait till they were back at the village.'

'Why not?'

'The *musiak*,' said Enrique, 'the avenging soul. It seeps out from the dead warrior's mouth and will avenge his death. First it kills the warrior who killed it, and then the others. The only way to destroy the *musiak* is to make the head into a *tsantsa*: the soul goes inside the *tsantsa* and is trapped there.

'As the head-taking party runs through the forest, the avenging soul goes with them. The warriors would rub charcoal on the head's face, to blind the avenging soul.'

The old hunter fell silent, as the demoniac screeches of a monkey echoed from the tallest branches of a nearby tree.

I asked Enrique about the avenging soul.

'A warrior could only get an avenging soul, when he had an *arutam* soul,' he said. 'The *arutam* was important for a Shuar warrior. It kept him alive. Without it, he could have perished easily. When I was just a boy my father took me to the waterfall and he waited for me to see the *arutam*.'

'Where do you see it?'

'In the mist,' said Enrique, 'in the spray which comes from the waterfall. It's there. The soul entered me as I slept. It came as a jaguar. It stared into my eyes, challenging me to kill it. I was not frightened, for I wanted to be a warrior like my father. So I stared back and, drawing near, I stabbed it with my knife.'

Enrique puffed his chest full of air.

'That was many years ago,' he said. 'But I will not forget that night, the night I became a warrior.'

The old Shuar's tales were from another time, a time before missionary Bibles and makeshift churches flooded the Pastaza.

'There was so much killing,' said Enrique, repeating himself. 'And when one of our clan was killed, we would have to avenge the death. It led to a cycle of death. There were assassins everywhere. They waited until night, then attacked the village. Children were snatched for slaves, and young women as brides. They set fire to the *malocas*, driving everyone into their trap.'

Again, the hunter paused, as he recalled the gruesome scenes of butchery.

'When the raiding party came to attack our village,' he said, 'I was protected by my *arutam* soul. When they struck, everyone was asleep. I remember the hunting dogs howling at the dark. Then the first screams, as the assassins ran into houses and started to kill. They were wild, desperate to take heads. They were hacking people who weren't even dead.

'My father was one of the victims that night. We buried his headless body under the floor of our house,' said Enrique. 'Of course our village raided theirs and took more heads. Soon after that the missionaries came. They taught us that evangelism was right, and that cutting heads of our enemy was wrong. They baptised me, Enrique, and made me a Christian.'

The hunter touched a callused hand to his brow.

'We no longer need to fear an enemy,' he said softly, 'for we have something very good – even better than an *arutam* soul.'

Enrique looked at me through the flames of the campfire. His cheeks were flushed.

'We have Jesus,' he said.

26

The Avenging Soul

Richard said the jungle was the womb from which all men had come. Emerging from it was like being reborn. Few sights could have been so welcome as the thatched roof of a *maloca* peeking out from between the rosewood trees. As we walked into the clearing in single file, I thanked God for delivering me from the green hell. The thought of traversing it again was almost too much to take. Perhaps, I mused, I would live out my days with Ramón, and become an honorary Birdman.

The village was well-proportioned, and set in a sprawling grassland. Along one edge, it was bordered by a small river, its water dark brown, like tea. A huddle of women were washing clothes on the bank. A rag-tag band of children and hunting dogs were darting about, enjoying the late afternoon sun.

Alberto, still holding the sloth under its arms, led us to a proud, towering long-house at the far end of the village. It was the tallest one I'd seen, lying east-west, and roofed with *kampanaka* palm thatch. A space of more than four feet stood between the raised bamboo floor and the ground. Unlike those at San Jose, and elsewhere, the *malocas* at Ramón's village were oval in shape.

In the days of head-taking raids, no one would have dared enter a Shuar house until welcomed by the host. Unexpected guests were sometimes mistaken as assailants and killed. Indeed, in the Shuar world any action out of the ordinary could be regarded as hostile gesturing. My own Afghan ancestors, from the wilds of the Hindu Kush, are famed for their love of bloodshed. They were once known for dressing their women in red, so that they weren't killed during 'friendly' bouts of warfare. But the Shuar made my own progenitors seem tame in comparison.

Without waiting to be invited into the longhouse, Alberto led us up the tree trunk ladder. The central chamber was about 25 metres long, with a sturdy bamboo floor and plenty of light from the open sides. The roof had been newly thatched, but was already lined with cobwebs. At the far end, a separate area was set aside for cooking. There was no furniture, save for a simple cloth hammock, strung at the near end of the room. A few possessions had been stowed under the eaves; and a large number of bottles and bowls lined one of the walls.

The house was empty, leading me to wonder whether Ramón was at church. But, as Richard pointed out, the village bore no signs of Christianity.

'They are not evangelists,' said Enrique ruefully, 'the Word of the Lord has not come here yet. But with the help of Jesus, they *will* see the light. They will build a church, a big one, with a great cross on the roof. And the sound of hymns will be heard.'

Enrique might have endured a Shuar childhood, complete with *tsantsa* feasts, but it had been swamped by the woolly-speak of the evangelists. His elation at the thought of a missionary crusade, was matched by our disapproval.

'Screw the missionaries,' said Richard, 'they think they're spreading religion, but what they're spreading is a disease.'

Before I could add my own vitriolic remarks, the great *aya-huasquero* climbed the ladder into the house. He received Alberto first, thanking him for the sloth. Then, he welcomed the rest of us to his *maloca*.

As he extended his hand towards me, I regarded Ramón's face. It was mischievous, adorned with flame-red lines painted with *achiote*. His cheeks were unwrinkled, despite his age, which was certainly the far side of fifty. A shine of sweat lit up the end of his nose, and his teeth were darkened by the black nut *nushumbi*. Upon his head was the finest feather *corona* I had seen. Crafted from a single scarlet macaw, its wings wrapped around the shaman's head, like the winged head-dress of Apollo. Ramón's wife, a large-boned woman, with a broad face and a square jaw, sported a smaller crown made from feathers and porcupine quills.

I admired his crown. He replied that great care is needed to make such a thing.

'If you cut the bird open,' he said, 'the feathers will start falling. So, when you have killed the bird with a single dart, you place it in an ants' nest. After five days all the flesh has been eaten away, leaving the bones and the feathers.'

When the creamy *masato* had been passed around, I opened my pack and withdrew a selection of gifts. I had brought some old clothing, some flour, rice, and a box of shotgun shells. The cartridges were clawed away, and stuffed in the eaves of the roof. Pleased that they had gone down so well, I gave Ramón's wife two of the Fanta bottles. She was so delighted that she brought out more *masato*. When I commented on the beverage, she invited me to watch her prepare it. In the cooking area, I looked on as she chewed handfuls of boiled manioc, spitting them back into the bowl. The woman's deteriorated dentistry severely hindered the process.

I illustrated the merits of the Fanta bottle as a kitchen appliance, making random crushing and rolling movements. Ramón's wife was very pleased with her new tool. She spoke no Spanish, but explained in sign language that she would make a toad and turtle stew for dinner. She was an adventurous cook, with a well-stocked larder. Her kitchen contained a number of animals, some live, some dead, others hanging in limbo between the two. They included the giant turtle, which had retracted its head and limbs; a gold and blue macaw, a pair of dead peccaries, and the hind legs of an unidentifiable hoofed mammal.

Sitting miserably beside the fire was a baby red-faced monkey, tethered by a short string. Its hands were furry, the size and shape of tarantulas. Richard identified it as an extremely rare Red Uakari. He said it hadn't had malaria, as the illness tends to bleach the redness from the face. The creature, he went on, would probably be kept as a pet for a while, then cooked for food.

Suspended above the fire from rattan hooks were three heads. I assumed they were being dried. They weren't human, but sloth heads, and had been shrunk. Despite their dreadful state, I recognised them immediately. For I'd seen sloth *tsantsas* before in Oxford's Pitt-Rivers Museum. They're no larger than oversized key fobs, with scrunched up features and a mass of woolly hair.

The Shuar supposedly regard sloths as their cousins. As such a close relative they're said to be capable of having a *musiak*, an avenging soul. Kill a sloth and, in revenge, it will send a falling tree to crush you in the jungle. Some say sloths can even acquire an *arutam* soul as well; others insist that they cannot, and that's why they are easy to kill.

Fearing that Alberto's sloth would shortly be served up by Ramón's wife, and his head turned into a *tsantsa*, I cajoled Richard to come to his rescue. The sloth, he told Ramón, had been a valuable companion during the journey from San Jose. And, as a weary traveller, he deserved freedom.

The shaman called his son. He told the boy to take the sloth to the edge of the forest, and to free it.

'Take what you need and there will always be enough,' he said.

I thanked him for his generosity of spirit.

'I killed another sloth this morning, when I saw it swimming in the stream,' he replied. 'Later, we will eat it.'

A second round of *masato* came and went. Keen to get down to business, I asked Ramón about *ayahuasca*. The old *maestro* was seated on a block of wood, carved in the shape of a turtle. He held his palms out at arm's length, and whistled through his blackened teeth.

'*Aya-hu-as-ca* is the key to life,' he said. 'Drink it, and you will find answers.'

'Will I fly?'

Ramón lit a pipe of *mapacho* and rearranged himself on the stool.

'You will fly if that is what you want,' he continued, 'but flying isn't important.'

I felt my lower lip tighten with worry. Was the chief of the Birdmen telling me to forget about flight?

'The flight is the journey ...' said Ramón, 'the journey from this world to the other world.'

'But if you fly, you are with the spirits,' I said.

Shaking his head slowly, the *maestro* drew on the pipe. The quid of burning tobacco crackled in its bowl.

'You do not have to fly to be with them,' he said. 'The spirits are all around us in the air, they *are* the air.'

*

The toad and turtle stew sat heavily on my stomach. So fearful was I of offending our hosts, that I consumed three helpings of the curious dish. It tasted like a greasy, gamey *coq au vin*.

Before we turned in for the night, Ramón went behind the long-house and broke off a section of dry termite mound. He placed it under the floor and set fire to it. The resins in the nest burned, keeping away insects. Richard told me to sleep away from the walls. The blood sucking assassin beetle, which carries Chagas' disease, would sure to be lurking there, he said. The disease, which brings faintness, swelling and vomiting, is reputed to have killed Charles Darwin.

Ramón agreed to prepare a special batch of *ayahuasca*. Residing so deep in the jungle as he did, he could get his hands on mature vines. The older the vine, the stronger the *ayahuasca*. No shaman ever grows the vines near his house, for *ayahuasca* vines are too powerful.

Soon after first light, Ramón took me into the jungle to search for a suitable piece of *caapi* vine. He told me to beware of falling trees. The avenging soul of the sloth he'd killed the day before may come after us. All around animals and insects were feeding. I felt fortunate to be at the top of the food chain.

Early morning was the best time to cut the *ayahuasca* vine, the *maestro* said, as the juices are concentrated in the bark. Selecting an old gnarled liana, he started to chop. Like other shamans I met, Ramón was an expert with a machete. His arms seemed wasted of their muscle, but they could strike with an immense force. Until a century ago, metal blades were almost unknown to the Shuar, who still hacked off heads and cut vines with stone axes. I would always see the hunters carefully cleaning and sharpening their machetes before going into the jungle. All their weapons were kept in a state of readiness, perhaps a legacy of the head-hunting days.

Cut into foot-long sections, the vine looked very ordinary. Its thin mottled bark and cornsilk-coloured wood hardly smelled of anything. The jungle abounds with plants, some no bigger than a light-bulb's filament, others stretch up two hundred feet. Every leaf, every tree trunk and seed pod are quite unique. Most are more attractive than the *caapi* vine. So how on earth did the peoples of the Upper Amazon ever come across it, and work out the process of brewing *ayahuasca*? It's one thing to break off the leaf of a plant and chew it for particular relief, like coca. But it's a giant leap to mix it with other plants, for an entirely new effect. The reductionist theory, wheeled out by intellectuals, says that centuries of trial and error explains it all. Just as infinite monkeys with typewriters could come up with *Hamlet*, the Amazonians had worked out *ayahuasca*.

Ramón must have cut about six feet of the liana. He kept repeating that such mature vines were very powerful. But perhaps even he didn't realise the enduring strength of *Banisteriopsis caapi*. In 1851, the first botanical specimens of the *ayahuasca* vine were taken to Kew Gardens by the celebrated British explorer Richard Spruce. In 1969 they were tested, and found to still contain high levels of the active ingredient, harmaline.

An alkaloid, harmaline is similar to mescaline, the active ingredient in many other hallucinogens (including the peyote cactus, the psilocybe mushroom, as well as LSD).

When he had collected enough *caapi*, Ramón gathered leaves from other plants, careful not to take more than he would require. These admixtures contained the actual hallucinogens which would enter our blood thanks to the effects of harmaline on the digestive tract. The specific hallucinations depend on the blend of admixtures used by a particular shaman. There are more than seventy-five plants commonly used as admixtures in the region. Most contain tryptamine derivatives which, as I understood it, lead to the sensation of flight.

Ramón wrapped the leaves and chunks of *caapi* vine in a cloth, before leading me through the labyrinth of trees and vegetation, back to the village. He was a man of few words, not given to idle chatter. Only once on the way home did he speak.

'We will take the *ayahuasca*,' he said. 'We will take it together. And we will die. The *ayahuasca* will kill us.'

I didn't know what to make of the remark, but hoped he was referring to allegorical death.

As soon as we returned to the *maloca*, the shaman's wife collared me. Sheepishly, she held out an enormous gourd. It was filled to the brim with the usual vile saliva-based beverage. Thanking her, I took a sip. I had sometimes managed to offload the drink on Richard. He had a far stronger stomach than me, and was always mindful to respect hospitality. But he had gone spear fishing with Ramón's youngest son. I explained that I felt a bout of malaria coming on. I'm not sure why, but as all Shuar know, you must never drink *masato* if you have malaria.

It was then that I remembered about my precious beetles. They were still in my pack and hadn't been fed in two days. I opened up the Tupperware containers. Thankfully, both were still alive. Ramón's wife showed great interest in the insects. She motioned with her hands, admiring their size.

I should have looked after them myself; they were my responsibility. But given the woman's enthusiasm, I asked her if she could take them to the kitchen, indicating in sign language that they were partial to rotten wood. She whisked the beetles away.

At the far end of the *maloca*, the *maestro* began to make the *ayahuasca*. Using the end of a Fanta bottle, he smashed the chunks of vine. The harmaline is contained just beneath the bark, and it must be crushed in order to release the alkaloids. Ramón was meticulous. He counted out five *chacruna* leaves (four inches in length, oval in shape), four leaves of *sanango*, and a few *bobinsana* leaves, and eight roughly made *mapacho* cigarettes. When the ingredients were ready, he laid a few pieces of vine in his cauldron, layering on top a few leaves. Then another layer of *caapi* and more leaves, more of the vine and, lastly, a handful of scrapings from the *sanango* root.

We carried the cauldron down to the water, filled it up and placed it on a special fire. Ramón did not use the cooking area in the *maloca* for making *ayahuasca*. The concoction was left to brew and the shaman turned his attentions to another matter.

The sloth he had killed the day before was being made into lunch by his wife. Its meat was considered a delicacy. Many Shuar, he told me, no longer ate sloths, for they feared retaliation. Unlike others, Ramón had not forgotten how to capture the creature's avenging soul – by making a *tsantsa* from its head. He said that one must never go out to hunt a sloth, but if one crosses your path, you're entitled to kill it.

Ramón fetched the head from the kitchen, and held it in his hands, gazing at it. He observed the lifeless features, the copper-brown hair, and the hole where its neck had been severed. Using a home-made blade, a sliver of steel, he started to peel the skin away. The shaman was skilled in the art of scalping, just as the Andean *maestro* had been in skinning the guinea pig. As the sloth had been dead for some time there was no blood. The skin came away from the bone remarkably easily.

The shaman said he always used the same red earthenware pot to boil sloth heads. He lit a fire behind the house, kindling it with banana leaves. The pot was dipped into the river.

When the water was boiling, the head was carefully dropped in. Raiding parties would sometimes carry a smouldering hornets' nest with them, to light fires. The smoke had the added advantage of keeping other insects at bay. The Shuar could also light a fire quickly using a bow and a hardwood stick. Ramón demonstrated the technique. But the other Shuar I met, had lost the art, since the missionaries had brought them matches.

The sloth's head was pulled from the water after about ten minutes. Longer than that, Ramón said, and the hair would start falling out. I saw none of the oily yellow grease which is said to exude from a human *tsantsa*. The sloth's head had shrivelled noticeably, and was ready to be sewn up.

Taking some fibre and a splinter of wood, the shaman darned the two flaps of skin together. A sloth is far smaller than a human, so its head requires far less shrinkage to turn it into a *tsantsa*. Ramón had heated a pan full of sandy gravel on the fire. When it was sufficiently hot, he funnelled it through the sloth's neck. Time and again, the sand was replaced. As Ramón agitated it inside the tiny pouch of skin, a smell of burning hair and meat mingled with the banana leaf smoke.

Satisfied that the sloth's *musiak* had been controlled, Ramón went to the *maloca* to hang the head up with the others. He left them above the fire for a week or so, he said, after which he buried them in the jungle. On the few occasions that missionaries had cut their way through to the village, they had offered to buy the heads. As Ramón saw it, *tsantsas*, whether human or sloth, had no intrinsic value, and could therefore not be sold.

During the afternoon, the cauldron of *ayahuasca* boiled down. The shaman refilled it with water and placed it back on the fire. Richard returned from the river with seven good-sized fish. They were flat fish, similar to plaice. He gave them to Ramón's wife, who hurried to the kitchen.

Soon after, she ferried several dishes into the main room of the *maloca*. Richard, Alberto, Enrique and I waited for the famous shaman to sit. He came up the tree trunk ladder, and said that, if I was to take *ayahuasca* that night, I should not eat. The stomach had to be empty. Even *masato* was off limits.

I edged back from the food, thankful that I could pass up the bowl of sloth goulash. Richard wolfed down two helpings of the stew. He picked at one of the roasted fish. Ramón's wife then offered her guests the third dish. It was common at a Shuar meal to have no idea what the food actually was. But the dish, which was sitting on a cactus-green banana leaf, was unlike any other jungle food I had come across. It consisted of two hard black lumps, a little smaller than golf balls. Richard passed up the dish, saying he could eat no more. Alberto ate one of the lumps, after peeling off its shell. Ramón's wife popped the other one into her mouth. When she had swallowed it, she looked over at me. And, in sign language, she thanked me.

I was just about to ask Richard what was going on, when it hit me. I sensed a jabbing pain in the base of my stomach, and acidic saliva in my throat. Ramón's wife had mistaken my precious *Titanus giganticuses* for food.

27

Flight of the Birdmen

Just before he died, Ramón's father had called his young son to where he was lying. The old man had been in a trance for many days, getting weaker and weaker. Even though he was a respected shaman and a healer, his family knew he was about to die. He had finished his work in this illusory world.

Moments before he slipped away, he filled his lungs for the last time, and blew into Ramón's face.

'That breath ...' said Ramón, squinting, 'that breath passed on to me *la sabiduría de la ayahuasca*, the knowledge of *ayahuasca*.'

'How long ago did your father die?'

Ramón thought for a moment.

'*Hace mucho tiempo*, a long time ago,' he said. 'I was no more than a child. I still had much to learn.'

'Without your father, who taught you?'

'The *ayahuasca* taught me,' he said, 'and it told me to speak to the trees and plants in the forest. They welcomed me, telling me how to use them. *Ayahuasca* is the pass which opens all secrets,' Ramón said. 'It's the most powerful medicine there is.'

When the third batch of water had more or less evaporated from the cauldron, Ramón filtered away the remaining liquid. It was the colour of caramel.

'We will leave it to cool,' he said, 'and when there is darkness, we can drink.'

I asked Ramón about the rumour that he could fly.

He widened his eyes and put a hand to the nape of his neck.

'*Ayahuasca* is very strong,' he said. 'I have already told you that. It can be used in many ways – as a purger of evil, as a medicine, a solver of problems ... It can take you back in time, or into the future, show you miracles, transform you into a boa constrictor or a leopard.'

'What about flying ... if you take *ayahuasca* can you actually fly?' Ramón looked through me with his gaze, but said nothing.

I found myself thinking about *ayahuasca* and hallucinogens. I knew that my friends would give me pointed looks if they heard I was about to consume a mind altering substance. In the West there's an extraordinary misunderstanding. Most people forget or merely ignore the link between plants and society. They may be condemning you while they're smoking a cigarette, or drinking a bottle of beer – both, of course, are made from plants which when smoked or fermented alter the state of the mind.

In our world we have grown away from the land and scorn natural preparations. Hallucinogens have a bad reputation, and rightly so. They are constantly misused by us in societies which are almost incapable of using anything correctly. Active ingredients are stripped out from plants and taken in massive doses for stimulation's sake. But the Shuar's use of *ayahuasca* is different. It is a medicinal plant used in the context of a specific culture. It is employed in unison with a rigid structure of ritual, which supports it as a framework. It is taken for answers, not to get high.

In the West people are preoccupied with the vision or sensation they may get by taking a drug. They don't give thought to the role of the concoction in healing, or its use as a tool. The shamans of the Amazon only take *ayahuasca* or any other hallucinogen when there's a reason to take it. When I hear of people in Europe experimenting with *ayahuasca*, it turns my blood cold. The plant-derived experience is only part of the equation, the other part being the ritual.

Our short-sighted approach is not entirely our fault. Compared with Asia or the New World, Europe has very few plant species. North America has a wide variety of remarkable species but, tragically, when the Europeans slaughtered their way across that continent, they destroyed the Native American knowledge which understood them, and replaced it with a crippled European system, touted by snake-oil salesmen. It must have put American medicine back centuries.

*

On a moonless night, a clearing in the jungle is very dark indeed. Save for the glint of the fireflies, or the odd flicker of a home-made wick burning in kerosene, there is blackness. Those who are not evangelists and have late night prayer sessions, go to sleep soon after dusk. They rise long before it gets light.

Alberto sloped away to find a place to sleep. He had been feeling queasy since eating my beetle. The misunderstanding had cost me a great sum but, as I pondered it, I had got my just deserts. I should have released the insects when I'd had the chance.

Once Enrique had prayed quietly for our salvation, he followed the others to bed. Richard said to call him if I became distressed during the *ayahuasca* session. It struck me then that he had always appeared reluctant to talk of his own *ayahuasca* experiences while, at the same time, regarding the brew with the utmost gravity. I think he felt that *ayahuasca* was something which had to be tried to be understood. There was no point in him offering his own tales until I had been initiated. Without another word he wandered down to the tannin-brown water to swim. Only a man of Richard's resolution would have dared swimming there in the darkness.

Ramón and I were suddenly alone. We were sitting at the far end of the *maloca*. It was a still night lit by a crescent moon. A pair of candles were burning before us, their flames perpendicular. In their light I saw the objects of ritual lying by the shaman's knee. A gourd of *ayahuasca*, a white enamel mug, a cloth bag, and a *chacapa*, the dried leaf rattle which I'd seen being used near Iquitos.

Ramón lit a pipe of *mapacho*, and drew on it until his chest was filled to capacity. He blew the smoke at me. I tried to relax. The *maestro* opened up the cloth pouch and fished out a skull. It had such long, threatening fangs at the front. I recognised it as a jaguar's skull. Sucking on his pipe a second time, Ramón blew down onto it. I watched as the swirls of grey smoke swept over the bone, before diffusing into the night.

Then, wiping his mouth with his hand, Ramón dipped the tin mess mug into the *ayahuasca*. He stirred the liquid with the cup, filling it almost to the top. I swallowed hard. The shaman put the mug to his lips and, taking small sips, drank the liquid. He leaned back, closing his eyes for a moment, breathing in through his nose. Stirring the cup in the brew a second time, he filled it again. I watched him in the dimness. With the brilliant macaw feather *corona* wrapped around his head, his face painted red with *achiote*, and the jaguar skull at his ankles, he made for a fearful sight.

He looked across at me, and then tipped a little of the dark liquid from the cup, back into the gourd.

'This *ayahuasca* is special,' he said softly. 'I have made it with *toé*, *datura*. *Volarás muy lejos*, you will fly far.'

'But *maestro*,' I faltered, '*datura* will kill me. It is too strong.'

'I told you,' he replied, 'when you take *ayahuasca*, you die.'

He handed me the cup. I drank it in sips, as he had done. It tasted bitter, like the sap of a tree. Although not pleasant, it was bearable. As the last drops of *ayahuasca* made their way down into my stomach, the shaman blew out the candles. There was no light now, only the glow of his pipe when he inhaled.

Taking up the *chacapa*, he rattled it; at the same time breaking into a soft whirring chant. The tone was like an old gramophone player stuck on a single note. I knew it took time for the *ayahuasca* to take effect. At first I tried to keep up with the chemistry of the reaction. The harmaline would be inhibiting the monoamine-oxidase, I thought, allowing the hallucinogens to enter my blood. The illusions would begin shortly.

I took a series of deep breaths, relaxing my shoulders and arms, leaning backwards. Then I focused on the sound of the leaf-rattle and the smell of the *mapacho* smoke. My senses were heightened. I could hear the sound of Ramón's youngest child snoring at the far end of the *maloca*. The sound was almost deafening.

A few more minutes drifted by. I tried to think of the chemistry again. But I was no longer alert. The base of my spine felt warm, as if a hand was pressing on it. I could not focus my mind now, and I was losing a sense of space. A few more minutes passed, filled with the hum of the shaman's chant, the smoke, and the rustle of dried leaves. With every second I became more disorientated. My eyes had adjusted to the darkness. I gazed up at the eaves of the thatch, which seemed bowed inwards and cruelly distorted. So I peered out from the long-house, up at the stars. They were bright; and they were constant. I thanked the stars for being there.

Then the *ayahuasca* took effect.

My stomach was signalling to my mind. I was about to be violently sick. I had been poisoned and had to get out of the long-house.

Scrambling on my hands and knees, I crawled haplessly to the ladder. I was beginning to panic. My chest muscles were tense with fear. I could no longer trust my eyes. What they showed me was a distorted mess of colours and shapes. I closed them, feeling my way down the tree trunk ladder.

My bare feet were now treading in the mud. Rejoicing that I was on the ground I staggered, crawling, stumbling, into the undergrowth. Poison was in my blood. It was killing me. I was dying. The *ayahuasca* had tricked me. Fear took over. My chest sucked in air and I retched. I retched like I have never retched before. A flood of liquid spewed from my mouth. Panting hard, I reassured myself. The *ayahuasca* had been a mistake, I told myself. As soon as it was light I would hurry away from Ramón and the jungle. Within a few days I'd be back in a big city.

The reassurances did nothing to stop the reaction. I retched again, my stomach twisting itself in knots to purge the hideous brew. As I retched, my mind warned of more purging. This time from the rear end. In the nick of time I ripped down my shorts, just as my bowels opened.

Crouching there in the undergrowth of a Shuar village, unable to control my alimentary canal, I felt that this must be as bad as life can get. As I vomited, I crapped. And, as I crapped I vomited. All the while the undergrowth's night-life was wondering what was going on. Frogs were jumping up, touching my buttocks with their heads. Moths and other winged insects were impaling themselves on the flow of faeces.

Yet, while in the undergrowth, I knew I was safe. There may have been frogs and moths, but I could lie low there and regroup. I coaxed myself to relax and, when the worst of the purging was over, I crawled back through the mud and up the ladder.

Ramón's chanting hadn't waned. The rustling of his *chacapa* and the low platform of his voice dispersed. I took my place again, cross-legged on the hard bamboo floor. Soon after, a second bout of purging overcame me. Scurrying fitfully across the floor, down the ladder and through the mud, I found sanctuary back with the frogs. I glanced up at the stars, drunk and off-balance, questioning how they could allow such a predicament.

Back on the bamboo floor, as Ramón's smoke enveloped me, I sensed the *ayahuasca* moving on to the next phase. The hallucinations had begun. I leaned back, my eyes closed, my lungs breathing the dastardly *mapacho* smoke. It began with my arms sensing warmth, as the base of my spine had done. I questioned how anyone could take *ayahuasca* for pleasure. As I lay there, wondering, my body changed.

My shoulder sockets were growing warmer, as my arms evolved. They transformed from being feeble, feckless limbs. The bones altered first. I could see them. I watched astounded, as they grew more delicate, shedding themselves of my sunburnt skin. After the bones, came the muscles – colossal ones, like those of a body builder. Only then, when my arms were fleshed with tremendous arteries and veins, did the final covering emerge – feathers. White, fluffy feathers.

I might have panicked, but the shaman's chanting gave a framework to the experience. His song was mournful, like the dirge at a funeral. Appropriate, for I was dead. I could not distinguish the words, the individual sounds. But, despite this, they made perfect sense. The incantations were beyond a language. They were protecting me … comforting, teaching. I breathed in the sound, inhaling it until my diaphragm was taut.

The song was speaking to me in a language without a voice. It was ordering me to thrust my wings outwards, to soar up, high into the air. I called back that I did not know how to fly. The sound of the *chacapa* touched my wings and dragged them up on a cushion of air. I laughed maniacally. I was flying. My wings moved with unequalled ease. There was none of the frantic, feverish motion of a man emulating a bird in flight.

This flight was natural, an obvious sensation. Glancing down, I saw the desert far below. I saw *el colibri*, the hummingbird. I was at Nazca. Circling round the symbols on that plain I understood the stupidity of the Western mind. *Ayahuasca* was the key which decoded the etchings, just as *datura* explained the witches' flight. Without one, the other had no meaning.

I flew on, guided by the *chacapa*'s sound, soothed by a spray of saliva from the shaman's lips. The colours were bright – purples and blues, yellows and pinks. I was on the far side of a magnificent wall, flying in a no man's land of illusion. I felt the rush of air on my face, and learned to control my wings by tilting their edges up and down. Ramón was with me. He said this was no illusion, but was the real world. We had died and come to life. I was alive for the first time. I was meant to fly, to be a part of the air. I sensed the shaman's energy, the force of his knowledge. I could not see him, but I knew he was there. I was Icarus and he Daedalus. But our wings were not made of wax and feathers. They were living. We were birds, yet we were men; we were men, but birds.

*

We flew for many hours. I do not remember when the journey ended, or the moment I awoke. Sunlight streamed through the morning rain. I strained to open my eyes, retched and rolled onto my back. The *maloca*'s chonta palm floor was as hard as quartz. At my sides, my arms ached, as if they had been flayed with a whip. I roused the fingers of my left hand. They were grasping something. Still lying on my back, I raised the hand to my face. In its grip was a long feather. Three triangular notches were missing from the leading edge. It had been dipped in blood.

Appendix 1

AMAZONIAN FLORA-BASED HALLUCINOGENS

Few native medicinal preparations have caught the West's imagination so strongly as *ayahuasca*. The deluge of recent publications on the use of this mysterious hallucinogenic decoction, reflects its unique role in an Amazonian shaman's arsenal. Traditional healers revere the *Banisteriopsis caapi* vine for its ability to transport them to another spiritual dimension. They brew it up with a mixture of leaves from other plants, using it to provide answers to questions and to effect cures. The Western preoccupation with *ayahuasca* is derived less from its curative capacity, and more from its extraordinary pharmacological formula.

The *Banisteriopsis caapi* vine is not itself a hallucinogen. Rather, it is a matrix which allows hallucinogens and other compounds to be absorbed by the body. The active ingredient contained beneath the vine's woody surface is harmaline. It's not dissimilar to mescaline, the active ingredient in the peyote cactus, the psilocybe mushroom and LSD. The harmaline alkaloid is a monoamine oxidase (MAO) inhibitor. Essentially, this means that it stops the digestive tract from screening out a range of toxic chemicals and, as a result, allows the hallucinogens to enter the body.

For the anthropological community, the main question regarding *ayahuasca* is how a supposedly primitive people could have ever deciphered the harmaline alkaloid. The range of admixtures added to the *ayahuasca* brew varies enormously in the Upper Amazon. Most contain tryptamine derivatives, such as DMT. The number of admixtures implies that considerable experimentation must have taken place throughout history.

Western chemists are interested in the possible uses for *ayahuasca* in formulating consumer drugs. A number of *ayahuasca* analogues have been prepared in the laboratory, most of which are free from the severe side-effects existent in the majority of *ayahuasca* brews. They contain DMT or similar alkaloid, together with an MAO-inhibitor, such as harmaline. One popular analogue is *pharmahuasca*. Other pharmaceutical corporations are attempting to take control of *Banisteriopsis caapi* itself. On 17 June 1986, a patent was granted to Loren S Miller of Palo Alto, California, for *Banisteriopsis caapi*. The patent's citation, which alludes to Loren as the 'inventor', notes that the plant is a 'new and distinct *Banisteriopsis caapi* plant named *Da Vine* which is particularly characterised by the rose color of its flower petals which fade with age to a near white, and its medicinal properties'.

Generally speaking, *ayahuasca* is a shamanic concoction used in the Upper Amazon – encompassing jungle regions of Peru, Colombia, western Brazil and northern Bolivia. More than 22 species are known, the two most common being *Banisteriopsis caapi* and *Banisteriopsis inebrians*. In addition, species have been found to occur in south-eastern parts of the United States, as well as in Mexico. The vine is usually cultivated, although rarely grown in the vicinity of residential dwellings. It is customarily boiled to form a tea-like drink with a variety of admixtures. The vine can also be chewed by itself. But adding a variety of other leaves is thought to make the decoction more potent, and to bring on hallucinations.

Through my research, I have found myself wondering whether the Spanish chroniclers, or their assistants, might have tried *ayahuasca*. I think it's more likely that a general devolution and mis-translation took place, occurring over centuries. Their research-gathering process must have led to gross inaccuracies, especially with the endless rewritten drafts and so forth. Perhaps an informant had told the chroniclers' assistants that there existed people who could actually fly, just as I was told by the shaman Alberto that Ramón could fly through the air. The chroniclers, like me, may well have not believed the claim. To the informant there could have been little or no difference between true and allegorical flight. After all, historically, flight meant different things to different people.

Ayahuasca is one of the best known hallucinogenic compounds used by shamans in the New World. It is, without doubt, one of the strongest and easiest ways to embark on a spiritual journey. Plotkin

(1993) has made note of the 'giant leap' between chewing an individual leaf, and mixing it with one or more leaves to alter the specific effect. The scope for a shaman to manipulate the range of visions, by altering the combination of admixtures, is another reason for its popularity. Visions depend on the chemicals present in the *ayahuasca*. Common admixtures include *chacruna* (*Psychotria viridis*); Lantana flowers (*Lantana camara*), *bobinsana*, and tobacco.

Some people experience bright colours and frequently gain a strong sensation of flight or levitation. Many of the hallucinogenic sensations incorporate a sense of the mind being detached from the body. Some see wild creatures, or sense themselves transforming into a particular animal. Others see places or people they are acquainted with at a great distance; others see their own death, or are taken back in time. Some users have mentioned seeing places or people which they have not encountered before, but which do exist. After viewing a place, or 'meeting a person in their vision', they encounter it for real soon after. We must, of course, remain sceptical with regard to such assertions.

Manuel Villvicencio (1858), the Ecuadorian geographer, was the first 'outsider' to study *ayahuasca* and to publish a report on it. He speaks of the ability to give the sensation of flight, of having been 'lifted into the air', saying, 'I've experienced dizziness, then an aerial journey in which I recall perceiving the most gorgeous views, great cities, lofty towers, beautiful parks, and other extremely attractive objects.' Harner (1973) writes of the Conibo-Shipo Indians of Peru's Ucayali River, who take *ayahuasca* before turning into a bird and flying away with the intention of killing a victim. Before committing the murder they return to human form. Harner himself wrote of meeting 'bird-headed' people when under the influence of *ayahuasca*.

The Chilean psychologist Claudio Naranjo conducted exhaustive trials with *ayahuasca*. The speed of the flight in his studies seems important. A third of the patients reported the sensation of flight and soaring. One man said he had the sensation of growing wings; and instead of fear, he sensed the freedom which goes with flight. He was no longer 'imprisoned to the ground'.

The English botanist Richard Spruce was, like Villvicencio, one of the first scholars to study and identify *Banisteriopsis caapi*. His important two volume work, *Notes of a Botanist on the Amazon and the Andes* (edited by Alfred Russel Wallace and not published until 1908), includes Spruce's initial report on *ayahuasca*, written for Geographical Magazine in 1853. He explained how a cold infusion was made, saying, 'the taste is bitter and disagreeable'. He also remarked that just two minutes or less after taking the brew the 'effects begin to be apparent. The Indian turns deadly pale, trembles in every limb, and horror is in his aspect'. This speed seems implausible. Perhaps Spruce had been witnessing *ayahuasca* mixed with *datura* or another strong admixture, which may have brought on such fast effects.

Spruce goes on to explain how he guzzled down half a dose of *caapi*, when the chief eagerly sent over a large calabash of *caxiri* (madiocca beer, similar to *masato*) of which he took a copious draught: 'as I knew the mode of its preparation, it was gulped down with secret loathing.' Then immediately after this 'a cigar two feet long and as thick as a wrist' was given to him, a confirmed non-smoker. Spruce never completed the *ayahuasca* ceremony though, because he had only taken half a dose. He says that, in May 1857, he reached the 'great forest of Canelos, at the foot of the volcano Coptopaxi', where he saw *caapi* again.

Spruce admitted that 'I regret being unable to tell what is the peculiar narcotic principle that produces such extraordinary effects. Opium and hemp are its most obvious analogues, but *caapi* would seem to operate on the nervous system far more rapidly and violently than either.'

Ayahuasca is true to the ancient systems of shamanic healing, in that one preparation can treat virtually every ailment. In many cases, the *ayahuasquero* will take the *ayahuasca* himself, when searching in the other world for a solution to the patient's problem. Illness is not seen merely as the result of a medical disease, but it is the result of a curse or some supernatural affliction.

Dobkin de Rios (1972) shows surprise that traditional societies use *ayahuasca* or other hallucinogens for a wide range of situations (eg for healing, religious practices, black and white magic, pleasure and initiation). In my view, there are no boundaries between magic, illness and other parts of community life: all these areas are one and the same in a primitive society.

Some anthropologists have noted the limiting of *ayahuasca* rites to the male members of society. One report states: 'ego [ie *ayahuasca*] is the only mind enhancing concoction that has been absolutely taboo on occasion for women. When a trumpet signalled the start of the puberty rites for the Yurupari, female members of the tribe fled into the jungle to avoid a death penalty for their seeing the ceremony or even the drink. In other regions it was thought that if a woman set eyes on prepared *caapi*, it would be rendered 'ineffective'. My own experiences are quite the opposite of this. Women know all about the preparation and partake freely. The prohibition may have surrounded male puberty rites rather than the brew.

The use of *ayahuasca* in cities and urban areas across Latin America is increasing rapidly. A number of religious sects have incorporated the hallucinogen into their systems of belief. Many of these were established initially in Brazil. The most recognised is currently the Santo Daime faith; others are the Barquinia and Hoasca religions. As with Santo Daime, other *ayahuasca* faiths have developed a myth which explains how they came to understand the hallucinogenic brew.

In using *ayahuasca*, the shaman will tend to say that the vine's spirit draws their attention to its medicinal and healing uses. I have been told that the trees whispered, telling the *curandero* how to prepare the drink. *Ayahuasqueros* believe that it's not the plant which actually heals, but the spirit of the plant. Through his songs, known as *icaros*, the shaman invokes the spirit of the vine, requesting that it heal or provide a solution.

Although *Banisteriopsis caapi* is a plant of the New World, it has been likened to Syrian rue (*Peganum harmala*), which grows throughout western Asia. Known for millennia for its powers, its seeds also contain harmaline. There is evidence that DMT-rich plant admixtures were added to the Syrian rue brews, in antiquity, to bring on the hallucinogenic effects.

Rudgley (1998) notes that Syrian rue's seeds, which produce a rich red dye, may have been used to dye carpets in Persia. He wonders whether the geometric designs of the carpets might have been inspired by the hallucinogenic content of Syrian rue (harmine and harmaline). He also points to the legends of 'flying carpets', questioning whether the link can be taken further. Textile designs have undoubtedly been inspired in various cultures by hallucinogens. The ecstatic representations of shamans and Birdmen in the Paracas and Nazcan textiles are one example of this. Andrew Sherratt (1995) has also queried whether the patterns of central Asian carpets and the idea of flying carpets might have derived from hallucinatory visions.

There is nothing new about hallucinogenic preparations. *Aya-huasca* is one of many which has been employed for millennia. Devereux (1997) talks of the discovery of a cave in northern Iraq, in 1975, containing a Neanderthal skeleton. Along with the 60,000 year old remains were 'clusters of pollen from 8 kinds of flowering plants'. At first they were thought to be funeral offerings, but later it was realised that they – eg ephedra – were known nerve stimulants and had been used in herbal curing in the region millennia before. Both Hofmann and Schultes have discussed the role of hallucinogens in the ancient Old World, from a cultural point of view. Despite this, the number of known Old World hallucinogens is limited when compared to those in the New World.

Schultes (1992) says that there are about 150 species of plant hallucinogens. 130 of them are located in the New World, especially in its tropical region. Some experts contend that they have played a key role in the development of New World religious beliefs.

Like the Incas, the Aztecs made use of numerous hallucinogenic plants. Not all provided visions. For example, the shrub Sinicuichi (*Heimia salicifolia*) gives intense auditory hallucinations. Sounds are distorted or seem far away. The plant has also been credited with supernatural powers. The Sinicuichi bird appeared on the Aztec statue depicting Xochipilli, the Prince of flowers.

The Aztecs were also known to use a certain 'round pellet' to achieve states of ecstasy. They called it *Ololiuhqui*, and attributed to it divine status. It was addressed with songs and the seeds were put on altars, and made into drinks. Hallucinations and delirium followed. The Spanish tried to prohibit the use of the plant, and largely succeeded in doing so. Schultes identified the seeds as Morning Glory (the species *Rivea corymbosa*). They have been found to contain a form of LSD.

Psychedelic mushrooms were also used by the Aztecs. *Encyclopaedia Britannica* records that the Spanish priest-historian Bernardino de Sahagun wrote of his disapproval of the cultic use of mushrooms in Mexico in the 16th century. There were reports of widespread use of hallucinogenic mushrooms during the coronation of the Aztec Emperor Montezuma in 1502.

Psychoactive snuff was thought to be the first native American hallucinogen discovered by the Spanish. Snuff has been found in 1200 year old mummy bundles in the New World. Virola snuff is made from the inner bark of various species of the *virola* tree, in the western Amazon. Its snuff contains trypamines, and is similar to nutmeg. The bark is stripped off the tree trunk in the early morning. (The resin exuded from the inner surface of the bark can be used as an arrow poison.) The exudate is a resin which darkens when exposed to the air, becoming reddish-brown. The bark is cut into slivers and is boiled for an hour or more, creating a paste. Some tribes ingest the *virola* orally, but most take it as snuff.

The fly agaric mushroom (*Amanita muscaria*), with its bright red cap, is another strong hallucinogen. It has been used by the nomads of Siberia for millennia, and leads to potent hallucinogens, as well as increasing strength and endurance. It may be the basis of the mysterious beverage *Soma*, drunk in antiquity in south Asia. Others think it may be the secret of the *Hoama* elixir of the Zoroastrians. Fly agaric is thought by some scientists to be the answer to the petroglyphs on the north-east coast of Siberia, found in the 1960s. They show humans and 'human-mushroom' figures with mushrooms growing out of their heads. Lapps in Scandinavia's Arctic Circle have traditionally used hallucinogenic mushrooms as well.

One remarkable quality is that the active ingredient in fly agaric passes through the bladder into the urine. Plotkin (1993) says that in 4000 BC the Aryans in southern Iran developed a ritualist fraternity based on the hallucinogen. They believed, as some Siberian peoples still do, that it would transport their souls into another realm. Two thousand years on, when the Aryans' descendants invaded northern India, they took the mushrooms with them. Once again the mushroom cult came to prominence and burgeoned in India. Various ancient Hindu texts, such as the Rigveda, give mention to the hallucinogenic properties of fly agaric.

For as long as they have been known, the West's establishment has persecuted the use of mind altering flora. Witches in Europe were using various solanaceous plant-hallucinogens like *datura* in the 16th and 17th centuries. Just as the Spanish Conquistadors persecuted the Incas and native peoples for their plant hallucinogen uses, the European Christians (Spaniards included) persecuted the medieval witches in Europe and in North America, because these people had visions which (a) couldn't be explained and (b) were at odds with Christian dogma.

We tend to overlook the extraordinary knowledge and experience that ancient society relied on. Much of this must have been deduced through experiences with hallucinogenic flora. Their encounters, which are so distinctly out of the ordinary, are absorbed into their lore and myth, often with the catalyst – the psychotropic substance – being lost in the process. Hallucinatory substances may well have contributed to the epic and fantastic tales extant in religious and cultural texts.

Ethnobotanists have suggested that the reason jungle plants have had to develop such an astonishing array of defences from fauna, is that they exist in highly threatening environments. Predators come in all forms: fungi, mammals, insects and viral diseases. Thousands of years of evolution has provided plants with extraordinary characteristics, none more so than the hallucinatory flora.

With the destruction of the rain-forests and the even speedier obliteration of tribal plant knowledge (a result of rampant westernisation, missionary activity and so forth), the race to learn ancient medications is being lost. A few companies, such as Shaman Pharmaceuticals, are actively attempting to learn from indigenous peoples about the plants in their societies, and their medicinal uses. One of the problems they face is that, since the early 1980s, there has been a decrease in fieldwork and an increase in plant medicines synthesised in the lab', as scientists learn to control genes etc. Shaman Pharmaceuticals sends teams of trained ethnobotanists into the jungle to work with and learn from indigenous shamans. They compensate indigenous groups who teach them about medicinal plants. The problem is time: plant cures take years, even decades, to get to the market.

One ethnobotanist, Mark Plotkin (1993), has developed a small-scale solution, called the 'Shaman's Apprentice Program'. His notes, which are based on tribal knowledge, are translated back into the tribal language and are studied by a young member of the tribe. Once written down, they are less likely to be lost, despite the fact that the plants themselves are liable to be made extinct if things continue as they are.

Appendix 2

THE SHUAR

Dozens of tribal societies worldwide have historically taken trophy heads. But the curious practice of shrinking heads has set the Shuar apart from other tribes. No other known peoples have treated their trophy heads in this way, with the possible exception of the ancient Nazcan, and other coastal civilisations of the Atacama. As discussed in the text, the reasoning for making *tsantsas* was clear. It was a means of controlling the *musiak*, the avenging soul. The *tsantsa* itself had no intrinsic value and was discarded once made and honoured, that is, until western souvenir hunters came looking for them.

The ability to shrink human heads has brought the Shuar widespread attention. While being captivated by the *tsantsa*-making technique, the outside world has often classified the Shuar as a barbaric people. From the earliest interaction with the tribe, Western observers dubbed them *Jivaro*, their own word for 'savage'.

There is no doubt that, until the post-war era, the tribe lived by an ancient tradition of warfare and *tsantsa* raids. But despite their eagerness to take heads, the Shuar were historically a people with a strong sense of ethics and a well-developed social framework. The ancient ways of the tribal society have almost entirely come to an end in the last handful of years. Small-scale petroleum projects in the deep jungle are one reason for this. But the overbearing responsibility must be assumed by a variety of missionary groups who have sought to cast the Shuar into the modern world, and to save their souls.

Landing in remote jungle enclaves, in flying-boats, the missionaries have wrought change on an unknown scale. Their intentions may be worthy, but they have led to the stripping away of a distinct tribal identity. Like a house of playing cards, a traditional Shuar community was extraordinarily fragile. Small changes affected the entire unit, causing it to collapse.

As mentioned earlier, the missionaries seem to have steered clear of prohibiting or condemning the use of *ayahuasca*. This point gives hope in the face of absolute uncertainty. With the continued use of *ayahuasca*, the shamanic tradition – although diminished in strength – can remain in place. The continuing existence of shamans ensures that, for the time being at least, the ancient knowledge of medicinal plants is able to survive.

Further weakening of the community occurred in the early years of the 20th century. The Shuar peoples have been devastated by the white man's introduction of Old World diseases, like whooping cough, measles, tuberculosis, venereal diseases such as gonhorrea, and so forth. Malaria, generally classified as an Old World affliction, has decimated Shuar numbers since the 16th century. In addition, the common cold has culled the Shuar's numbers. The only positive factor in terms of population, is that the cessation of *tsantsa* raids has led to a reduction of death through warfare.

It is fortunate that a range of scholarly ethnographic studies were made of the tribe before the curse of change ravaged the Shuar lands. By far the best and most accurate published study is Michael Harner's (1972). Many of the other works fell victim to the pitfalls of poor ethnographic research. However fascinating one finds the *tsantsa* tradition to be, it is a shame this one facet of Shuar life has been grasped by western observers virtually to the exclusion of all else.

Thankfully, the Shuar's use of *ayahuasca* allows them to continue with their central belief: that the world is an illusion, and that only by taking the hallucinogen can they enter the *real* world. One wonders how this fundamental philosophy would change if *Banisteriopsis caapi* was prohibited by missionary groups in the region.

Until the 19th century, when explorers came searching for the head shrinking people, the tribe had been largely left alone since the initial Spanish incursions into the region. The Spanish, of course, had no interest in *tsantsas* or the Shuar. They were concerned only with finding gold. The tribe's partial enslavement and subsequent rebellion, mentioned in the text, occurred in 1599. The size of the Spanish casualties may have been (in my opinion) grossly exaggerated. But, without doubt, the Shuar insurrection dissuaded the Spanish from exploring the area further. Harner (1972) notes that perhaps no other tribal people on the Latin continent has had so much written about them, with so little still known of them.

In traditional Shuar society every man, woman and child, was on constant guard, watching for raiding parties. The *tsantsa* raids were their *raison d'être*. They proved a warrior's bravery and the community's superiority. Feuding kept the tribe strong and alert. Like animals in the wild, those who were incapable of keeping up, were picked off.

A visitor was always in fear of being butchered. For this reason, guests would never enter another's *maloca*, without being expressly invited to do so. And, even then, they would never travel to an acquaintance's abode unarmed. A bowl of *masato* might be pushed aside, until the hostess – the woman who had prepared it – had taken a sip.

During the night the house would be barricaded against attack. Anyone wishing to defecate or urinate would do so within the house, and remove their waste in the morning. After reading the standard works on traditional Shuar society, I was surprised to see for myself the openness of the houses. There are no barricades now, nor are there watch-towers. People leave their *malocas* at night and wander freely through the village.

These days, when a man dies, he is buried in a cemetery area at the edge of the village. Traditionally the Shuar would bury dead members of the family (especially the head male) under the dirt floor of the house. In some cases, the *maloca* was then abandoned out of respect. The dead man was buried in a shallow grave, not more than about two and a half feet from the surface. If married, his widow would cut her hair short as a sign of mourning.

In cases where the house was to be abandoned because of its owner's death, the body may have actually been interred in the house at ground level (the Kafirs of Nuristan had a similar tradition of above ground burials). The body would be inhumed in a *kanu* (from which we derive our word 'canoe'), a balsa wood coffin made from a hollowed-out log, erected on a scaffolding. Some of the *tsantsas* he had made during his lifetime may have been buried with the warrior. These would be placed in the small of his back. Also buried with him would be clothing, weapons and other artefacts and his monkey skin travelling bag. The tradition is almost identical to the Nazcan and Paracas funeral techniques, discussed in the text.

Many of the Shuar's thatched *malocas* that I encountered were much like any other Upper Amazonian houses. The traditional oval design has been largely forsaken for a simpler open-sided square house. But *malocas* are still built on high ground, near a river, surrounded by a garden area. They tend now to face inward to a football field. Houses are of course communal, with one area belonging to the women, and one to the husband. With less polygamy (which is frowned on by missionaries) there is more commonly only one wife, and so the house is less often subdivided along gender lines.

In the past, in addition to barricades, there was frequently a secret passage leading to the jungle, for escape in times of attack. Houses were routinely abandoned after about ten years; partly because the house would be rotting by then, and partly because the gardens would be overworked, and the hunting grounds depleted. With more permanent missionary-built schools, water tanks, churches and other communal buildings, villages are now less likely to be abandoned.

Until head-taking feuds were eliminated, houses had to be large enough to hold the *tsantsa* feast. Garden areas, growing *yuka* and other vegetables would also have to be big enough to grow sufficient food for the feasts.

The Shuar did not wage war to gain territory. Feuding was regarded as a means of taking as many heads as possible, or to capture women. Revenge would help to select the village targeted which, in all likelihood, would have made an attack of their own previously. A *kakaram*, a great warrior, would usually lead a warring party. To be considered a *kakaram* the man must have taken at least three or four heads. Before the raid, spies would be sent to stake out the enemy village. Men were recruited for the attack: usually about thirty took part. One problem of a warring party was that some of its warriors would invariably be the enemies of others. So parties were loosely arranged into pairs, mutual friends covering each other's backs.

Warring groups would first combine forces to attack one or two houses in the enemy village, often setting the thatch alight to drive the occupants out. The enemy were butchered regardless of age or sex. If a man snatched a girl as a wife, she may well have been butchered en route home by the rest of the group, in order to make another *tsantsa*.

The world of the Shuar was based, as we have seen, on the premise that apparent reality is illusion. The importance of the soul to this premise cannot be over-emphasised. Only by understanding this complex idea, can one gain a rudimentary grasp of the working of traditional Shuar society. The belief was founded on the notion that one could enter the supernatural world by using *ayahuasca*, and acquire a soul there.

Three distinct types of soul could be acquired, known accordingly as *arutam*, *musiak* and *nekas wakani*. The soul depended on the person and his circumstance. Once someone had attained a single soul, he was immune to all murderous forces, such as sorcery, assassination and poisoning. However, he wasn't immune to the scourge of contagious disease brought by the white man. But when he had acquired two souls he would be immune to even these Old World afflictions.

Nothing, traditionally, was so important to a Shuar man as acquiring an *arutam* soul. It ensured his survival. It was not so important for a woman, largely because females were not exposed to such danger during their lives. They did not take part in *tsantsa* raids. Harner (1972) asserts that an *arutam* soul was sought when a son was as young as six years. The child was taken by his father to a waterfall (considered as a sacred place), where he paced up and down, in the hope of attracting an *arutam* soul. The soul was thought to exist in the spray at the base of the waterfall. If, after several days the boy had not seen an *arutam* soul, he was given *datura*, *Brugmansia arborea*, juice. The father would take *datura* as well as giving it to his son to drink.

In the dream which followed, the seeker would behold a pair of creatures, two giant anacondas, jaguars or even a pair of fire-balls. Taking all his courage, he had to go up and touch one of the creatures. Once he had done this they would explode and disappear. He spent the first night on the river-bank. While sleeping there, the *arutam* soul would come to him as an old ancestor warrior. The soul entered the child and resided in his chest. Imbued with great self-confidence, the *arutam* soul would give him inner strength.

The *musiak* (the avenging soul) could only be acquired by someone already possessing an *arutam* soul. The *musiak* was only manifested when the possessor of an *arutam* soul was slain. The avenging soul seeped out of the dead warrior's mouth, and set about avenging his death; ie killing the person who killed him. The Shuar believed that as the head-hunting expedition retreated, the slaughtered enemies' souls hovered alongside the party. The only way to dispose of them, to deactivate them, was to turn them into *tsantsas*. This forced the avenging *musiaks* or souls into the shrunken heads.

One of the processes in making a *tsantsa* was to rub charcoal into the skin so as to blind the avenging soul. When the shrinking itself was concluded, three consecutive *tsantsa* feasts were held: at the end of which the *musiak* spirit would be expelled from the *tsantsa* and sent on its way.

In the confusion of a *tsantsa* raid, the warriors would have to hurry to remove heads as carefully as they could. With a knife, the victim's skin was peeled back from the upper part of the chest, the shoulders and the back. Then the head was chopped as far down the neck as possible, close to the collar-bone, traditionally using a stone-edged axe. The warrior would remove his own headband and thread it through the neck and out of the mouth, making it easier to carry, slung over the shoulder. Heads had to be decapitated with great speed, as the *tsantsa* party was usually under attack at the time.

Once they were a distance from the village, the assassins would cut the skin away from the bone and throw the skull into a river, a gift for *pani*, the anaconda. The skin was boiled in plain water. Within half an hour it was removed. Any more time than that and the hair began to fall out. The skin had already shrunk by about half. It was allowed to cool and dry. Then it was turned inside out, and any flesh on the inner edges was cut away. After this, the fold of skin was turned the right way again, and the slit in the back was sewn up with string made from vine. The lips were sealed with pins made from chonta palm, or vine.

Small stones (no more than about two inches wide) were heated in a fire and, one at a time, they were rolled around the sack-like envelope of the *tsantsa*. Gradually it would reduce in size. When too small for stones, sand was heated and put inside. The *tsantsa* may have been wrapped in a large leaf to insulate the heat, keeping it in.

The party of assassins would pack up the heads after about an hour of hot-sand treatment, and run off into the jungle towards their village. Each day they would stop for three or four hours to work on the *tsantsas*. It was in their interest to complete the first stages, because of fears that the *musiaks* would attack them.

A machete blade was heated and pressed against the lips to dry them. Then the facial skin was repeatedly rubbed with balsa-wood charcoal. Sometimes a large red seed was placed beneath the eyelids, filling the hole, preventing the *musiak* from seeing. Between four and six days of treatment were needed for the basic *tsantsa* to be completed, at which time it was about the size of a man's fist. A hole was made at the top of the head, and a string was tied to it, so that the warrior could wear it around his neck at the tsantsa feast.

The feasts were huge occasions. To honour a *tsantsa* correctly, three separate feasts for the entire village would be held. In order that there would be sufficient food and drink for the celebration, crops of *yuka* were planted once the raiding party had returned. The first *tsantsa* feast may not have taken place until a year after the raid. Pigs would be raised, and the host may have even built a special new house for the occasion.

Several hunters would go out into the jungle to kill game. The Shuar would use unripe bananas to keep time. They and the guests would be given an unripe banana from the same stalk. Once it was ripe, they knew it was time to get to the feast. The celebrations would each last for as much as five days, the third feast being the longest. Up to about 150 guests would turn up. Only after the third banquet were the chonta palm pins removed from the *tsantsa*, and replaced with the long, intertwined cotton strings.

I felt fortunate to learn the ancient rituals first-hand from Enrique, the Shuar chief at San Jose village. He must be one of the last to remember the full spectrum of lore, ritual and hunting techniques.

Hadingham (1987) cites a report from 1527 by Miguel de Estete, who accompanied Pizarro on his third voyage. He described head shrinking on an island off the coast of Ecuador, and at first assumed that the heads were from a tribe of dwarfs on the island. This substantiates the probability that head shrinking was once practised throughout the Peruvian coastal area. Nazca pots and textiles are well known for their depictions of trophy heads. A *tsantsa* taken from a tomb at Pisco was supposedly presented to Queen Victoria's consort Prince Albert in the 19th century.

Missionary activity may have brought rampant change, but one aspect of Shuar life which appears to have altered little is a belief in witchcraft. The belief strengthens the need for a shaman. The Shuar still apparently believe that witchcraft is the source of almost all misfortune, including illness and death. Their society appears to still possess two distinct types of shaman – those who bewitch and those who cure. All shamans are either one or the other.

All Shuar shamans have *tsentak*, spirit helpers, who abide by their instructions. Bewitching shamans can enlist the help of the *wakani* spirit bird, as we have seen. The shaman calls these birds and he blows on them. They fly to the victim's house and circle, terrifying him. Death from madness can follow. Of course, if a member of society drops dead in accidental circumstances, it may be inferred that he died as a result of a shaman's magic.

Just as there was an unwavering faith in the soul, the Shuar traditionally believed in jungle spirits. For example *Yacumama*, the mother spirit of the river, was thought to exact revenge on any woman in menstruation who paddled across her. *Yacumama* could send a dolphin to upturn her boat. The spirit was only warded away if the woman wore a clove of garlic around her neck or arm. The river spirit was omnipresent. She could take many forms, including that of a Christian European. Her victims were carried to the bottom of a river, unable to ever escape from this realm: an enormous land populated with strange creatures. A reverse image of our world, it was thought to be upside-down. All the inhabitants had their heads on backwards. The spirit of the river lived in a crystal palace with walls fashioned from mother of pearl. She sat on a turtle throne fashioned from feathers, with one eye closed and the other open, always watching for the crocodile. Beliefs in such spirits of nature appear to continue, even alongside the belief in Christianity.

One aspect of life that has not changed, is the Shuar love of hunting. No longer does a warrior embark on raids for enemies' heads, but hunting for game is as popular now as ever. From the time that a male child can walk, he is encouraged to hunt. The boy would traditionally have been permitted to fire arrows or darts into the corpse of a slain victim, to give him practice.

Peccary and monkey are hunted, prized for their flesh and their skins. The armadillo and agouti are only valued for their meat. Most types of bird – with the exception of carrion-carriers – are hunted, especially parrots, toucans, doves and macaws. Harner (1972) asserts that rabbits and deer are never hunted for their meat. Rabbits are supposedly considered too much like rats; and deer are not hunted for they are regarded as human demons with supernatural powers. The Shuar believed that by eating a deer they may be eating a dead man's soul, which would then enter them. The Shuar hunters whom I met appeared to have no scruples about killing other rabbits or deer.

A 16-gauge shotgun is the ultimate status symbol for a Shuar man. However, the ubiquitous lack of ammunition ensures that blowpipes are still in constant use. Unfortunately, the younger generation are forgetting the skill of blowpipe use, considering the weapons to be old-fashioned.

These days the blowpipes are used mainly for tree-dwelling animals. The Shuar are regarded as great experts with blowpipes and poisoned darts. Most pipes are about seven feet long (those sold to tourists in Iquitos and elsewhere are shorter so they can fit in overhead lockers of jet aeroplanes). They are split down the middle, grooved and bound back together with fibre strips and a natural resinous glue, with a black beeswax coating.

When aged about four boys are given a hollow reed. They learn to blow small darts at insects, such as butterflies. A few years later they are given a miniature blowpipe. The child shoots hummingbirds, and progresses to larger birds. When he's about sixteen he kills his first sloth and would traditionally make a tsantsa from its head.

Women had their own special way of killing. They would poison their victims with a natural toxin, such as ampihuasca, mixing it in the masato they served. In addition to the two poisons mentioned, Shuar hunters also use poisons derived from various species of poison arrow frogs, and are experts in blending toxins. Mumatatchi ants are sometimes cooked over a low heat until they produce a poisonous juice, which is added to ampihuasca.

Most poisonings were traditionally done at tsantsa feasts. The big problem was locating the person responsible for the poisoning. The list of suspects was never a short one: everyone had a secret enemy who, given the right moment, he or she might want to slay. The matter fast became complex, framed by a hierarchy of death. If for example one couldn't kill an adulterer, because he had fled, one could kill his father, brother or cousin. If a relative had been killed by witchcraft, one would go after the perpetrator seen in an ayahuasca vision. This person, of course, was more than certainly innocent, as were the witches burned at the stake during the European witch trials. So, with a little time, it's not hard to see how everyone in such a society would be trying to avenge the death of others!

Glossary

Achiote: Plant whose oily red seeds are used as facial paints by Shuar and other Upper Amazonian peoples.

Agouti: See *Mahasse*.

Agua de florida: Perfumed water, used in shamanic ceremonies and for ritual purification.

Aguardiente: Potent jungle alcohol derived from the sap of the *aguardiente* palm.

Ajinomoto: Brand name of monosodium glutimate powder, popular in Peru.

AK-47: Russian-made Kalashnikov assault rifle.

Algonquin: Native American people of the Ottawa river valley.

Alpaca: Domesticated llama, prized for its wool.

Altiplano: High plateau of southern Peru and northern Boliva.

Amazons: Legendary tribe of warrior women, once thought to reside in the South American jungle.

Ambulantes: Street-sellers, common in Lima and other big cities.

Amigo: Spanish for 'friend'.

Ampihuasca: Jungle vine used as a poison, for hunting fish etc.

Anaconda: Large semi-aquatic species of boa constrictor.

Anamuk: Magical bewitching dart sent to destroy by a bewitching shaman.

Anopheles: Species of malarial mosquito.

Arutam soul: Most important of the three Shuar souls, it is acquired in childhood and protects a warrior from death.

Assagai: Short spear favoured by the Zulu tribe.

Assassin cult: Secret order of murderers once operating in the Middle East, under the effect of hashish.

Atacama Desert: South American desert, ranging from Peru to Chile on the Pacific seaboard.

Atropine: Powerful hallucinogenic alkaloid present in *datura* and other Solanaceous species.

Avatar: Incarnation of a Hindu deity; a holy man.

Ayahuasquero: A shaman skilled in the use of *ayahuasca*.

Ayamara: Native American people of the Peruvian Andes, and their language.

Aztec: Nahuatl-speaking people of Mexico, and their empire.

Azulejos: Blue glazed tiles introduced to Peru by the Portuguese.

Banda: Round hut, common in East Africa.

Banisteriopsis caapi: Vine containing harmaline used in preparing *ayahuasca*.

Banisteriopsis inebrians: Species of liana used for making *ayahuasca*; similar to *Banisteriopsis caapi*.

Barriada: Shanty-town; as found on the outskirts of Lima and other large cities.

Besom: Broom made of twigs, supposedly ridden by witches.

Bobinsana: Admixture sometimes added to *ayahuasca*.

Bora: Native Indian tribe residing close to Iquitos.

Boutu: Local name for the pink Amazonian river dolphin.

Brugmansia: Latin name for *datura*.

Brujo: Spanish for 'witch'.

Caapi: Alternative name for *ayahuasca*.

Caiman: Amazonian species of alligator.

Campesino: Spanish for 'country person'.

Capybara: Largest known rodent, it measures up to four feet and lives in the Amazon region.

Cassava: Edible starchy tuber native to the Americas; used to make flour, porridge, alcohol etc. Also called *yuka* and *manioc*.

Cecropia: Leafy jungle plant which induces drowsiness when eaten by sloths.

Centimo: One hundredth of a Peruvian *Sol*.

Ceviche: Dish of raw fish marinated in lemon juice; popular on the Peruvian coast.

Chacapa: Ritualistic rattle used by Amazonian shamans.

Chacruna: Admixture often added to *ayahuasca*, regarded as important in providing colourful visions (*Psychotria viridis*).

Chagas' disease: Infection carried by the Assassin beetle, causing heart palpitations and death.

Chancay: Pre-Incan civilisation of coastal Peru, famed for its pottery.

Charqui: Beef stew, popular in the Peruvian Andes.

Chicha: Maize-based liquor, popular in Andean communities.

Chigger mite: Six-legged fly which burrows beneath the skin to lay its eggs.

Chonta: Jungle palm, the heart of whose inner stem is regarded as a delicacy.

Chuchuhuasi: Intoxicating jungle liquor made from the *chuchuhuasi* tree.

Chullpa: Ancient funeral tower.

Chumpi: Ornamental woven wool belt, worn by people on Taquile Island, Lake Titicaca.

Cipó d'água: Vine containing fresh water.

Coca de maté: Tea made with coca leaves.

Cochineal: Red dye made from dried cochineal beetles.

Colibri: Spanish for 'hummingbird'; one of the major images at Nazca.

Collectivo: Shared Peruvian taxi.

Corona: Spanish for 'crown'; sometimes referring to Native Indian feathered crowns.

Crir: Ancient Aztec glider.

Cuandero: Healer; one who practises *ayahuasca*.

Curare: Resinous extract of the *Strychnos toxifera* vine, used by Amazonian tribes as a tranquilliser for hunting.

Cuscomys ashaninka: Recently-discovered Andean mammal the size of a domestic cat.

Cuy: Spanish for 'guinea pig'; a popular dish in Andean communities.

Deet: Synthetic insect repellent.

Dendrobates azureus: Indigo-coloured species of poisonous frog, used by native peoples for hunting.

Ekeko: Ancient Ayamara deity whose image is considered to bring good luck.

El Dorado: Mythical land thought to be made of gold.

Estofado: Thick chicken stew, popular in Andean communities.

Fly agaric: Poisonous hallucinogenic mushroom with a bright red cap.

Garimpeiros: Local self-employed gold miners.

Gaseouse: Peruvian word for a soft carbonated drink.

Guaje: Hard-shelled fruit, high in vitamin C, with yellow-orange flesh, popular in Upper Amazon.

Hacienda: Spanish word for a 'property', a villa.

Hardtack: Hard savoury biscuit once popular fare with expeditions.

Harmaline: Alkaloid compound found in *Banisteriopsis caapi*.

Hashish: Narcotic resin collected from the female hemp plant.

Huaquero: Spanish word for 'grave-robber'.

Icaros: Shamanic songs sung during an *ayahuasca* ceremony.

Iguachi: Shuar word for the Devil.

Jaca shoqpi: Andean divinaton technique based on the dissection of a guinea pig.

Jambiyah: Curved Yemeni dagger, traditionally with a handle fashioned of rhino horn.

Jivaro: See *Shuar*.

Kakaram: Shuar warrior.

Kapok: Tropical tree whose seed pods contain a silky fluff traditionally used for mattress stuffing etc.

Macumba: Brazilian religious sect founded on West African tribal beliefs.

Maestro: Master; a traditional healer or shaman.

Mahasse: Medium-sized tropical rodent, popular as food.

Mahicaris: Slang term for 'Devil Worshippers'.

Mal de ojo: Evil Eye; popular superstition brought to the New World by the Spanish.

Maloca: Traditional thatched hut or long-house.

Mandrake: Plant of the Deadly Nightshade family, once used by European witches in flying ointments.

Manguaré: Pair of hollowed logs used as signalling drums over the jungle.

MAO-inhibitor: (Monoamine oxidase) Chemical substance (such as harmaline) which restricts the body's natural ability to filter out specific toxins.

Mapacho: Strong jungle tobacco used in shamanic ceremonies.

Masato: Masticated cassava beverage prepared by Shuar tribe.

Matamata: Species of 'prehistoric' turtle found in the Upper Amazon (*Chelus fimbriatus*).

Maya: Ancient civilisation and their language, who resided in Mexico and Central America.

Mescaline: Hallucinatory alkaloid contained in the peyote cactus.

Mestizo: Person of mixed European and Native American ancestry.

Mololo: Local name for an infusion of Cramp Bank.

Mormodes rolfeanum: Species of jungle orchid thought by some to resemble a bird.

Motocarro: Three-wheeled motorbike taxi, as operated in Iquitos.

Motorista: Man in charge of driving a boat.

Mumatatchi ant: Species of jungle ant which secretes a toxin when disturbed.

Murrel: Oily sardine-like freshwater fish, commonly found in South Asia.

Musiak: Said by the Shuar people to be a warrior's avenging soul.

Naka-naka: Amazonian slang for 'lies'.

Namaste: Traditional Indian greeting.

Nape: Alternative name for *ayahuasca*.

Natema: Shuar name for *ayahuasca*.

Native American Church: Religious organisation founded on the ritual use of hallucinogenic peyote cactus.

Ocelot: Medium-sized wild cat, found in the Amazonian jungle and elsewhere in the Americas.

Paiche a la Loretana: Grilled fillet of piraruca, commonly served with roasted cassava.

Pampa: Extensive flatlands of western Peru, as at Nazca.

Peki-peki: Local name in the Peruvian Amazon for a dugout canoe driven by a crude motor.

Pele: Large balls of cured latex.

Peyote: Cactus-based hallucinogen; used in Native American Church rites.

Phyllobates terribilis: Most toxic species of poison arrow frog; resides in Surinam's jungle.

Pinde: Alternative name for *ayahuasca*.

Piraruca: Large primitive freshwater fish, found in Upper Amazon and prized for its meat.

Pisco: Grape brandy made in the coastal town of Pisco.

Pisco sour: Whipped beverage containing Pisco and egg white.

Pishtao: Mysterious – possibly erroneous – practice of melting human corpses to acquire fat.

Psyilocybe: Mushroom (*Psilocybe mexicana*) from which is derived a hallucinogen called psilocybin.

Punga: Local word for kapok.

Quechua: Ancient Andean language, supposedly predating the Incas.

Quenas: Pan-pipes; popular Andean woodwind instrument.

Quinua: Weed found in the Andes whose seeds are ground and eaten.

Rashed: Flying vehicle thought to be possessed by King Solomon.

Rub' al-Khali: The Empty Quarter of the Arabian Desert.

Ryuku Kempo: Style of martial art, originating in Okinawa.

San Pedro: Andean cactus used as a hallucinogen.

Sanango: Hallucinogenic nerve agent; sometimes taken alone as an infusion, or mixed with *ayahuasca*.

Santo Daime: Religious organisation of Brazilian origin, founded on the ritual use of *ayahuasca*.

Saqqara glider: Model of a supposed glider found in an Egyptian tomb, kept at Cairo Museum.

Selva: Spanish word for 'jungle'.

Sendero Luminoso: Shining Path, Marxist organisation which terrorised Peru from about 1980 until 1992.

Seringueiro: Traditional rubber tappers in Peruvian Amazon.

Shuar: Native tribe residing in the Pastaza region, near the Peruvian-Ecuadorian border. Formerly known as *Jivaro* which means 'savage'.

Siete raices: Amazonian tonic made from seven roots.

Sillar: Volcanic stone light in colour.

Sinicuichi: *Heimia salicifolia*; shrub used as an auditory hallucinogen.

Sirena: Spanish word for 'mermaid'.

Sol: Currency of Peru.

Solanaceae: Family of plants, which includes numerous hallucinogens and the potato.

Soma: Hallucinogenic beverage drunk in South Asia in antiquity.

Spider monkey: Agile South American monkey with slender limbs and long prehensile tail.

Susto: Literally 'fear'; idea that a sharp fright splits one's soul from the body.

Suyos: Agricultural and administrative divisions of Taquile Island.

Syrian rue: Middle Eastern plant containing harmaline.

Takpa: Ominous interruptuion during an Andean shamanic ritual.

Tia: Spanish word for 'aunt'.

Titanus giganticus: Enormous species of beetle with very powerful mandibles, growing up to 20 cm.

Tobacco water: Bitter water flavoured with an infusion of tobacco; used in shamanic ceremonies.

Toé: Shuar word for *datura*.

Totora: Type of reed found at Lake Titicaca, woven into simple boats.

Trachyte: Pale volcanic stone.

Tsantsa: Trophy head taken in a Shuar raid and shrunk to the size of an orange.

Tsentsak: Invisible magical dart regurgitated by a shaman.

Tumi: Sacrificial Incan dagger, sometimes fashioned from gold.

Una de gato: Literally 'claw of the cat'; a potent Amazonian aphrodisiac and healing potion.

Vimana: Mythical flying machine said to have flown in ancient India.

Virola: Hallucinogenic snuff related to nutmeg, taken in the Upper Amazon.

Volador: Aztec ceremony in which Birdmen swoop down around a towering pole, simulating flight.

Vulcanization: Process which makes raw rubber malleable.

Wak'a loom: Traditional collapsible loom found near Lake Titicaca.

Wakani: Spirit helping bird, faithful to a Shuar shaman.

Wawek: Bewitching shaman.

Wayuro seed: Red and black bean, acquired from the pods of a jungle tree, credited with mystical powers.

Yagé: Alternative word for *ayahuasca*.

Yarena: Common palm with long slatted fronds, commonly used for building jungle shelters.

Yuka: See *cassava*.

Bibliography

FLIGHT

The Prehistory of Flight, Clive Hart, 1985, University of California
 Press, Los Angeles
Interpretive History of Flight, M. J. B. Davy, 1937, Science Museum
 Press, London
Men in the Air, ed. Brandt Aymar, 1990, Wings Books, New York
Nazca, Flight of Condor I, Jim Woodman, 1977, John Murray, London
Vimana Aircraft of Ancient India and Atlantis, ed. David Hatcher
 Childress, 1991, Adventures Unlimited Press, Illinois
Flight Before Flying, David Wragg, 1974, Osprey Publishing, Reading
Wings, ed. H. G. Bryden, 1942, Faber and Faber, London
The Inventions of Leonardo da Vinci, Charles Gibbs-Smith, 1978,
 Phaidon Press, London
The Dream of Flight, Clive Hart, 1972, Faber and Faber, London

PERUVIAN HISTORY

The Conquest of Peru, William H. Prescott, 1896, George Routledge
 and Sons, London
In Search of the Immortals: Mummies, Death and the Afterlife,
 Howard Reid, 1999, Headline, London
The Incas and their Ancestors, Michael E. Mosley, 1992, Thames and
 Hudson, London
Peru: A Short History, David P. Werlich, 1978, Southern Illinois
 University Press, Edwardsville
The Ancient Civilizations of Peru, Alden J. Mason, 1957, Penguin
 Books, London.
Peruvian Prehistory, R. W. Keatinge, 1988, University of Cambridge
Shamanism, Colonialism and the Wildman: A Study in Terror and

Healing, Michael Taussig, 1987, University of Chicago Press, Illinois

TRAVEL & GUIDES
Exploration Fawcett, P. H. Fawcett, 1953, Hutchinson, London
Masks, Mummies & Magicians, Roger and Simone Waisbard, 1965, Oliver and Boyd, London
Inca Cola, Matthew Parris, 1998, Weidenfeld & Nicolson, London
The Inca Trail, Richard Danbury, 1999, Trail Blazer Publications, Surrey
Peru, E. George Squier, 1877, reprinted 1973, AMS Press Inc, New York
Eight Feet in the Andes, Dervla Murphy, 1983, John Murray, London
Insight Guide to Peru, 1999, Insight Guides, London
Footprint Guide to Peru, Alan Murphy, 1999, Footprint Handbooks, Bath

THE INCAS
Highway of the Sun, Victor Von Hagen, 1956, Victor Gollancz, London
History of the Inca Empire, Bernabe Cobo, reprinted 1991, University of Texas Press, Austin
Lost City of the Incas, Hiram Bingham, 1951, Phoenix House, London
Inca Land, Hiram Bingham, 1922, Constable & Co, London
The Conquest of the Incas, John Hemming, 1970, Bookclub Associates, London
The Incas, Empire of Blood and Gold, Carmen Bernand, 1994, Thames and Hudson, London
Peru Under the Incas, C. A. Burland, 1967, Evans Brothers, London
Everyday Life of the Incas, Ann Kendell, 1973, Dorset Press, New York
Popul Vuh, ed. Dennis Tedlock, 1985, Simon and Schuster, New York
The Incas and Other Men, George Woodcock, 1959, The Travel Bookclub, London
The History of the Incas, Pedro Sariento de Gamboa, 1573
Inca Myths, Gary Urton, 1999, British Museum Press, London

TEXTILES & ART
Ancient Andean Textiles, Rebecca Stone-Miller, 1994, Thames and Hudson, London

The Weavers of Ancient Peru, Moh Fini, 1985, Tumi, London

Culturas Precolombinas Paracas, 1983, Banco de Crédito del Perú en la Cultura, Lima

Textile Traditions of Mesoamerica & the Andes, Margo Blum Schevill, 1996, First University of Texas Press, USA

Arts of the Amazon, Barbara Braun, 1995, Thames and Hudson, London

Art of the Andes, Rebecca Stone-Miller, 1995, Thames and Hudson, London

Early Nazca Needlework, Alan Sawyer, 1997, Laurence King, London

SHUAR

Off With their Heads, Victor Von Hagen, 1937, The Macmillan Company, New York

Jivaro: People of the Sacred Waterfalls, Michael Harner, 1972, University of California Press, Berkeley

Jivaro: Among the Head-shrinkers of the Amazon, Bertrand Flornoy, 1953, Elek Books, London

Mission to the Head Hunters, Frank and Marie Drown, 1961, Hodder and Stoughton, London

Amazon Head Hunters, Lewis Cotlow, 1953, Henry Holt and Co, New York

Head Hunters of the Amazon, F. W. Up de Graff, 1923, Garden City Publication Company, New York

Historical and Ethnographical Material on the Jivaro Indians, M. W. Stirling, 1938, United States Govt. Printing Office, Washington

Blood Revenge, War, and Victory Feasts Among the Jibaro Indians of Eastern Ecuador, Rafael Karsten, 1923, United States Govt. Printing Office, Washington

AMAZON & ITS TRIBES

Across the River of Death, Jorgen Bisch, 1958, The Scientific Bookclub, London

People of the Amazon, Lilo Linke, 1963, Robert Hale, London

The Lost World of the Amazon, Franz Eichhorn, 1955, The Travel Bookclub, London

The Rivers Ran East, Leonard Clark, 1954, Hutchinson, London

Affable Savages, Francis Huxley, 1951, Rupert Hart-Davis, London

The Rivers Amazon, Alex Shoumatoff, 1979, William Heinemann, London
The Amazon, Alain Gheerbrant, 1992, Thames and Hudson, London
Among the Wild Tribes of the Amazons, Charles W. Domville-Fife, 1924, Seeley, Service and Co, London

FLORA & FAUNA

Insight Guide to Amazonian Wildlife, Hans-Ulrich, 1992, APA Publications (HK), Hong Kong
Poison-Arrow Frogs, Ralf Heselhaus, 1992, Blandford, London
The Encyclopaedia of Medicinal Plants, Andrew Chevallier, 1996, Dorling Kindersley, London
Notes of a Botanist on the Amazon and the Andes, Richard Spruce, 1908, Macmillan & Co, London
A Narrative of Travels on the Amazon and Rio Negro, Alfred Russel Wallace, 1892, Ward, Lock, Bowden and Co, London

AYAHUASCA

Amazon Healer, Marlene Dobkin de Rios, 1992, Prism Books
The Visionary Vine, Marlene Dobkin de Rios, 1984, Waveland Press Inc, Illinois
Ayahuasca, ed. Ralph Metzner, 1999, Thunder's Mouth Press, New York
Abismos Cerebrales/El Chamanisimo, Fernando Cabieses, 1999, Lima, Peru
The Spears of Twilight, Philippe Descola, 1997, Flamingo, London
Forest of Visions, Alex Polari de Alverga, 1999, Parkstreet Press, Vermont
The Three Halves of Ino Moxo, Cesar Calvo, 1995, Inner Traditions International, Vermont
The Yage Letters, William S. Burroughs and Allen Ginsberg, 1963, reprinted 1975, City Lights Books, San Francisco
The Alchemy of Culture, Richard Rudgley, 1993, British Museum Press, London
Vine of the Soul, Richard Evans Schultes, 1992, Synergetic Press Inc, Arizona
The Cosmic Serpent, Jeremy Narby, 1998, Victor Gollancz, London

HALLUCINOGENS & SHAMANISM

Plants of the Gods, Richard Evans Schultes and Albert Hofmann, 1992, Healing Arts Press, Vermont

The Long Trip, Paul Devereux, 1997, Penguin Arkana, New York

Phantastica, Lewis Lewin, reprinted 1998, Parkstreet Press, Vermont

The Shaman, Piers Vitebsky, 1995, Duncan Baird Publishers, London

Hallucinogens and Shamanism, ed. Michael Harner, 1973, OUP, New York

Wizard of the Upper Amazon, F. Bruce Lamb, 1974, North Atlantic Books, Berkeley

Dance of the Four Winds, Alberto Villoldo, 1995, Destiny Books, Vermont

Dreamtime, Hans Peter Duerr, 1985, Basil Blackwell, London

Tobacco and Shamanism, Johannes Wilbert, 1987, Yale University Press, New Haven

The Encyclopaedia of Psychoactive Substances, Richard Rudgley, 1988, Little Brown, London

Consuming Habits: Drugs and History and Anthropology, ed Jordon Goodman, Paul E. Lovejoy & Andrew Sherratt, 1995, Routledge, London

Narcotic Plants, William Emboden, 1972, Studio Vista, London

Tales of a Shaman's Apprentice, Mark J. Plotkin, 1993, Penguin Books, New York

A Witch-Doctor's Apprentice, Nicole Maxwell, 1962, Victor Gollancz, London

The Healing Journey, Claudio Naranjo, 1975, Hutchinson, London

Index